Popular Political Support in Urban China

Popular Political Support in Urban China

JIE CHEN

WOODROW WILSON CENTER PRESS
Washington, D.C.

STANFORD UNIVERSITY PRESS
Stanford, California

EDITORIAL OFFICES:

Woodrow Wilson Center Press
One Woodrow Wilson Plaza
1300 Pennsylvania Avenue, N.W.
Washington, D.C. 20004
Telephone 202-691-4010

Order From:

Stanford University Press
Chicago Distribution Center
11030 South Langley Avenue
Chicago, Ill. 60628
Telephone 1-800-621-2736; 773-568-1550

2 4 6 8 9 7 5 3 1

Library of Congress Cataloging-in-Publication Data
Chen, Jie.
Popular political support in urban China / Jie Chen.
p. cm.
ISBN 0-8047-4959-0 (hardcover : alk. paper)
ISBN 0-8047-5057-2 (pbk : alk. paper)
1. Political culture—China—Beijing.   2. Legitimacy of
governments—China.   3. Zhongguo gong chan dang—Public opinion.   4.
Allegiance—China—Beijing.   5. Political participation—China—Beijing.
6. China—Politics and government—1976–   7. Political
leadership—China—Public opinion.   8. Public opinion—China—Beijing.
I. Title.
JQ1516.C435 2004
306.2'0951—dc22   2003014594

ABOUT THE CENTER

The Center is the living memorial of the United States of America to the nation's twenty-eighth president, Woodrow Wilson. Congress established the Woodrow Wilson Center in 1968 as an international institute for advanced study, "symbolizing and strengthening the fruitful relationship between the world of learning and the world of public affairs." The Center opened in 1970 under its own board of trustees.

In all its activities the Woodrow Wilson Center is a nonprofit, nonpartisan organization, supported financially by annual appropriations from the Congress, and by the contributions of foundations, corporations, and individuals. Conclusions or opinions expressed in Center publications and programs are those of the authors and speakers and do not necessarily reflect the views of the Center staff, fellows, trustees, advisory groups, or any individuals or organizations that provide financial support to the Center.

To my wife, Yanping

Contents

List of Tables and Figures   xi

Acknowledgments   xv

Chapter 1: Introduction   1

Chapter 2: The Extent of Popular Political Support in Beijing   21

Chapter 3: Relationship between Diffuse and Specific Support   54

Chapter 4: Sources of Diffuse Support   76

Chapter 5: Sources of Specific Support   121

Chapter 6: The Behavioral Consequences of Political Support   154

Chapter 7: Conclusion: Empirical Findings and Their Implications   179

Appendix A: Reliabilities of the Diffuse and Specific
            Support Indexes   195

Appendix B: Supplemental Information about the Distribution
            of Diffuse Support and Specific Support   201

References   205

Index   225

Tables and Figures

Tables

1.1 The Expected Relationships between the Two Dimensions
of Political Support and the Three Categories of
Sociopolitical Correlates   7

2.1 Distribution of Diffuse Support   30

2.2 Correlations between Nationalism and Preference for
Stability and Items in Diffuse Support   33

2.3 The Level of Fear of Political Persecution   35

2.4 Correlations between Fear of Political Persecution and
Responses to Diffuse Support Index   35

2.5 Distribution of Specific Support   49

3.1 Correlation between Diffuse and Specific Support   66

3.2 The Relationship of Diffuse and Specific Support by
Partial Correlation Controlling for Sex, Age, Education,
and Income   68

3.3 Recast of the Correlation between Diffuse Support and
Specific Support   71

4.1 Diffuse Support for Political Regime by Age   79

4.2 Diffuse Support for Political Regime by Gender   82

4.3 Distribution of Self-Assessed Economic Status   91

4.4 Correlations between Democratic Beliefs and
Diffuse Support   100

4.5 Correlations between Interest in Politics and
Diffuse Support   102

4.6   Correlations between Need for Political Reform and
      Diffuse Support   105
4.7   Correlations between Preference for Stability and
      Nationalist Sentiment and Diffuse Support   108
4.8   Satisfaction with One's Life and Diffuse Support   112
4.9   Correlations between Interest in Issues and Assessment of
      Local Policy and Diffuse Support   113
4.10 Multiple Regression (OLS) of Diffuse Support by
      Sociodemographic Attributes, High-Politics Orientations,
      and Low-Politics Orientations   116
5.1   Specific Support by Age   124
5.2   Specific Support by Gender   125
5.3   Specific Support by Education   127
5.4   Multiple Regression (OLS) of Specific Support by
      High-Politics Orientations   138
5.5   Specific Support by Satisfaction with One's Material and
      Social Life   143
5.6   Multiple Regression (OLS) of Specific Support by
      Sociodemographic Attributes, High-Politics Orientations,
      and Low-Politics Orientations   148
6.1   Frequency of Political Acts   164
6.2   The Spread of Political Participation   166
6.3   The Expected Relationships between the Two Dimensions
      of Political Support and the Two Major Forms of
      Political Acts   168
6.4   Estimated Coefficients of Logistic Regressions of Voting
      Behavior by Diffuse Support and Specific Support   174
6.5   Multiple Regression (OLS) of Contacting Behavior by
      Diffuse Support and Specific Support   175
A.1   Reliability of the Diffuse Support Index   196
A.2   Reliability of the Specific Support Index   198
B.1   Distribution of Diffuse Support   202
B.2   Distribution of Specific Support   203

Figures

3.1   Trends of Diffuse Support Items   57
3.2   Trends of Specific Support Items   59

3.3	Levels of Consistency of Diffuse and Specific Support	62
3.4	Implications of the Interaction between Diffuse Support and Specific Support	70
4.1	Diffuse Support by Education	85
4.2	Diffuse Support by Occupation	87
4.3	Diffuse Support by Economic Status	93
4.4	Comparison of Diffuse Support among CCP and Non-CCP Members	95
5.1	Occupation and Specific Support	130
5.2	Economic Status and Specific Support	133
5.3	Party Membership and Specific Support	135
5.4	Relationships among Interest in Local Issues, Assessment of Local Public Policies, and Specific Support	147

Acknowledgments

At various stages of the research project reported in this book, I was so fortunate as to be helped by many people and supported by several institutions. First of all, I would like to express my heartfelt gratitude to my colleagues and friends for their invaluable guidance and assistance. Particularly, my gratitude goes to Yu Guoming and Liu Xiayang of People's University (*Renda*) of China for helping me design and implement the Beijing surveys on which the study is based; Robert Hathaway, Gang Lin, James Millward, L. Chris Reardon, Jihong Zhao, Yang Zhong, and Yongming Zhou for their critical and constructive comments on major arguments in and structures of earlier versions of the book; Joshua Behr and Robert Holden for skillfully and meticulously editing an early draft of my work; and Bruce Dickson, David Shambaugh, Wenfang Tang, and anonymous reviewers for providing me with insightful and concrete suggestions later incorporated into the final version of the manuscript.

I would like to thank several institutions that played important roles in facilitating my research. Acknowledgments are due to the Public Opinion Research Center of People's University of China, one of the most reputable survey research institutions in China, which executed the Beijing surveys with its high level of professionalism. I greatly appreciate the Woodrow Wilson International Center for Scholars and the Sigur Center for Asian Studies of George Washington University for providing me with generous fellowships and superb staff and facility support during the writing of this book; the Fulbright Scholar Program for its fellowship supporting my research activities related to the project in China; and Old Dominion University, University of Tennessee–Knoxville, and University of Wisconsin–River Falls for various faculty research grants during the entire course of this project.

My sincere gratitude also goes to editors of the two presses who have seamlessly collaborated on the publication of this book: Muriel Bell of the Stanford University Press and Joe Brinley of the Woodrow Wilson Center Press. Throughout the review and publication process, both enthusiastically supported me and this project. Moreover, they offered substantive as well as editorial suggestions, all of which were enormously helpful. I also thank Yamile Kahn of the Wilson Center Press for coordinating between the two presses and shepherding the book through the production process.

Finally, I would like to express many thanks to my wife for willingly putting up with my obsession with this project and for unreservedly supporting my research activities that sometimes compete with her professional career and with my obligations to our family. While I have indeed tried to balance the needs of my family and those of my research, my wife has not been fairly compensated for the sacrifice she endured during my research for this book. As I am deeply indebted to her, therefore, I dedicate this book to my wife, Yanping.

Chapter 1

Introduction

It is commonly assumed outside China that the government led by the Chinese Communist Party (CCP) lacks popular support and legitimacy and has serious difficulties maintaining sociopolitical stability in China. How much support does the Chinese government actually enjoy from its citizens in the post–Mao era? Why do Chinese citizens support or not support the government? How does Chinese citizens' support or lack of support for the government influence their political behavior and in turn affect sociopolitical stability? The answers to these questions are critical not only for our comprehension of the current popular base of CCP rule but also for our assessment of the prospects of such rule. This book seeks to address these crucial questions, based on a unique set of data drawn from a series of public opinion surveys conducted in Beijing from 1995 to 1999.

The importance of popular political support is not unique to democratic polities. Although popular support for the government is variably defined, many studies have suggested that such support is crucial for the functioning and persistence of any form of government (e.g., Easton 1965; Lujan 1974; Rigby 1982; Miller 1993; Chen et al. 1997; Citrin and Muste 1999; Rose and Mishler 2000). In democratic systems, the level of political support significantly influences both the functioning and the stability of governments (especially in crises), because democratic governments can exist and operate only with the consent of the people (e.g., Lipset 1959, 1960; Miller 1974a; Seligson and Muller 1987; Finkel et al. 1989). In nondemocratic systems, such as the current system in China, while order is usually maintained by coercion or monolithic ideologies or both, the prolonged absence of political support may eventually bring about political instabilities and even "revolutionary alteration of the political and social system" (Miller 1974b,

1

951). Such political instabilities and revolutions, for example, were witnessed in the former Soviet Union and East European countries in the late 1980s and early 1990s (see, e.g., Pakulski 1986; White 1986; Avery 1988; Palma 1991). In general, therefore, "societies with legitimate authority systems [i.e., ones enjoying popular support] are more likely to survive than those without" (Inglehart 1997, 15).

Given the political and theoretical saliency of the topic, a large number of survey-based empirical studies have investigated political support in a variety of democratic systems.[1] Nonetheless, regrettably, such studies of non-democratic systems are scarce,[2] and even scarcer for China—the most populous country in the world.[3] The purpose of this book is to reduce this gap by exploring the extent, sociopolitical sources, and behavioral consequences of popular political support in urban China. Since there tends to be a strong correlation between political support and the effectiveness of incumbent government, this study will lead to a better understanding of the stability and even the viability of the current Chinese political system and government. Consequently, the book will also shed light on the prospects of democratization in China, which has been one of the most common topics among China observers.

In this first chapter, I will discuss my theoretical approach to popular political support in contemporary China and then describe the empirical data on which the analysis of such support is based. A brief summary of each chapter will follow.

Theoretical Framework and Major Hypotheses

Analysis in this book is guided mainly by the Eastonian theoretical framework of political support, but also by empirical insights from various studies of both Chinese and non-Chinese settings. Although the theoretical framework, derived from Easton's classic works (Easton 1965 and 1975), has drawn some criticisms,[4] it has been continuously applied and refined by

---

1. For a comprehensive review of these studies, see Reef and Knoke (1999) and Citrin and Muste (1999).
2. There are only a handful of exceptions, including Lujan (1974), Miller (1993), Geddes and Zaller (1989), and Rose and Mishler (2000).
3. Thus far, the only exception is Chen et al. (1997).
4. These criticisms can be grouped into two categories—methodological and theoretical. In the methodological category, for example, Loewenberg (1971), Miller (1974a

many analysts (Muller 1970a and 1970b; Lujan 1974; Muller and Jukam 1977; Muller, Jukam, and Seligson 1982; Seligson and Muller 1987; Finkel, Muller, and Seligson 1989; Gibson and Caldeira 1992; Kornberg and Clarke 1992; Miller 1993; Gibson, Calderia and Baird 1998; Hetherington 1998). This book is not intended to disentangle the debates over the Eastonian framework. Rather, in this study I choose useful insights from this theoretical framework systematically to analyze political support in contemporary China. These insights will help lay the theoretical foundations for the conceptualization of political support, and for the investigations of both sociopolitical correlates and behavioral consequences of political support in China.

Defining Political Support

Political support, the key concept in this book, is defined according to an Eastonian conceptualization. Easton's definition of political support begins as follows: "We can say that *A* supports *B* either when *A* acts on behalf of *B* or when he orients himself favorably toward *B*. *B* may be a person or a group; it may be a goal, idea, or institution. I shall designate supportive actions as overt support and supportive attitudes or sentiments as covert support" (Easton 1965, 159). As to the "covert support," which is referred to as "political support" in this study, Easton further identifies three major objects toward which such support is directed—the *regime,* the *authorities,* and the *political community.* According to Easton (1965, chapters 11–13), the regime, which is usually considered the most important object, refers to the fundamental values, norms, and institutions of the government; the authorities incorporate not only the incumbent leaders but the political leadership in general; the political community denotes the group of persons bound together in a common political enterprise.

Subsequently, for political support ("supportive attitudes"), Easton makes a distinction between two dimensions—"diffuse support" and "specific support" (Easton 1965 and 1975). Diffuse support, often seen as the more

and 1974b), Citrin (1974), and Zimmermann (1979) pointed out the difficulty of distinguishing and measuring the two dimensions of political support empirically. In the theoretical category, for example, Rogowski (1983) contended that analysts in the Eastonian framework err in assuming that people can make cognitive connections between what they want from a political system and what that system actually delivers.

influential dimension, represents a person's conviction that the existence and functioning of the government conform to his or her moral or ethical principles about what is right in the political sphere. Of the three political objects mentioned above, the regime is the primary object of diffuse support. It is believed that citizens are linked to the regime by diffuse support stemming from their assessment of the fundamental values, norms, and institutions of the government. As Easton himself (1965, 278) points out, citizens' support for the regime is "the single most effective device for regulating the flow of diffuse support." Thus, diffuse support for the regime is also regarded as the "belief in legitimacy" of the political regime (Easton 1965, chapter 18). According to this conceptualization, specifically, diffuse support in this study refers to Chinese citizens' supportive attitudes toward the fundamental values that the current, post–Mao regime advocates, and the basic political institutions through which the regime rules the country.[5]

As distinct from diffuse support, specific support measures a person's satisfaction with specific policies and performance of the government. Of the three political objects, the authorities are considered to be the primary object of specific support. Citizens are linked to the political authorities through their specific support derived from their perceptions and evaluations of the actual policy outputs of the authorities. In addition, this dimension of support is "object-specific": "people are or can become aware of the political authorities—those who are responsible for the day-to-day actions taken in the name of a political system" (Easton 1975, 437). Based on this concept, specific support in this book denotes Chinese citizens' positive assessment of public policies made by China's incumbent central authorities in dealing with major socioeconomic issues (e.g., inflation, housing, job security, employment, social order, and corruption).[6]

In short, within the Eastonian framework, political support as a subjective entity includes both dimensions—diffuse support and specific support. And while these two dimensions of support may be directed toward the three political objects—the regime, the political authorities, and the political community—each dimension is designated primarily for one political object: diffuse support for the regime and specific support for the political authorities. This concept is applied to the definition of political support in this study of citizens' support for the government in China.

---

5. The measurement of such attitudes among respondents will be discussed in detail in chapter 2.

6. The measurement of specific support will be explained in chapter 2.

Political support is the major object of analysis in this book. Following the Eastonian framework presented above, I choose to focus on the two dimensions of political support—diffuse support and specific support, and emphasize two political objects—the political regime toward which diffuse support is manifested and the political authorities toward which specific support is directed. The analysis that follows in this book is anchored in two main conceptual tracks: (1) diffuse support for the political regime and (2) specific support for the political authorities. On the track of diffuse support for the political regime, the analysis is aimed at the public's general attitudes toward the predominant values, norms, and institutional structures of the current political regime in China. On the track of specific support for the political authorities, the investigation is targeted at the public's overall assessment of major policies and performance of the political authorities. These two conceptual tracks link the components together in the book.

The Relationship between Diffuse Support and Specific Support

Since diffuse support and specific support here are considered to be the two component dimensions of political support, it is important to examine the relationship between these two dimensions in order to better understand the internal dynamics of political support and hence the impact of such dynamics on citizens' political behavior. This relationship involves at least two critical political and theoretical questions: Can citizens' positive and negative evaluations of government performance (i.e., specific support) help to build or erode their beliefs in the legitimacy of the political system (i.e., diffuse support)? If citizens' evaluations do affect their beliefs in the legitimacy, is the impact felt immediately or is it delayed?

The relationship between specific and diffuse support has been tackled in a large body of the literature on political support. Theoretically, according to the Eastonian framework, the two dimensions "should not bear a close relationship to one another" (Gibson and Caldeira 1992, 1127). Although the two dimensions are not totally independent of one another, the relationship between them is weak or moderate. And change in one dimension should not translate into a one-to-one change in the other (Adamany and Grossman 1983). This is because, according to the Eastonian conceptualization, diffuse support and specific support differ in their formations and in the patterns of change, although they are somewhat related. Diffuse support, as an entrenched emotional attachment to the political regime, takes a long time to form and is shaped mainly by prolonged sociopolitical forces, such as ongoing socializations and accumulated assessments of government performance. Once shaped, this support tends to be firm and long lasting. Thus, diffuse support is relatively stable and changes slowly, if it changes at all (see Finkel, Muller, and Seligson 1989; Gibson, Caldeira, and Baird 1998). In contrast, specific support is formed in a relatively short period of time, usually as the result of spontaneous response to specific policies and performance of the political authorities. "This kind of support [specific support] varies with perceived benefits or satisfactions," and "when these decline or cease, support will do likewise" (Easton 1975, 439). Therefore, specific support is relatively volatile and changes swiftly.

In short, because diffuse support and specific support differ in their formations and the patterns of change, they can be only weakly associated. Because specific support can gradually be converted into diffuse support (as the former accumulates over time) (Easton 1965, 275), however, these two dimensions can never be completely disconnected. With few exceptions,[7] this kind of weak association between the two dimensions of support has also been confirmed by empirical findings from earlier studies (Finkel, Muller, and Seligson 1989; Chen et al. 1997; Gibson 1992; Calderia and Gibson 1995; Gibson, Caldeira, and Baird 1998). Thus, in this study, I expect that there is a weak or moderate relationship between diffuse and specific support among respondents.

The Correlates of Diffuse and Specific Support

To understand fully the nature, intensity, and behavioral consequences of political support in contemporary China, one must have a grasp of the sociopolitical origins or correlates of political support. In this study, it is assumed that impacts of a set of sociopolitical factors differ on each of the two component dimensions of political support. Conceivably, this is because, as described above, these two component dimensions have distinct psychological properties and political objects: that is, diffuse support is characterized as entrenched emotional attachment and directed mainly toward the political regime; specific support is regarded as spontaneous and directed mainly toward the political authorities.

7. For example, Cusack (1999) has found a strong relationship between "satisfaction with government performance" and "satisfaction with political regime" in Germany.

Table 1.1

The Expected Relationships between the Two Dimensions of Political Support and the Three Categories of Sociopolitical Correlates

Category of Correlates	Diffuse Support	Specific Support
Sociodemographic attributes	Strong relationship	Weak relationship
High-politics orientations	Strong relationship	Weak relationship
Low-politics orientations	Weak relationship	Strong relationship

While each of the correlates of both dimensions of support will be specified in detail in the chapters that follow, several principal categories of the correlates of both dimensions are outlined here. In this research, I focus on three principal categories of the sociopolitical correlates: sociodemographic attributes, high-politics orientations, and low-politics orientations. Table 1.1 summarizes the hypothesized relationships between each of the two component dimensions of political support and the three categories of the sociopolitical correlates. It indicates the expected degree of the relationships: strongly related or weakly related, while the direction of the relationship between each dimension of political support and every component item within each of the three categories will be specified and tested in the chapters that follow.

Sociodemographic Attributes

Here, the category of sociodemographic attributes includes such items as gender, age, education, occupation, income, and the CCP membership. On the one hand, I expect that in our surveys, there should be strong relationships between most, if not all, sociodemographic attributes and diffuse support. This is because the sociodemographic attributes may capture some of the effects that family, peer groups, generations, social classes, and political memberships have on political socialization processes; the socialization processes tend to have a strong and lasting impact on people's political values and beliefs that in turn become the bases of diffuse support (see Lujan 1974, 24–5; Kornberg and Clarke 1992, 22; Miller 1993). As Easton (1975, 445) argues, diffuse support arises typically "from childhood and continuing adult socialization." In the case of China, for example, people from the Great Leap generation, the Cultural Revolution generation, and the post–Mao reform generation may have quite different views about the current communist regime because their socialization processes were influenced by such distinct sociopolitical factors as dramatic political events and various government-sanctioned political campaigns in the tumultuous history of the PRC (Jennings 1998, 967).

On the other hand, I assume that there is a weak relationship between the sociodemographic attributes and specific support, compared to the strength of the relationship between these attributes and diffuse support. Unlike diffuse support, which is composed of a set of entrenched emotional attachments, specific support is made of spontaneous responses to and evaluations of policies and performance of the political authorities. Such responses and evaluations may vary with sociodemographic attributes since some policies and performance can benefit people in one sociodemographic grouping or another at any given point in time. Thus, these attributes should not be completely disconnected with specific support. Nonetheless, the connections between the sociodemographic attributes and specific support should not be strong, due to the fact that, while the sociodemographic attributes remain relatively stable or unchanged, the policies and performance to which people respond tend to be relatively unstable and change frequently from time to time. Because of this discrepancy between the sociodemographic attributes and evaluations of policy and performance as specific support, one can expect the relationships between most, if not all, of the sociodemographic attributes and specific support to be weak, if they exist at all.

High-Politics Orientations

The category of high-politics orientations refers to a set of citizens' attitudes toward so-called high-politics issues and principles. The concept of high-politics issues involves "the principal political issues of society, the abstract ideas and language of politics, and the decisions and actions of the society leadership" (Bialer 1980, 166). In this research, high-politics orientations include such items as citizens' democratic values, belief in the need for a further reform of China's political system, interest in national and international affairs, and nationalist/patriotic sentiments. On the one hand, it is assumed that these high-politics orientations strongly associate with diffuse support. This is because (1) diffuse support itself is a set of attitudes toward a critical part of high politics—namely, the fundamental norms/values and structure of the political regime—and (2) this set of attitudes is naturally associated with attitudes toward other parts of high politics. In other words, people judge whether the structure and norms/values of the regime are morally right according to their high-politics orientations, such as political ideologies. Such high-politics orientations as political ideologies "provide a context within which . . . the political structure and related norms may themselves be tested for their legitimacy" (Easton 1965, 289). In contemporary China, for example, those who strongly believe in democratic values are very likely to regard the current, one-party rule under the CCP as illegitimate, since the norms/values and the institutions of this rule go against democratic values. As a result, these democratic believers in China tend to have a low level of diffuse support for the current political regime.

On the other hand, it is expected that there should be a weak relationship between high-politics orientations and specific support. The reason for this expectation is that specific support is derived primarily from positive assessments of specific policies and performance of the authorities, and such assessments are based mainly on cost-benefit calculations rather than abstract sentiments within the category of high-politics orientations (Easton 1965). In urban China, for instance, when people judge such specific policies as combating local environmental pollution and maintaining community security, they tend to respond spontaneously to these policies based on perceived costs and benefits of the policies. Therefore, the high-politics orientations are not likely to influence, at least strongly, people's judgment of specific policies and performance of the authorities.

Low-Politics Orientations

The category of low-politics orientations means a set of attitudes toward so-called low-politics issues. The concept of low-politics issues concerns the government's or political authorities' decisions that "directly touch the citizen's daily life, the communal matters, and the conditions of the workplaces" (Bialer 1980, 166). Low-politics orientations include such items as citizens' satisfaction or dissatisfaction with personal living conditions and social status, interest in local issues, and assessment of public policies dealing with local affairs. It is expected that these low-politics orientations strongly relate to specific support. While specific support comes from the evaluations of macro policies and performance of the political authorities at the national level, the low-politics orientations concern the assessments of micro public policies and their effectiveness at the individual and local levels. But in most cases, the micro public policies and their effectiveness result from the macro policies and performance of the political authorities at the national level. This is especially the case in such an authoritarian country as China where the central authorities at the national level have almost unlimited political and policy prerogatives to influence and control local affairs and individual life, although the effectiveness of such prerogatives has been undermined significantly since the onset of the post–Mao reform. Citizens in China, therefore, may be more likely than their counterparts in the West to link the evaluations of their personal living conditions and local affairs to the perceptions of policies and performance of the political authorities at the national level. For example, residents in any given locale—especially in such a major city as Beijing—may conceivably attribute the conditions of local public order at least in part to the periodic, nationwide crime-combating campaigns, which are launched by the national authorities and variably implemented by the government units and neighborhood organizations at the local level (Smith 2001).

Yet it is supposed here that the relationships between diffuse support and low-politics orientations should be much weaker than those between specific support and these orientations. Unlike specific support that is directly and almost instantaneously associated with people's evaluations of the public policies directly touching their everyday lives and their living standards, diffuse support, as Easton (1975, 446) specifies, may be influenced only by "spill-over" effects from evaluations of such policies and living conditions "over a long period of time." In other words, people may not change their views about the fundamental structures and norms or values of the political regime (i.e., diffuse support) just because of some changes in their income or living conditions at any point of time. Nonetheless, as these changes in their income and living conditions become consolidated over a long period of time, people may accordingly change their attitudes toward the political regime as a whole. This could be the case in China: the ordinary citizens have not shifted and will not shift their views about the current communist regime in a one-to-one knock-on manner according to the ebb and flow of order and living conditions in the entire course of the post–Mao reform. And only over a substantial period of time can changes in people's living conditions and the local environment influence their fundamental views about the regime. In short, due to this time lag of transformation between the assessment of personal daily life and local affairs and the views about the fundamental political system, there should be weak connections between low-politics orientations and diffuse support.

In summary, it is assumed that diffuse support and specific support should each be variably affected by a different combination of sociopolitical variables mentioned above. Diffuse support may be influenced strongly by sociodemographic attributes and high-politics orientations, but only slightly by low-politics orientations. Specific support is likely to be influenced strongly by low-politics orientations and only slightly or indirectly by sociodemographic attributes and high-politics orientations.

Behavioral Consequences of Political Support

Does political support affect citizens' political behavior? If so, how? The answer to these questions should have direct implications for the stability, viability, and future of the incumbent government and, probably, of the political system. Most studies of political support basically agree that political support significantly influences individuals' behaviors that may in turn affect the stability and survival of the incumbent government or the political system as a whole (Lipset 1959 and 1960; Easton 1965 and 1975; Muller 1970a; Miller 1974b; Muller 1977; Muller and Jukam 1977; Muller, Jukam, and Seligson 1982; Miller 1993; Chen 2000). Nonetheless, scholars may differ as to how political support (especially each of its two dimensions—diffuse and specific support) variably influences different kinds of political behaviors.

For the Western settings, many studies of behavioral consequences of political support focus on the behavioral effect of diffuse support. The empirical findings from these studies overwhelmingly suggest that a low level of diffuse support is likely to result in "antisystem" or "unconventional" political behaviors (e.g., protest and demonstration), while a high level of such support tends to bring about "compliant" or "conventional" behaviors (Muller 1970a and 1970b; Miller 1974b; Muller 1977; Muller and Jukam 1977; Muller, Jukam, and Seligson 1982).[8] By contrast, only a few studies focus on the behavioral effect of specific support. In them, one can discern two opposite views: (1) there is virtually no connection between the level of specific support and unconventional behaviors (Muller and Jukam 1977); and (2) low specific support is a catalyst of unconventional behaviors (Erber and Lau 1990).

For the communist societies, there are almost no survey-based empirical

---

8. There are only a few exceptions to these predominant findings. For example, Citrin shows that "there is neither a strong nor even a consistent association" between trust in government (similar to diffuse support) and unconventional behaviors, such as various forms of political protest (Citrin 1974, 980).

studies that directly deal with the behavioral consequences of political support.[9] Yet there is a substantial body of literature focusing on the impact of general subjective orientations on mass political participation or behaviors. Some of the subjective orientations tackled in this literature are similar or closely related to the two dimensions of political support defined here. Thus, in this analysis I draw some useful insights from the findings presented in that literature when developing major hypotheses about the behavioral consequences of political support in China.

Within the literature on communist political participation, there are at least two distinct approaches that are heuristic for the inquiry into behavioral consequences of political support in China. One is the so-called mobilization model that describes mass participation as "almost entirely a product of regime-directed mobilization" (Bahry and Silver 1990, 821) and little individual subjective motivations (Townsend 1967; DiFranceisco and Gitelman 1984; Barghoorn and Remington 1986; Roeder 1989). The other is the "motivation" model that sees mass participation in those societies more as a result of individual subjective motivations (Falkenheim 1978; Burns 1988; Bahry and Silver 1990; Manion 1996; Shi 1997). The mobilization approach is more applicable to mass participation and political behaviors in prereform, orthodox communist societies such as the Stalinist USSR and the Maoist PRC. This is because, in these systems, "not only were . . . political institutions authoritarian, but society itself seemed inhospitable to democratic values" (Bahry and Silver 1990, 822). The motivation approach is more suitable for political participation in reform, nonorthodox communist societies such as the USSR under Gorbachev and the PRC under Deng and his current successors. In these societies, not only do more legitimate channels and opportunities become available for mass participation, but the public itself becomes more open-minded and critical about public policies and politics in general (Shue 1988; Pei 1994; Shi 1997).

Relevant to this study is that while there is a consensus among the motivation analysts themselves that individual subjective orientations significantly influence political participation especially during the reform period, the question of which kinds of subjective orientations influence what types of political acts has not been settled. Some analyses (Friedgut 1979; Di-

9. An exception to this is Miller's (1993) study of the regime legitimacy in the former Soviet Union under Gorbachev.

Franceisco and Gitelman 1984), including recent studies of China's mass participation (Shi 1997; Jennings 1997) within the motivation model downgrade or neglect the impact of individual attitudes toward high-politics issues (which are considered in this study to be strongly associated with diffuse support) on most of the legitimate and conventional forms of participation. Instead, these studies focus on the effects of orientations to low-politics issues (which are regarded in this study as closely related to specific support). In his study of mass participation and political behaviors in China even during "the most liberal period" (the late 1980s), for instance, Shi (1997) suggested that because the communist regime prevented the public from directly engaging high-politics, those who participated in politics were presumably not motivated by their orientations to high-politics issues. Other motivation analysts (Bahry and Silver 1990; Liu 1996; J. Chen 2000), however, have found that individual attitudes toward both low-politics and high-politics issues make a significant difference in mass political participation and behaviors. In their study of Soviet mass participation "on the eve of the Gorbachev era," for example, Bahry and Silver (1990) found that such high-politics orientations as individual attitudes toward "fundamental values of the Soviet regime" (which are very similar to diffuse support in this study) significantly and variably influenced conventional and unconventional forms of political behaviors in the former Soviet Union. Thus, they concluded that various subjective motivations including both orientations toward high-politics and low-politics issues should be given at least equal attention in the study of mass participation and political behaviors in a nonorthodox, reformist communist society.

Considering the various approaches to the behavioral consequences of political support in the Western settings and to mass political participations in the communist settings, what kinds of relationships should we expect in this study between both diffuse and specific support on the one hand and various forms of political participation and behaviors on the other? A basic assessment of the sociopolitical environment for mass political participation and behaviors in contemporary China can help us answer this question. Since the late 1970s, China has experienced a gradual political reform or liberalization.[10] Due to the reform and liberalization, people now have more

10. For detailed discussion of the serious yet temporary setback in the gradual liberalization in 1989 and its reversal under Deng Xiaoping in the early 1990s, see Baum (1994).

opportunities as well as more incentives to articulate their interests in various political issues. For instance, people in the urban areas may feel more rewarded when voting in local and work-unit competitive elections because deputies to local People's Congresses and work-unit leaders tend to be more responsive to public demands (as these officials seek to win these elections) than they were in the Mao era and even in the early reform period (Pei 1998). Although people still cannot directly influence high politics by electing their national leaders, they now have such opportunities as local competitive elections to express their opinions and exert their influence indirectly on some public and administrative issues.[11] Moreover, due to the liberalization and sustained influence from the West, people in China are more likely to have diverse views about the fundamental norms and values of the political regime (i.e., diffuse support) as well as specific policies of the government (i.e., specific support), which in turn motivates the people to engage in various forms of political activities.

As a result of these significant changes in the sociopolitical environment, ordinary people now have more opportunities and incentives than they did before the post–Mao reform to express their views about both high-politics and low-politics issues. Thus, when considering the central hypothesis, I am inclined to draw on one of the two arguments within the motivation model: in general, people's attitudes toward both high-politics and low-politics issues significantly influence various forms of mass political participation in such a reform, nonorthodox communist society as contemporary China. From this argument, one can extrapolate the central hypothesis that both diffuse support (closely related to high-politics orientations) and specific support (closely associated with low-politics orientations) may affect political participation and behavior in contemporary China. Furthermore, drawing on the above-mentioned empirical findings from both Western and communist settings, one may refine this central hypothesis by assuming that each of the two dimensions of political support might variably influence different forms of political participation and behavior. The question of how exactly each dimension of political support influences each form of political participation and behavior will be addressed later.

---

11. Since people are no longer coerced into voting in these local elections, even nonvoting becomes a legitimate option for those who object to the electoral system and CCP rule as a whole (Chen and Zhong 2002).

Data

In general, the second half of the 1990s witnessed the emergence of the so-called third-generation of the CCP leadership under Jiang Zemin, the gradual consolidation of power of this leadership at least at the national level, and the deepening of the post–Mao reform that had both positive and negative effects on Chinese citizens' lives.[12] These were the underlying sociopolitical circumstances under which the data used in this book were collected. Specifically, the data came from three longitudinal representative-sample surveys conducted in Beijing in cooperation with the Public Opinion Research Institute (PORI) of the People's University.[13] How were these surveys conducted? To what extent can the data be generalized? These two important questions are addressed in this section.

The Beijing Surveys

The three longitudinal surveys were cross-sectional trend studies, instead of panel studies,[14] which drew three random samples from the same population of the adult residents in Beijing at three different times. Although different persons could be included in each of the three samples, the results from all these samples were representative of trends in the same population in Beijing because each properly selected sample was equivalent to every other sample from that population. The main reason to choose trend studies over panel studies in Beijing was that, since the early 1990s, people's residences in Beijing had become increasingly mobile because of the unprecedented pace of urban housing development in that city. Such high mobility made it extremely difficult, if not impossible, to track many household respondents and therefore very high attrition from the same sample could have

12. A detailed discussion on the sociopolitical and socioeconomic conditions in the second half of the 1990s will be presented in chapter 2.

13. The Public Opinion Research Institute of the People's University in Beijing, which was set up in 1986 as the first of its kind in the People's Republic of China, has done numerous surveys for both Chinese and foreign organizations.

14. In theory, trend studies draw random samples from the same population at different times and each of the samples may include different respondents. By contrast, panel studies require interviews of (or at least most of) the same sample at different times. For a more detailed discussion on the differences between trend studies and panel studies, see, for example, Manheim and Rich (1986).

occurred had panel studies been implemented. This kind of high attrition could severely compromise the validity of potential panel studies. Therefore, trend studies seemed to be the best survey strategy to cope with these special circumstances in Beijing. In addition, the methods of cross-sectional trend study have been successfully applied in some earlier analyses of political attitudes for various sociopolitical settings (McDonough, Barnes, and Pina 1986; Seligson and Muller 1987; Miller, Hesli, and Reisinger 1994; Miller, Reisinger, and Hesli 1996; Gibson, Caldeira, and Baird 1998; Tang and Parish 2000).

The first survey with a sample of 700 respondents was completed between November and December 1995. The second and third surveys, with equivalent sample sizes of 720 each, were conducted in December 1997 and December 1999, respectively. The response rates for the three surveys range from 93 percent to 96 percent.[15] Most of the questions in all three surveys were identical, which enables us to detect changes in variables and relationships between and among the variables in a span of about four years.

Respondents in the three surveys were chosen through a multistage random sampling procedure. In the 1995 survey, seven urban districts were randomly chosen in the first stage of sampling. Five residential neighborhoods (*juweihui*) were randomly chosen in the second stage of sampling. The third stage of random sampling produced a sample of twenty households from each of the five residential neighborhoods of the seven urban districts. One individual was randomly chosen from each household as the respondent in the final stage of sampling in our 1995 survey. The 1997 and 1999 surveys were both conducted in eight randomly selected *urban* districts of Beijing. Thirty-six residential neighborhoods (*juweihui*) were randomly chosen in the second stage of sampling. The second stage of random sampling produced a sample of twenty households from each of the thirty-six residential neighborhoods of the eight urban districts. One individual was randomly chosen from each household as the respondent in the final stage of sampling in these two surveys.

The three samples were divided almost evenly between the two sexes (51.7 percent, 51.6 percent, and 50.8 percent males in the 1995, 1997, and 1999 samples, respectively). All age groups (from eighteen years old to

15. These response rates are considered high by Western standards but are quite similar to the response rates from some other surveys conducted in China and the former Soviet Union (Gibson, Duch, and Tedin 1992; Nathan and Shi 1993; Shi 2001).

over sixty-five) and major urban occupation sectors are represented in the samples. The education levels of the respondents ranged from elementary, middle school, high school, to college. The sampling error is less than 4 percent for all three surveys.

In these surveys, college students of journalism and sociology were employed as field interviewers. Before each of the actual surveys was carried out, the interviewers were trained by the project leaders in field interviewing techniques. Each field interviewer delivered the questionnaire to the randomly chosen individual respondent, who filled it out. Then the field interviewer brought the questionnaire back to the survey center.

Care was taken to minimize linguistic misinterpretations and respondent effects. The original wording of the questionnaire (originally designed in the United States) was reviewed by the PORI to fit the Chinese social and cultural context and to provide for seamless translation from English to Chinese. Respondents were offered confidentiality and encouraged to provide answers that best captured their true feelings. In general, circumstantial evidence and evidence from other similar surveys (e.g., Shi 1997) suggest that Chinese respondents feel much freer to express their views in such public opinion surveys as ours than is typically assumed in the West. This is partly because, since reform, the Chinese government has not effectively censored or regulated survey research, owing to weakened Party control at the grassroots level and the lack of any consistent, applicable official rules governing survey research.

Generalizability of the Data

Like many other public opinion surveys, the three Beijing surveys produce two kinds of results: descriptive and relational.[16] These two kinds of results to be presented in this book can offer at least two general lessons for the study of popular political support in contemporary China. First, although the descriptive results from the surveys—such as those about the extent of both diffuse support and specific support among our respondents—cannot be directly applied to the entire country, they do help to establish some needed statistical baselines against which the findings from other areas of the country can be compared. These baselines are especially relevant to

16. For detailed discussion on the distinction between these two kinds of survey results, see, for example, Manion (1994).

subsequent studies conducted in large metropolitan areas, such as Shanghai, Guangzhou, Tianjing, Chengdu, and others, which not only share many socioeconomic similarities with Beijing, but also—together with Beijing— significantly influence the socioeconomic and sociopolitical development of the country.

Second, the findings from the three surveys about the relationships between variables can be directly generalized to other parts of China, especially urban China, since most, if not all, of these relationships are generic in nature.[17] These relationships are mainly between the two dimensions of political support and between each dimension of support and the three categories of sociopolitical factors and mass political behavior (respectively, as sources and behavioral consequences of political support). In fact, some recent empirical studies based on data collected from single-locale or multiple-locale samples have generated insightful, generalizable inferences about the patterns of the relationships between sociopolitical variables in both urban and rural China.[18] When discussing the generalizability of the data from local samples (single- and multiple-locale) in the study of contemporary China, therefore, Manion (1994, 747) argues that "data from local samples can yield reliable answers, generalizable to a population beyond the sample, to a crucial category of questions—those about relationships between variables."

An Overview

I start my analysis with a detailed and multidimensional examination in chapter 2 of the extent of political support and the trends of such support in

17. For more detailed discussion on the generalizability of findings about relationships between variables from single-locale samples in the study of contemporary China, see, for example, works by Manion (1994) and Walder (1998).

18. For example, using data from a single-locale sample of Tianjing, Walder (1995) demonstrates the existence of two distinct career paths that lead to a divided elite in China. Drawing on data collected in Beijing, Shi (1997) explores the correlation between citizens' political participation and various socioeconomic factors in urban China. Based on a survey carried out in four counties, Manion (1996) and Jennings (1997, 1998) have identified the patterns of electoral connections and the correlates of political participation in rural China. Finally, a group of China scholars tap into data from a single county, Zouping, and offer important general arguments about the economic transformation of rural China (Walder 1998).

Beijing over the time period covered in the three surveys. I first explain how the empirical measures of both diffuse support and specific support are based on the results of various measures from studies of both Western and non-Western settings. Using these measures, I gauge the extent of both diffuse and specific support within the three samples. Subsequently, I compare the extent of the two dimensions of political support in each of the three surveys. All these analyses are intended to shed light on such important questions as: How much popular political support does the current communist regime enjoy in urban China? Which kind (or dimension) of political support does the regime rely on more?

Chapter 3 is devoted to the exploration of the complex yet important relationship between diffuse support and specific support. I first examine differences between the two dimensions of political support in terms of their consistencies and the patterns of changes. Then I examine the bivariate relationship between these two dimensions of political support and the impacts of sociodemographic and sociopolitical factors on the relationship between the two dimensions. This chapter is intended to address several crucial theoretical and political questions, such as: Which dimension of political support is more stable or volatile? Can the public's positive and negative evaluations of government performance (i.e., specific support) help, respectively, to build or erode their beliefs in the legitimacy of the government (i.e., diffuse support)? If they can, what can be said about the timing of the effects?

The sociopolitical sources of diffuse support and specific support are examined, respectively, in chapters 4 and 5. As mentioned above, I focus on three principal categories of the sociopolitical correlates: sociodemographic attributes, high-politics orientations, and low-politics orientations. In each chapter, I specify and test the relationship between each dimension of political support and each component factor within every one of the three categories of sociopolitical sources. Some general inferences about the sources of political support in contemporary China are drawn from the findings about the relationship. The exploration in chapters 4 and 5 of the sources of political support will help us address such critical questions as: Who are more likely to support the incumbent government and/or the communist system in contemporary China, especially in today's urban China? What social, economic, and political factors motivate people to support the government or the system? Do the relationships between the three categories of sociopolitical sources and political support change as the society changes during the post–Mao reform? And if so, how?

The behavioral consequence of political support is the analytical focus of chapter 6. The analysis of this issue is important because, as mentioned earlier, such behavioral consequences have direct implications for the stability, viability, and future of the political system as well as of the incumbent government in contemporary China. In chapter 6, I will first examine the forms and intensity of political participation in such an urban setting as Beijing. Then I will closely examine how each of the two dimensions of political support variably influences each form of political participation and behavior. Some important general implications for the sociopolitical stability of today's China will be drawn from the empirical results about the correlation between each dimension of political support and mass political participation. The important theoretical and empirical questions to be addressed in that chapter include: Does political support as a set of attitudes really affect how people behave politically in post–Mao China? If it does, which dimension of political support, diffuse or specific support, is more closely associated with political behaviors and hence more consequential for political stability in that country?

Finally, in chapter 7, I summarize all major findings, and then discuss their theoretical and political implications. The summary is carried out around the three fundamental questions addressed by this book, which deal with the extent, sources, and consequences of political support in China. The discussion of the implications of my findings will also shed some light on the prospects for political changes in contemporary China.

Chapter 2

The Extent of Popular Political Support in Beijing

Do most people in Beijing support both the political regime (or fundamental political system) and the incumbent authorities? If so, how much do they support each? The answers to these questions will help establish the popular bases of the rule of the Chinese Communist Party (CCP), regardless of the nature of such rule. As the first step in addressing these questions, I will begin this chapter discussing the measurement of both dimensions of political support—diffuse support for the political regime and specific support for the political authorities.

The Measurement of Political Support

As noted in chapter 1, there is almost no survey-based, empirical research on popular political support in China. Thus, the measurement of political support in this study is mainly derived from three other major sources: (1) theoretical justification and empirical results from studies in non-Chinese settings, (2) insights from non-survey-based, field observations by China observers, and (3) empirical results from the analysis of our own data. The measurement of each of the two dimensions of political support is established separately as follows.

The Measurement of Diffuse Support for the Political Regime

An Important Principle Guiding Measurement Design

When developing survey instruments to measure diffuse support, I follow the principle of ideological neutrality, which has been successfully implemented in several important studies of political support in various, non-Chinese sociopolitical settings (Citrin et al. 1975; Rose and Mishler 2000). By ideological neutrality, I mean that the face content of survey instruments should not predispose someone with a given ideological orientation to accept (or reject). According to this principle, the investigator must "guard against the use of terms [in survey questionnaires] that are so laden with ideological symbolism and associations that people ignore their actual intellectual content and instead respond reflexively to symbolic cues" (Citrin et al. 1975, 5).

Using this principle of ideological neutrality to guide questionnaire designing has at least two advantages for our survey studies. One advantage is methodological: ideological neutrality can enhance the validity of survey instruments. The object of study here is people's (relative) generic support for the current regime, whatever the ideological nature of the regime. Although there could be a relationship between people's support for the regime and their ideological orientations, such a relationship should not result in any way from ideologically charged language in the questionnaire items. For example, in contemporary China, those who strongly support democratic values are more likely to respond unfavorably to such ideologically loaded phrases as "authoritarian regime" and "proletarian dictatorship," while those who prefer centralized political control and hierarchical order are more likely to turn away from such terms as "free society" and "pluralistic institutions." In all these cases, people's attitudes toward the regime are tainted by some ideologically loaded terms in the questionnaire. Therefore, valid measures of support for the regime must use language "as ideologically neutral as possible" (Citrin et al. 1975, 5) so that respondents with various ideological backgrounds can all have, in principle, a fair chance to register their level of support for the current regime.

The other advantage of employing the principle of ideological neutrality is sociopolitical: ideological neutrality can reduce (though not totally eliminate) the political sensitivity of survey instruments and hence improve the truthfulness of interviewees' responses. Although contemporary Chinese society in general is much freer than it was during the Mao era and early reform period, the government does not hesitate to suppress the public expression of attitudes threatening the government-defined "social and political stability." Thus, respondents in China are likely to conceal their true opinions of the political regime if their opinions seem to be deemed by the government as threatening. Conceivably, this is even more likely to be the case if respondents are asked questions loaded with strong ideological terms, such as "authoritarian regime" and "communist government," since theses questions are more politically sensitive. Therefore, in order to acquire respondents' truthful opinions regarding the political regime, the investigator should avoid using ideological terms in questionnaires in China.

Indicators of Diffuse Support

To operationalize the concept of diffuse support for the political regime or regime legitimacy, many scholars have identified several major components of the concept. For Lipset (1981), regime legitimacy is tied to affect for the prevalent political institutions in a society. Easton (1965; 1975) sees regime legitimacy (or "diffuse support" in his original term) as affect primarily for values, norms, and institutions of the regime. Combining these two approaches, Muller and Jukam (1977, 1566) locate three major operational components for the concept of regime legitimacy: (1) "affect tied to evaluation of how well political institutions conform to a person's sense of what is right"; (2) "affect tied to evaluation of how well the system of government upholds basic political values in which a person believes"; and (3) "affect tied to evaluation of how well the authorities conform to a person's sense of what is right and proper behavior [or conduct]."

Following Muller and Jukam's operationalization of regime legitimacy,[1] I measure popular diffuse support for China's current political regime by asking the respondents in all three surveys to assess six items (or statements) as follows:

1. I am proud to live under the current political system.
2. I have an obligation to support the current political system.
3. I respect the political institutions in China today.
4. I feel that the basic rights of citizens are protected.
5. I believe that the courts in China guarantee fair trials.
6. I feel that my personal values are the same as those advocated by the government.

Specifically, items 1 and 6 are designed to detect the popular affect for the values and norms of the regime. Items 2 and 3 are intended to tap into affect

---

1. Their operationalized measure of regime legitimacy or diffuse support has been used in several cross-nation and single-nation studies of political support (Muller 1977; Muller and Williams 1980; Seligson and Muller 1987; Finkel, Muller, and Seligson 1989).

derived from respondents' generalized feelings about major political institutions and the current political system as a whole. Items 4 and 5 relate to
a person's evaluations of political authorities in terms of whether the authorities have functioned and wielded their power in accordance with one's
sense of fairness and basic interests. Respondents were asked to rate each
of the six items on a 4-point scale, where "1" indicates respondents' strong
disagreement with a statement, and "4" indicates their strong agreement
with the statement. These six items were then combined to form an additive
index to capture a collective profile of a respondent's diffuse support for the
political regime, ranging from 6 (indicating the lowest level of regime
support) to 24 (indicating the highest level of regime support). This index
is used in the multivariate analyses that follow. The reliability of this index
is discussed in appendix A.

The Measurement of Specific Support for the Political Authorities

An Important Principle Guiding Measurement Design

When developing survey instruments to measure specific support, I focus
on people's evaluations of major policies that are made and implemented
by the incumbent political authority rather than of any specific leaders. This
survey strategy has been successfully implemented in several important
studies of political support in some non-Chinese sociopolitical settings (Citrin et al. 1975; Muller and Jukam 1977; Finkel, Muller, and Seligson 1989;
Kornberg and Clarke 1992; Miller 1993).

There are two important reasons for adopting this principle in our surveys. First, theoretically, the evaluations of government policy and performance are "the manifestation of . . . attitudes toward the political authorities
in response to outputs which satisfy [or dissatisfy] members' performance
demands or wants" (Muller 1970b, 393). Therefore, in general, citizens are
linked to the incumbent political authority through their perceptions and
evaluations of the actual policies (made by the authorities) and their outcomes (Lujan 1974, 26). In addition, most ordinary citizens cannot and do
not need to know or remember each or most of political leaders who are
responsible for specific public policies at the both national and local levels.
Thus, any meaningful connection between the citizens and the incumbent
leaders is most likely to be established through citizens' evaluation of public policies. Such evaluation serves as one of the ongoing, sociopsychological media between the citizens and the leaders. This is especially the case

in China where national leaders who possess real power to make and implement policies are not popularly elected, and the so-called local elections apparently do not function as the connecting mechanism between the citizens and the leaders. As a result, citizens in China judge the incumbent authority as a whole mainly through the policies made and implemented by the authority. Thus, I chose this policy-focused principle when designing questionnaire items about citizens' specific support for the incumbent authorities.

A second reason is that, politically, this principle of questionnaire design protects the respondents in our samples from potential political troubles from the government. As a China-survey researcher, Tianjian Shi, has pointed out, "officially, there is one rule governing public opinion surveys in China: researchers cannot ask about people's perceptions and images of the leaders of the CCP and the state." This is because, according to the government, "the information on people's perception and image on these political leaders are 'state secrets'"(Shi 1996, 217).[2] Under this rule, even if respondents were asked about specific leaders, the respondents would be more likely to conceal their true feelings (if the feelings were critical of the leaders). Therefore, considering respondents' safety and the truthfulness of their responses, I chose this policy-focused (as opposed to leader-focused) principle to guide the design of the questionnaire on specific support.

Indicators of Specific Support

Drawing upon indicators from some previous cross-country survey studies of political support (Muller and Jukam, 1977, 1565–7; Finkel, Muller, and Seligson, 1989, 336–7, 346–7), I have fashioned nine items to capture respondents' evaluations of specific policies and their outcomes. These items are linked to the following public policy areas:

1. Controlling inflation
2. Providing job security
3. Minimizing the gap between rich and poor
4. Improving housing conditions for all
5. Maintaining order in society

---

2. According to Shi (1996, 217), "this rule was stated in an internal document issued jointly by the State Bureau of Security Regulations and Propaganda Department of the CCP."

6. Providing adequate medical care for all
7. Providing welfare services to the needy
8. Fighting official corruption
9. Combating pollution

The relevance of these policy areas to our Beijing samples was assessed in several interviews conducted prior to the administration of formal surveys. The results from these presurvey interviews indicated widespread interest among interviewees in each of these policy areas.

The relevance of the items in this index of specific support has been also confirmed by some earlier field observations by China observers. From a systemic perspective, for example, Tang and Parish (2000) have correctly noted that since the post–Mao reform, the sociopolitical base of the relationship (or what they call social contract) between the state and the population has been transformed from citizens' acceptance of Maoist idealist goals to constant evaluations by them of government policies dealing with their daily socioeconomic life. In this context of social-contract change, these analysts (Tang and Parish 2000, chapter 5) have identified fifteen areas of the "government's outputs" about which the public in urban China was concerned between the late 1980s and the early 1990s. Among these fifteen areas, the public was most worried about inflation, housing, medical care, official corruption, and social (or community) order (Tang and Parish 2000, 108). In addition, the issues of most concern by the public during the late 1980s and the early 1990s either persisted or reemerged during the mid 1990s (Baum 1994, chapter 16, epilogue; Lieberthal 1995, 267–91) when our surveys commenced. These earlier findings from field observations by China scholars indicate that the policy issues covered in our specific support index are at the core of the public's concerns.

For each of the items in the specific-support index, respondents were asked to grade government-policy performance based on the grading scheme commonly used in China's schools: that is, on a 5-point scale, where "1" stands for failure and "5" stands for excellence. In order to capture a collective profile of the respondents' evaluation of government performance, the nine items were then combined to form an additive index, ranging from 9 (indicating very poor policy performance) to 45 (indicating excellent policy performance). This index constitutes one single measure of government-policy evaluation and is employed in the multivariate analyses that follow. The reliability of the index is dealt with in appendix A.

How Much Diffuse Support Is There in Beijing?

Sociopolitical Context and Mainstream Views

Before 1989 most Western observers of China were optimistic about the prospects for the post–Mao reform and popular support for the political regime. After the Tiananmen crackdown, however, most China scholars believed that the political regime led by the CCP had lost its popular support and legitimacy, and hence had become nonviable. Goldstein (1994, 727) has summarized this pessimistic mood among China scholars:

> Prior to the late 1980s, scholars documented trends and changes, but did not question the continued existence of the Communist regime. The events of 1989 in China and elsewhere shattered this assumption and analysts embraced the task of diagnosing the condition of what most came to view as moribund system. This sea change raised questions about the fate of the country's Communist political elite and institutions, whatever their present profile, that had not been on the agenda of mainstream Chinese studies since the 1950s. Although scholars continue to disagree about the probable life-span of the current regime, the disagreement now is usually about when, not whether, fundamental political change will occur and what it will look like.

After the dramatic political events of 1989, the widespread, mainstream view among China scholars was that the communist regime had lost its popular support and would eventually collapse. China scholars also identified at least two major areas in which the regime had lost its support of the population. First, the regime had lost its ideological appeal to the population, especially the intellectuals and the younger generation (Rosen 1991; Link 1993; Ding 1994; Chen and Deng 1995; Chen 1995; Tang and Parish 2000; Teiwes 2000). For example, these analysts often cited the so-called crisis of faith as evidence of how much moral support the regime had lost in the face of dramatic socioeconomic and sociopolitical changes since the beginning of post–Mao reform. The crisis of faith meant that many people in China felt that "there is more or less nothing to believe in. They don't believe in Marxism-Leninism and Mao Zedong Thought, the leadership of the Chinese Communist Party, the superiority of socialism, or the brilliant prospect of Communism" (Burton 1990, 5). In fact, these scholars pointed out, even many Party members had lost their "spiritual pillar," the core beliefs that have been promoted by the Party and had guided them to support and even sacrifice for the regime under Mao (J. Chen 1995, 27).

Second, some China analysts argued that the regime had lost its moral appeals to the population. Due to rampant official corruption and misconduct in the post–Mao era, they asserted, ordinary people in China became more skeptical about basic moral standards and motivations of the Party and government leaders, and doubtful about their leadership (Meaney 1991; Kwong 1997, chapter 3; Gong 1997; Liu 1998, chapter 2; Wu 1999; Whyte 2000, 158–9; Lu 2000; Chen 2000). As Baum (2000, 22) has pointed out, even the top government leaders themselves, such as then-President Jiang Zemin of the PRC, admitted that official corruption threatened "the very existence of the Party and the state" (Jiang 1997). To substantiate their views, for example, some observers cited a salient case of official corruption that involved then-mayor of Beijing Chen Xitong and his associate Wang Baosen (a ranking official in the Beijing Municipality), who were alleged to have embezzled a large amount of public funds and to have received bribes.[3] Such scholars used this case, among others, to illustrate how serious official corruption became in the reform era, how discontented ordinary people were with Party and government leaders, and how much trust the people had lost in the moral sense of the leaders. In short, according to these observers, in the eyes of the public, the current regime did not deserve the right to rule since it had become immoral.

But these conventional views, summarized above, on popular support for (or the legitimacy of) the regime have not been systematically verified against the empirical evidence of representative-sample surveys. This study seeks to verify the conventional views against the data collected from our three longitudinal samples of Beijing residents.

The Empirical Results from the Three Beijing Surveys

Table 2.1 presents the distributions of all the items within the index of diffuse support for the political regime for the three samples. Two important findings emerge from the distributions. First, the overall results of the distributions tend to contradict the mainstream views mentioned above: a clear majority of our respondents apparently supported the current political

3. For a detailed description of this case, see Baum (1994, 385–7).

regime. Specifically, the percentages of those who either agreed or strongly agreed with each of the six statements (which collectively measure diffuse support for the political regime) ranged from a low of 66 percent for item 6 regarding congruence between personal and regime values in 1999 to a high of 97 percent for item 2 about a citizen's obligation to support the political system in 1995. This finding is also reinforced by the fact that the mean scores of all six items within the diffuse support index in each year were higher than "2" (which indicates "disagree" with the item statement and hence lack of support for the object to which the statement refers), ranging from a low of 2.51 for item 6 in 1999 to a high of 3.59 for item 2 in 1995. These findings suggest that, in general, the respondents in the three samples had positive feelings about all the six objects that the six items were designed to measure.

Furthermore, as table 2.1 shows, the mean scores of the diffuse support index in three surveys were found to be well above the midpoint ("15") of the 6-24 scale: 19.45, 18.92, and 18.23 in 1995, 1997, and 1999, respectively. These summary scores for the index apparently suggest that the respondents in these three samples offered strong support for the political regime as a whole, or considered the current regime legitimate. All in all, the results from our three surveys contradict the mainstream view that the regime has lost its ideological and moral appeal.

A second important finding from the results presented in table 2.1 is that there were significant variations in respondents' assessments of the items in the diffuse support index. Specifically, the respondents gave substantially higher scores for one subgroup of the items (items 1–3) than they did for the other subgroup (items 4–6) in each survey: the mean scores for items 1–3 were all clearly above "3," while those for items 4-6 were generally below "3" (with only one exception for item 4 in 1995).

What unique factors caused such a difference between respondents' evaluations of the two subgroups of the six items, which are all designed to measure one general concept? The answer to this question will provide a better understanding of the internal dynamics and hence the uniqueness of diffuse support for the political regime in China. To provide an initial answer to this question, I will first look at the differences between the two subgroups and then explore some sociopolitical factors that could cause respondents to assess one subgroup more positively than the other.

A close look at the two subgroups of the diffuse support items suggests a discernible conceptual difference between them. In one subgroup, items

Table 2.1

Distribution of Diffuse Support, 1995, 1997, and 1999

	Positive Responses (%)c			Mean Score			Standard Deviation		
	1995	1997	1999	1995	1997	1999	1995	1997	1999
1. Proud of system (1–4)a	95.4	91.9	87.3	3.48	3.38	3.31	.62	.69	.71
2. Obligated to system (1–4)a	97.5	92.6	85.4	3.59	3.39	3.24	.54	.64	.68
3. Respect institutions (1–4)a	93.2	90.4	87.7	3.37	3.31	3.23	.65	.67	.68
4. Basic rights protected (1–4)a	86.7	78.5	67.0	3.08	2.97	2.67	.65	.74	.74
5. Fair courts (1–4)a	82.2	74.9	77.5	2.94	2.88	2.92	.67	.75	.68
6. Personal vs. government values (1–4)a	80.0	71.9	65.9	2.97	2.72	2.51	.67	.72	.68
Entire index (6–24)b	—	—	—	19.45	18.92	18.23	2.63	3.15	3.08

Note: The supplemental information about the distribution of diffuse support in the three surveys is presented in appendix B.

a "1" to "4" are the numerical scores assigned to responses to each item in the diffuse support index: 1 = strongly disagree, 2 = disagree, 3 = agree, and 4 = strongly agree.

b The six items above were combined to form an additive index to capture a collective profile of a respondent's diffuse support for the political regime, ranging from "6" (indicating the lowest level of regime support) to "24" (indicating the highest level of regime support).

c The percentage of positive responses is the combination of the percentages of those who "agree" and "strongly agree" with the questionnaire statement.

1-3 deal with the political system (items 1 and 2) and political institutions (item 3) as a whole at the national level; in the other subgroup, items 4-6 tackle some factors mainly at the individual level, such as "personal values" in relation to the regime values (item 6) and individual experience with "basic rights" protection (item 4) and the court system (item 5) in China.

Given this discernible conceptual difference, what factors made our respondents' assessment of one subgroup more positive than the other? I suspect that at least two salient, almost universal, sentiments within the population could make most respondents feel more positive about the subgroup of items regarding the national government and institutions as a whole. These two sentiments are nationalism/patriotism and a strong preference for sociopolitical stability. While the impacts of these sentiments on the entire index of diffuse support will be systematically examined in the chapters that follow, here I will offer preliminary explanations of the effects of these sentiments on the variations among the items within the index.

First, nationalism has increasingly gained currency in almost all sectors of the population. In our three surveys, for example, over 80 percent of the respondents either believe or strongly believe that "China should play a more important role in Asia and the world," and "China should and will be a stronger power in the world in the next century."[4] Such a strong nationalist sentiment results not only from the relentless promotion of nationalism by the post–Deng leadership to buttress its own legitimacy but also from ordinary citizens' need for this sentiment to cope with their loss of faith in the old official ideology of Maoism (Downs and Saunders 1998; Zheng 1999, chapters 2 and 3). More important, nationalism in China has been considered to be closely associated with "the interests of the state," and it has strongly emphasized the loyalty to the national government (Hunt 1994; Duara 1996; Fitzgerald 1996; Zheng 1999; Zhao 2000; Chan 2001). Thus, I suppose that those who strongly believe in nationalism tend to give higher scores for items 1-3 since these items concern the national government and its institutions as a whole.

Second, according to some earlier studies, a majority of the people have accepted the "stability first" argument advocated by the CCP (Zhen 1994;

---

4. Respondents were asked to rate each of the two statements on a 4-point scale where "1" indicates respondents' strong disagreement with a statement, and "4" indicates their strong agreement with the statement. These two items are combined to form an additive index for nationalist sentiment in each survey.

Zhong 1996; Chen et al. 1997; Schoenhals 1999; Teiwes 2000). In our three surveys, over 90 percent of respondents preferred a stable and orderly society to a freer society that could be prone to disruption.[5] This deep fear of chaos has mainly resulted from people's perception of negative political and economic consequences stemming from the turbulent political changes in the former Soviet Union. Exploiting Chinese people's fear of political chaos, the post–Mao leadership has repeatedly urged Chinese people to believe that "only the Communist Party could provide" sociopolitical stability in China (Chan 2001, 162). Popular acceptance of this "stability first" argument has in effect provided "potent support for even an unloved Party-state" (Teiwes 2001, 87). Thus, I expect that those who strongly believe in the importance of sociopolitical stability are more likely to give higher scores for the items (items 1–3) about the national Party-state system.

To test the two above-mentioned propositions about the impact of nationalism and a preference for stability on the variations of the items within the diffuse support index, I examine the bivariate correlations between these two sentiments and each of the items. As table 2.2 indicates, nationalism and preference for stability were positively correlated with all six items in the three surveys. Nonetheless, the relationships between nationalism and preference for stability on the one hand, and the first three items (about the political systems and institutions at the national level) on the other hand were stronger than those between these two sentiments and the last three items. Specifically, the correlation coefficients for the relationships between the two sentiments and the first three items ranged from a low of .117 to a high of .261, while those for the relationships between these two sentiments and the last three items ranged from a low of .041 to a high of .103. These results support my earlier proposition that the respondents who had strong nationalism and preference for stability are more likely to give higher scores for the items closely related to the national government and institutions. Since, as mentioned above, a clear majority of our respondents in all three surveys had strong beliefs in nationalism and stability, the assessments of the items (items 1–3) associated with the national government had to be higher than those of the other items.

---

5. The actual wording of this questionnaire item is: "I would rather live in an orderly society than in a society in which people enjoy so many freedoms that they can become disruptive."

Table 2.2

Correlations between Nationalism and Preference for Stability and Items in Diffuse Support, 1995, 1997, and 1999

	1995		1997		1999	
	Nationalism	Preference for Stability	Nationalism	Preference for Stability	Nationalism	Preference for Stability
1. I am proud to live under the current political system.	.187**	.165**	.146**	.120**	.261**	.193**
2. I have an obligation to support the current political system.	.216**	.226**	.213**	.117**	.208**	.216**
3. I respect the political institutions in China today.	.173**	.151**	.160**	.118**	.172**	.143**
4. I feel that the basic rights of citizens are protected.	.052	.041	.049	.039	.083*	.080*
5. I believe that the courts in China guarantee fair trials.	.075*	.087*	.084*	.040	.061	.075*
6. I feel that my personal values are the same as those advocated by the government.	.085*	.103*	.097*	.081*	.067	.101*

Note: All entries are the Pearson correlations (r). * $P < .05$. ** $P < .01$.

The Truthfulness of the Responses to the Diffuse Support Index

Did our respondents give generally positive responses to the items about the political regime in our surveys simply because they were afraid of potential political persecution by the government? This question raises legitimate concerns over the truthfulness of the responses and the validity of the items within the diffuse support index in our surveys. To rule out these concerns, I will first measure the level of the fear of potential political persecution among the respondents and then examine the correlations between such fear and the respondents' responses to the items in the index.

To measure the fear of political persecution, I used the following statement in all three surveys: "I would not criticize the government and/or leaders because I might get into some potential political trouble due to my criticism." The respondents were asked to assess the statement on a 4-point scale, where "1" represents a strong disagreement and "4" refers to a strong agreement with this statement. Those who scored higher were more afraid of political persecution when considering the expression of opinions on the government and leaders.

Table 2.3 shows the distributions of responses to this statement in the three surveys. The distributions indicate that about the same number, a little over half, of respondents (in both "agree" and "strongly agree" categories) in all three surveys said they would not criticize the government and leaders because of their fear of potential political persecution. The results presented here correspond to the findings on a similar issue from an earlier nationwide survey that was conducted in China at about the same time as our first survey.[6] All these results manifested a serious concern over political persecution.

But did the fear of potential political persecution actually affect how the respondents responded to the questions within the diffuse support index in our three surveys? If so, those who were more afraid of potential political persecution were supposed to give more positive responses (higher scores) to the items in the index, in order to avoid such potential persecution. As a result, there would be strong and positive correlations between the level of

6. Based on his nationwide survey conducted between 1993 and 1994, Shi (2001, 405) found that over 40 percent of the respondents in the PRC were concerned about "the possibility of being reported to the authorities if they criticized the government."

Table 2.3

The Level of Fear of Political Persecution, 1995, 1997, and 1999

	(1) Strongly Disagree (%)	(2) Disagree (%)	(3) Agree (%)	(4) Strongly Agree (%)	Mean Score (1–4)	Standard Deviation
1995	6.0	42.1	30.9	21.0	2.01	.87
1997	7.8	41.0	28.7	22.5	2.16	.88
1999	8.1	40.8	29.1	22.0	2.08	.85

Note: The actual statement used to measure the fear of political persecution was: "I would not criticize the government and/or leaders because I might get some potential political trouble due to my criticism."

the fear and respondents' scores for the items in the diffuse support index. To test this proposition, I examine these correlations.

Overall, the correlations between the fear of potential political persecution and all six items in the diffuse support index were very weak (though positive), ranging from a low of .04 for item 6 in 1997 to a high of .096 for item 1 in 1995 (table 2.4). These results indicate that the respondents' fear of potential political persecution as a variable could explain only less than 1 percent of the variance of each item within the diffuse support index. Furthermore, only one of these correlations, which is between the level of fear

Table 2.4

Correlations between Fear of Political Persecution and Responses to Diffuse Support Index, 1995, 1997, and 1999

	Fear of Political Persecution		
	1995	1997	1999
1. I am proud to live under the current political system.	.096*	.071	.080
2. I have an obligation to support the current political system.	.052	.069	.058
3. I respect the political institutions in China today.	.048	.051	.046
4. I feel that the basic rights of citizens are protected.	.073	.032	.068
5. I believe that the courts in China guarantee fair trials.	.049	.046	.047
6. I feel that my personal values are the same as those advocated by the government.	.047	.040	.041

Note: All entries are the Pearson correlations (r). * $P < .05$.

and item 1 in 1995, was significant. All in all, the magnitude of the effect of the fear was too small to undermine the validity of the items within the diffuse support index in all three surveys. These results of the insignificant impact on responses to regime-related questions also coincide with those from Shi's (2000, 405–7) nationwide survey study on "political trust" (which is closely related to the concept of diffuse support in this study), conducted between 1993 and 1994 in China. Based on the above-mentioned empirical evidence, therefore, one may conclude that the fear of potential political persecution in general did not assert any consequential impact on the re-spondents' assessments of the component items within the diffuse support index in our three surveys.

How Much Specific Support Is There in Beijing?

As distinct from diffuse support, specific support refers to a person's satis-faction with specific government policies and performance. It is mainly through citizens' perceptions and evaluations of the actual policy outputs of the government that citizens are linked to political authorities. This is espe-cially the case in such a nondemocratic country as China, since there is no popular, meaningful election for the national leaders in that country, which could serve as another important connection between the authorities and the citizens. Therefore, to study people's evaluations of government policies is to examine their support for the incumbent political authority.

Sociopolitical Context and Conventional Views

How has the post–Mao, reformist leadership performed in various public policy areas? How effective have its policies been in meeting the needs of the population and addressing urgent socioeconomic problems? Most China analysts agree that the reformist leadership should be credited with the sustained high growth rates of the national economy and the improvement of living standards for a majority of the population in the reform era (Lieberthal 1995, chapter 5; Dreyer 2000, 145–61; Dernberger 1999; Tang and Parish 2000). "Although the reforms followed a sometimes tortuous course, the outcome was remarkably successful in some key areas," notes Lieberthal (1995, 125). To support this assessment, for example, these an-alysts often point out that, since the early 1980s, the average annual growth rate of China's GDP has been as high as about 10 percent, and the per capita disposable income has been tripled (adjusted for inflation).[7]

Nonetheless, many China analysts have also pointed out various socio-economic and sociopolitical problems during the reform, with which the incumbent political authority has tried to grapple through their public policies. Although these analysts disagree on how effectively the problems have been coped with, they all recognize the severities and sociopolitical consequences of these problems—especially those directly touching people's daily lives. As mentioned in chapter 1, these problems include official corruption, inflation, job security, medical care, inequality, the environment, welfare for the needy, and so on. I will describe the sociopolitical background of each of these issues and summarize analysts' views on government policies in each area.

Corruption

Recognizing that official corruption has threatened the very existence of the Party and the state, the central government has taken several policy measures to fight corruption. For example, in the mid 1980s, the government issued two documents to ban Party and state organizations from engaging in profit making "businesses." In addition, according to these documents, Party and government cadres and their family members were not allowed on the payroll of any business firm (ZGFLNJ 1993, 290–2). Again, in 1993, reiterating and emphasizing some of the regulations issued during the late 1980s, the Party's Central Committee and the State Council jointly issued another document to ban Party and government cadres at and above the county level from running businesses, buying and selling stocks, accepting gifts, or using public funds for club membership (ZGFLNJ 1994, 574). Furthermore, since Jiang Zemin succeeded Deng Xiaoping as the leader of both the Party and the state in 1997, Jiang has repeatedly called for anticorruption campaigns at such important events as national Party congresses.

How effective were their regulations and campaigns to fight official corruption? While it is very difficult to measure objectively the extent of corruption, available official statistics (which could give us only a part of the picture of official corruption) indicate that the number of official corruption

7. See also *China Statistical Yearbooks* published by the State Statistical Bureau of the People's Republic of China (1991–2000).

cases has increased rapidly since the reform. While from 1982 to 1988 about 2,600 cases of corruption were reported each year by the public to the prosecutors at the national level for investigation, from 1989 to 1999 the number of such cases each year increased up to 17,400 (Liao 2000). It has been widely known that such official statistics show only a small part of the overall magnitude of official corruption. Nonetheless, they do suggest a soaring trend of official corruption despite the central authority's anticorruption regulations and campaigns since the early 1980s. Thus, many earlier studies have argued that the incumbent authority's anticorruption measures have not been effective, and ordinary citizens' complaints about official corruptions at various levels have increased since the mid 1980s (e.g., Gong 1997; Manion 1998; Tang and Parish 2000, 178–82).

Inflation

Before the post–Mao reform, the term "inflation" was used in the PRC as an abstract yet negative concept to describe an economic problem in the so-called old society under the Nationalist government (before 1949). This is because in the Mao era before the reform, prices for most consumer goods had remained very stable, if not unchanged. As Lieberthal (1995, 269–70) has observed, the top leadership of the Party in the Mao era had "viewed holding the line on inflation as necessary for maintaining social stability," and for demonstrating the "superiority" of the "new society" under the CCP. In addition, the planned economy under Mao was a structural factor that was prone to stable price.

But the post–Mao economic reform aimed at establishing a "socialist market economy" entailed lifting price controls, and thus created a structural condition for inflation. Moreover, in the reform era, the central government often called for high growth rates, which were often fueled by government investment and spending, and no longer imposed strict control over the money supply, an excess of which could cause inflation (Wong 1994, 50). In short, the post–Mao reform created an inflationary environment. China has experienced a roller-coaster pattern of inflation since the beginning of reform in 1978, with two peaks in the late 1980s and the mid 1990s.

How effective has the incumbent authority's policy been in dealing with inflation? Some scholars suggest that the central authority has not been very successful, because it has been constrained by some structural factors such as a "semireformed economic system" (Lieberthal 1995, 272) and the lack of the macroeconomic institutions required to manage a market economy.[8] Other analysts believe that the central authority has done reasonably well in dealing with such a macroeconomic problem as inflation, especially in the late 1990s (Naughton 1996; Bottelier 2000). For example, one analyst of China's economy argues that:

> The high inflation (economic overheating due to excess investment in real estate and many industries) of 1992/93/94 was successfully overcome with a macro-stabilization program that started mid-1993. As part of this process, China shifted the emphasis in economic control from direct administrative intervention to reliance on indirect instruments of macroeconomic management. A "soft landing" was accomplished in 1996 after wrenching domestic policy adjustments and power shifts. Inflation has dropped out of sight since the middle of 1997. . . . The successful macro-stabilization program has contributed significantly to China's current stability, and external economic strength. If China had not made the difficult internal policy and institutional adjustments that permitted a "soft landing" in 1996, the Asian financial crisis would probably have dragged the economy down in a much more serious way (Bottelier 2000, 67).

In terms of ordinary people's assessment of the central authority's policies dealing with inflation, some earlier empirical studies indicated that most citizens were not satisfied with government performance in this area, especially in the late 1980s (Tang and Parish 2000, 108) and the mid 1990s (Zhong, Chen, and Sheb 1998) when inflation went up.

Job Security

One of the most salient "superiorities" of the socialist system under Mao was job security for all in the urban areas. This superiority, known as the "iron rice bowl" employment system, provided work for all with lifelong tenure and remained until the end of the 1980s. By the early 1990s, however, unemployment (or *xiagang,* the term coined by the government) began to increase.[9] Financial and efficiency problems of state-owned enterprises (SOEs) have been major sources of the increasing unemployment rate.

---

8. For a brief summary of this view, see Naughton (1996, 122–3).

9. For a summary of the transition from the "iron rice bowl" system to current contractual employment, see Solinger (1999, 635–7).

Under economic reform, SOEs have been gradually separated from direct control by the government, and governments at all levels have moved away from direct financial responsibility for performance of the SOEs or for labor insurance for SOE workers. In addition, SOEs now face market competition, in accordance with the central authority's call for the establishment of a market economy. Most SOEs, however, are unprepared for such competition due to their awkward management systems, obsolete technology and facilities, and, in most cases, uncompetitive products. In face of the increasingly severe competition in the market, many of these enterprises have had either to lay off a large number of their employees in order to improve their productivity or to close down. As a result, troubled SOEs have produced a large part of the unemployment army in China, especially in urban areas.

The Institute of Economics of the Chinese Academy of Social Sciences estimated that by the late 1990s, the overall unemployment rate had reached about 7 percent in the urban labor force, which was the highest rate since 1949.[10] In some large cities with more SOEs in heavy and military industries, the rate was close to 20 percent (Bottelier 2000, 71). Even many of those who are currently employed in SOEs were "quasi-unemployed—that is, still on the books, but receiving only partial wages or none at all—or semi-employed (working only intermittently)" (UNDP 1999, 65). Due to this cruel reality, most urban dwellers, even those who currently have jobs, have become increasingly worried about their job security or employment opportunities. One of the government-controlled media admits that there is a widespread "job security panic" within the urban population (Chan and Senser 1997, 111). Sometimes this panic sent tens of thousands of workers into mass demonstrations in the streets in several major cities (e.g. Chan and Senser 1997; Bottelier 2000).

How did the central authority deal with this job security panic and its root, the high unemployment rate associated with SOEs? On the one hand, since the early 1990s, the authority had tried to reform SOEs in order to revitalize these enterprises. In 1997, the Fifteenth National Congress of the

---

10. According to the State Statistical Bureau, the average unemployment rate was about 3 percent in 1995 and 1999 (State Statistical Bureau 2000, 115). This figure is considered by many China observers to be a gross underestimate. Even the figure reported by the Institute of Economics could substantially underestimate the real magnitude of unemployment in China, since there is a large, yet unknown number of unemployed migrant workers who do not have a valid urban residence permit needed for unemployment status.

CCP specified policy measures and goals for the transformation of SOEs, moving the transformation into a new phase. The Congress adopted the "control the big, while releasing the small" (*zhua da fang xiao*) strategy to reform SOEs (Jiang 1997). The strategy was intended to establish highly competitive large-enterprise groups with transregional, intertrade, cross-ownership, and transnational operations. The strategy called for relaxing control over small SOEs and strengthening them through reorganization, association, merging, leasing, contract operation, shareholding partnerships, or sell-offs. This strategy was designed to invigorate SOEs by building up their capacities and competitiveness, and hence to alleviate unemployment in SOEs. But some China analysts believe that the strategy was too optimistic and unrealistic (Tian and Liang 1999; Dernberger 1999; Baum 2000). Some analysts suggest that the policy could not be sustained due to lack of financial resources and structural bases (e.g., mature labor market) (Tian and Liang 1999, 87–8). Therefore, they do not believe that this strategy was effective in addressing the problem of "job security panic" among the urban residents, especially those in the SOEs.

Welfare for the Needy

Closely related to the problem of unemployment in SOEs, the issue of welfare for the needy has become increasingly crucial for political stability. In the urban areas, the unemployed constitute the major portion of the poor (UNDP 1999, 91). From 1988 to 1995, the number of urban residents in poverty rose from 23.5 million to 28.1 million, an increase of 20 percent (Khan and Riskin 2001, 73)! Some incidents of social unrests resulted from discontent among the poor and the urban unemployed (Chan and Senser 1997).

The government tried to address the socioeconomic needs of those who were laid off from the SOEs in order to prevent political unrest. Then-Party leader, Jiang Zemin, pledged that "the Party and the government will . . . show concern for laid-off workers, help them with their welfare, organize job training, and open up new avenues of employment" (Jiang 1997). In general, the incumbent authority promoted the establishment of non-SOE based social safety nets at the national and regional levels through unemployment assistance, health insurance, direct subsidies, temporary public work schemes, job retraining programs, and labor market information and placement services. It was hoped that these policy measures could help the poor cope with stresses from unemployment and to be reemployed eventually.

But so far, according to some China observers, while there were some suc-
cesses, the overall results of these policies have not been very impressive
(Schoenhals 1999, 601–2; Dreyer 2000, 159–60). For example, some analysts pointed out that there were still a large number of the unemployed who
were below the poverty line and had not received any of the financial assistance and unemployment services promised by the central authority (Tian
and Liang 1999). Thus, these analysts believed that there was still a great
potential for unrest by the unemployed in urban areas.

Medical Care

Before the post–Mao reform, most urban residents were employed by SOEs
or government units, which provided them with social welfare services including virtually free medical care. The entire old social welfare system in
general as well as medical care in particular, however, has encountered great
financial and social challenges during the reform era. The challenges for
medical care in urban China have come mainly from three sources. First,
the cost of medical care has grown rapidly due to the aging population and
the rising cost of medicine. As a result, for instance, total medical expendi-
tures increased by 706 percent from 1978 to 1992 for SOE/government employees (UNDP 1999, 69).

Second, while the costs of medical care have rapidly increased, the financial resources of SOEs and government units to cover the costs have
decreased. Since the beginning of the post–Mao economic reform, governments at all levels have gradually moved away from direct financial responsibility for SOE employees' welfare, including medical care. Now,
SOEs must use their own profits to cover a large portion of employees'
medical costs. Thus, how much payment for the costs of medical care employees can receive depends mainly on how competitive and profitable each
SOE is. Since most SOEs have been neither competitive nor profit making,
they usually do not have enough funds to pay for employees' medical care
(Croll 1999, 688). Thus, "many state and collective units have experienced
a payment crisis for health care" (UNDP 1999, 69). Many employees have
received only partial payment for medical costs, and many others have not
received any payment for a long time (Croll 1999, 688).

Third, even if some SOEs and government units manage to cover their
employees' medical-care payments, an increasing proportion of the urban
population no longer belongs to these enterprises and units. In Beijing, for
example, the percentage working in SOEs and government units declined

from 74 percent in 1997 (when our second survey was conducted) (Beijing Municipal Statistical Bureau 1998, 97) to 64 percent in 1999 (when our last survey was completed) (State Statistical Bureau 2000, 118–9). These figures indicate a current trend of more and more urban dwellers shifting their employment from SOEs and government units, which are together referred to as "state units," to nonstate units—such as collectively owned, joint-venture, private, and foreign enterprises—and even becoming self-employed. Conceivably, this trend has been mainly caused by the financial difficulties of SOEs and new opportunities in the reformed economic system. However, the trend, as Croll (1999, 687) points out, also "has led to an increasing number of urban residents . . . who are now excluded, partially or completely, from the previous unit-based [i.e. state-unit-based] welfare system and for whom there are no alternative forms of social security" that includes medical care. This increasingly large group has faced even more uncertainty in their medical care, since government regulations governing provision of medical care are far from complete and not adequately enforced.

By the late 1990s, the central authority had tried to promote a so-called cost sharing scheme to deal with these challenges. Under this plan, the state, employees, and employers would share the costs of medical care (UNDP 1999, 68). Meanwhile, the authority called on the governments at provincial and local levels to explore their own resources and methods to deal with the difficulties and challenges in medical care. In response, some provinces and cities have introduced risk pooling funds for serious diseases and social risk pooling funds for retirees, and several pilot studies from individual cities have been widely popularized in the effort to find a new financial basis for providing medical care.

To assess the incumbent authority's responses to the challenges in the medical care system, some scholars point out that the central government has not yet developed a coherent and consistent nationwide strategy (White and Shang 1996; Croll 1999). Therefore implementation of any plan has been at the mercy of the political will of local governments and the financial resources of individual enterprises. Consequently results have been uneven: some urban residents have adequate medical care, some do not have any at all, and perhaps most stand in the middle (Li 1997, 72).

Inequality

In general, the issue of equality or inequality may have critical economic as well as political implications for sociopolitical development in any type of society. Nonetheless, the issue has been even more politicized in China because the population was indoctrinated with "the virtue of egalitarianism" under Mao for almost four decades and traditionally believed in it (Riskin 1987, chapter 10; Tang and Parish 2000). The results from our three surveys indicate that most people in China also believe that the government has the responsibility to narrow the gap between rich and poor.[11] In the Mao era, while the actual socioeconomic inequality between the political elite and the masses presumably existed, inequality within the masses was relatively minimal (Khan and Riskin 2001).

But in the reform era, the top leadership of the CCP abandoned the Maoist virtue of egalitarianism, and advocated the new Party lines of "to get rich is glorious" and "allow a portion of the population to get rich first" (Deng 1993, 23). As economic reform has been carried out under these new Party lines and a market economy has gradually prevailed, the economic and social inequalities have become widespread throughout society rather than limited to the gap between the political elite and the masses. Among all kinds of socioeconomic inequalities, income inequality has been the most visible and contentious among the people since the beginning of re-form. Using the Gini coefficient[12] as a measure of inequality, the World Bank reports the overall trend of income inequality in China in the reform era (UNDP 1999, 54). According to this report, in the early reform years (the late 1970s and the early 1980s), inequality changed little. But, in the second half of the 1980s, income inequality rose sharply—the Gini co-efficient increasing from 0.30 in 1984 to 0.35 in 1989, while average personal income grew little. In the first half of the 1990s, while average personal incomes have grown fast, income inequality continued to increase rapidly—the Gini coefficient reaching 0.42 in 1995. Using a comprehensive measurement, a group of international social scientists estimates the level of income inequality based on the data collected from two nationwide sur-veys conducted in the late 1980s and the mid 1990s (Khan and Riskin 1998; Khan and Riskin 2001). Their estimate indicates somewhat greater income inequality: the Gini coefficientgrew from 0.38 in 1988 to 0.45 in 1995. Based

11. The results from the three surveys show that over 90 percent of respondents in all three surveys considered the government to be "responsible for narrowing the gap between rich and poor."

12. The Gini coefficient, used by development economists, is a common measure of inequality. It ranges in value from "0" indicating perfect equality to "1" referring to absolute inequality.

on a more straightforward indicator, the income ratio between the rich and the poor, some Chinese economists has also identified the drastic widening of income inequality:

> In 1990, the average income of the top 20 percent of households was only 4.2 times higher than that of the bottom 20 percent. By 1998, the ratio had jumped to 9.6 times. . . . The richest 10 percent of households were the biggest winners in the recent reforms. Their share of the total income increased from 23.6 percent in 1990 to 38.4 percent in 1998. On the other hand, the bottoms 20 percent of households were losers big time: their share of the total income declined from 9 percent in 1990 to 5.5 percent in 1998.[13]

According to a World Bank report, by the mid 1990s the magnitude of income inequality in China had already exceeded the levels of income inequalities in most East and West European countries as well as those in other Asian developing countries, such as India, Pakistan, and Indonesia (World Bank 1998). In short, in the reform era, as Khan and Riskin (2001, 121) observe, "China's income distribution has undergone a qualitative transformation from being one of the most equal among the developing Asian countries to being one of the more unequal."

As mentioned above, the post–Mao leaderships, from Deng Xiaoping to Jiang Zemin, have abandoned egalitarianism as one of the ideological and policy obstacles to economic efficiency. To a large extent, they have deemed inequality, particularly income inequality (or "differentiation" in their term), as a desirable outcome of the reform program. Consequently, the central authority has not been systematically concerned over such populationwide income inequality per se, and it has never had a consistent policy to deal with this kind of inequality (Khan and Riskin 2001, 121).[14] Some analysts have pointed out that more and more people in China have become discontented with the lack of government policy to minimize the gap between the rich and poor, and such discontent is a potential source of political instability in China (Wu 1999, 26–27; Li 1997).

---

13. This passage comes from Shaoguang Wang (2000, 385), which summarizes the findings of Chinese economists, Xu Xinxin and Li Peilin (1999).

14. Nonetheless, the central authority has begun to address the problems of the increasing income gap between the relatively advanced coastal provinces and the more backward central and western ones, and of absolute poverty in rural areas (UNDP 1999, 45–62; Gustafsson and Zhong 2000; Khan and Riskin 2001).

The Environment

Since the post–Mao reform, environmental conditions in both urban and rural areas have seriously deteriorated (UNDP 1999, 73–84; Edmonds 1999, 644–7). Briefly, the environmental deterioration has been mainly caused by such systemic factors as "a large population, rapid economic growth, industrial structure geared to heavy industry, and limited natural resources" (Lieberthal 1995, 276). Among various forms of the environmental deterioration, air and water pollution most directly and commonly affects the life of the urban population and hence is most relevant to this study.

The magnitude of air pollution in China has been ranked very high on a world scale. According to the World Health Organization (WHO), 60 to 90 micrograms per cubic meter of suspended particulate matter are an acceptable range of air quality. In the 1980s, however, the average total of suspended particulate matter was 520 and 318 in north and south China, respectively (World Bank 1991). And by 1999, China had 9 of the 10 most air-polluted cities in the world (Edmonds 1999, 644).[15] These nine Chinese cities had 700 or nearly 700 micrograms per cubic meter of suspended particulate matter in the air (Reuters 1999). According to a report in 1994 (Biers 1994), in Beijing, our survey site, the figure was never below 220 micrograms, which was far above the WHO acceptable standard. In addition, acid rain has affected about 40 percent of China's territory, especially major cities (Vermeer 1998, 977). The major sources of the air pollution in China have been industrial sulphur dioxide emissions, which mainly come from the heavy consumption of coal as energy. The level of such emissions was doubled between 1982 and 1997 (Edmonds 1999, 644).

As for water pollution, according to a report in China's official media, most of China's rivers as well as its underground water has been contaminated (Li 1999). In cities, for example, 78 percent of the urban river sections are unfit for use as drinking water sources, while over 50 percent of the urban underground water is heavily polluted (Vermeer 1998, 970). About 60 percent of all Chinese drinking water has a higher fecal coliform count than the WHO drinking water standard (Qu and Li 1990). The main pollutants

---

15. In 1999, the ten cities were listed in order of total suspended particulate, as follows: Lanzhou, Jilinshi, Taiyuan, Jiaozuo, Rajkot (India), Wan Xian, Urumqi, Yichang, Hanzhong, and Anyang (Edmonds 1999. 644).

are from wastewater discharges from industrial enterprises and fast growing populations in both rural and urban areas. These alarming levels of water
pollution have been further exacerbated by the general shortage of water
all over the country. More than 300 cities in China lack sufficient water. For
instance, the level of underground water in Beijing fell from 5 meters below the surface in 1950 to 50 meters in 1994 (UNDP 1999, 75). Due to the
shortage of water in general, many people in both rural and urban areas are
forced to use water below the conventional health standards for their daily
needs.

Air and water pollution has caused real health problems within the population. While there is hardly any nationwide, scientific data available to
establish the link between sickness and deaths and air pollution, some sophisticated regional studies have proved such links in certain locales. For
example, a study conducted in Beijing linked higher particulate concen-
trations in the air with increased mortality from pulmonary heart disease.
Another study in Shanghai showed that the incidence of lung cancer was
highest in industrial parts where air pollution was the most severe in the city
(Johnson, Liu, and Newfarmer 1997). Some studies indicated dangerous
levels of lead poisoning among children in many cities, which were caused
in large part by air pollution from leaded gasoline, industrial emissions, and
coal combustion (Shen et al. 1996). In terms of the effect of water pollution
on health, the number of cases of waterborne diseases has increased. For
example, by 1996, the number of cases of such diseases as dysentery and
diarrhea in China either remained the same or increased (Chen 1997, 67).
Some analysts believe that these diseases were caused by water pollution
(Banister 1998, 996).

Facing such mounting environmental problems, the post–Mao leadership
has taken some actions in two major areas. First, it has attempted to strengthen
the organizational apparatus in environmental protection. In 1984, the
central authority raised the status of the Office of Environmental Protection
to commission-level within the State Council. In 1998, the central authority
upgraded the bureau to the ministerial level, the State Environment Protection Administration (SEPA), which is charged with coordinating environmental protection policies among and between central and local government
units. In addition, the SEPA is replicated as Environmental Protection Bu-
reaus (EPBs) down through the county level, which are responsible for implementing policies made by the SEPA (Jahiel 1998). Second, the central
authority has enacted a body of environment protection laws. For example,

the latest law, Environmental Protection Law of 1998, is considered the most comprehensive legislation to protect the environment and combat various pollutants (James C. F. Wang 2002, 187).

Some China analysts believe that the post–Mao leadership's initial steps to remedy environmental problems have been held back by administrative deadlocks and a higher priority for economic growth. Some researchers have suggested that due to the inferior bureaucratic status of the SEPA and its local agencies at all levels, they have found it difficult to obtain active support and cooperation from other bureaucratic authorities in charge of economic development to tackle environmental problems. (Edmonds 1994, 255–6; Smil 1993; Sinkule and Ortolano 1995; Jahiel 1997, 1998). Strong and influential government agencies such as planning commissions (*jiwei*), economic commissions (*jingwei*), construction commissions (*jianwei*), and industrial and commercial authorities are known to be reluctant to endorse and enforce stringent environmental measures for fear that they might slow down economic growth. "With a strong pro-growth orientation, both central and local governments have usually sided with these economic agencies and have subordinated environmental protection to economic interests when the two have been in conflict" (Lo and Leung 2000, 677). Thus, enforcement of environmental regulations in China has been often compromised by the priority of economic development.

In sum, all the issue areas described above are critical to the sociopolitical life of ordinary people, especially urban residents, in contemporary China. In general, the incumbent political leaders have from time to time made various policies to cope with problems in these issue areas. And these policies have been variably evaluated by many China analysts. But how did our respondents assess the incumbent authority's policies in these issue areas? This question is answered in the section that follows.

The Empirical Results from the Three Beijing Surveys

Table 2.5 presents the distributions of the items in the specific support index for the three surveys. At least two important findings stand out from these distributions. A first finding is that, in general, our respondents gave mediocre "grades" for the incumbent authority's policies in most of the nine issue areas in each of the three years. Specifically, the mean scores for seven issue areas (corruption, job security, inequality, housing, medical care, social order, and pollution) were below the "so so" level (or point 3), while only in two areas (inflation and welfare for the needy) were mean scores at

Table 2.5

Distribution of Specific Support, 1995, 1997, and 1999

	Mean Score			Standard Deviation		
	1995	1997	1999	1995	1997	1999
1. Controlling inflation (1–5)[a]	2.6	3.2	3.6	.93	1.0	.90
2. Providing job security (1–5)[a]	2.8	2.6	2.3	.83	.95	.91
3. Minimizing inequality (1–5)[a]	2.4	2.3	2.2	.98	.97	.96
4. Improving housing (1–5)[a]	2.8	2.6	2.4	.96	1.0	1.1
5. Maintaining order (1–5)[a]	2.7	2.8	2.4	1.1	1.0	1.1
6. Providing medical care (1–5)[a]	2.5	2.7	2.6	.94	.96	.93
7. Providing welfare for the needy (1–5)[a]	3.0	3.0	2.9	.92	1.0	1.0
8. Combating pollution (1–5)[a]	2.7	2.6	2.3	1.1	1.1	1.0
9. Fighting corruption (1–5)[a]	2.2	2.3	2.0	.98	1.1	.98
Entire index (9–45)[b]	23.7	24.5	22.8	7.0	6.4	6.8

Note: The supplemental information about the distribution of specific support in the three surveys is presented in appendix B.

[a] For each of the items in this index, respondents were asked to grade government-policy performance based on the grading scheme commonly used in China's schools: on a 1-5 scale, where 1 = very poor, 2 = poor, 3 = so-so, 4 = good, and 5 = very good.

[b] The nine items above were then combined to form an additive index, ranging from 9 (indicating very poor policy performance) to 45 (indicating excellent policy performance).

or above that point for some years. This general finding is further confirmed by the results of the mean scores of the entire specific support index in the three surveys. All these mean scores are substantially below the midpoint (27) of the index scale (from a minimum of 9 to a maximum of 45): from a low of 22.8 in 1999 to a high of only 24.5 in 1997.

A second important finding from the distributions of the items in the specific support index is that respondents' evaluations of the incumbent policies in the issue areas studied here were far from uniform. The mean scores for some issue areas presented in table 2.5 were distinctly higher or lower than those for the rest of issue areas. At the high end, the average mean scores for two issue areas, inflation and welfare for the needy, in the three surveys were above 3. At the low end, the average mean scores for the other two issue areas, inequality and corruption, in the three surveys were only about 2.2. These findings suggest that, while the incumbent authority fared relatively well in dealing with inflation and welfare, it failed in narrowing the rich-poor gap and fighting official corruption. Interestingly, these findings coincide with those from an opinion survey of intellectuals and cadres, which was conducted jointly by the Secretariat and the Policy Research Office of the CCP Central Committee in 2001.[16]

As for the two issue areas at the high end, while the mean scores for the inflation area had gradually yet steadily increased from 2.6 in 1995 to 3.6 in 1999, the mean scores for the area of welfare for the needy remained about 3 in all three years. This difference suggests that although the incumbent authority's policies in these two issue areas earned higher evaluations on the average in the three years of our surveys, such evaluations were earned in the two areas in different ways. While the incumbent authority earned the higher evaluations gradually for "controlling inflation," it was perceived to have better performed consistently in "providing welfare for the needy." The findings about the area of inflation control apparently correspond to those from earlier studies mentioned above, and to the overall trend of inflation in the 1990s. People did complain about high inflation in the mid 1990s (Zhong, Chen, and Sheb 1999), but they felt quite relieved in the late 1990s when the central government's so-called soft-landing economic strategy (Bottelier 2000, 67) finally resulted in much lower and even negative inflation rates. But the findings for the area of welfare for the needy contradict some earlier observations. A possible reason for such discrepancy could be that most of our respondents did not have personal experience with government policies dealing with the needy and learned of such policies only from the official media, which constantly gave positive news about government policies.

In terms of the two issue areas at the low end, government policies dealing with both social inequality and official corruption earned the lowest scores. This evidence confirms the above-mentioned arguments from earlier studies that these two areas have been considered to be the most troublesome and persistent socioeconomic problems faced by the post–Mao leaderships since the late 1980s (Lieberthal 1995, 269–73; Chen and Deng 1995, 113–8; Wu 1999, 26–7; Li 1997). This finding also coincides with the result of an early opinion survey conducted in Beijing in 1994, in which most respondents ranked corruption and the gap between the rich and poor as China's worst problems in need of immediately governmental solution (Yu and Liu, 1994, 85–7).

16. This Party-sponsored survey was designed to provide the top Party leaders with information about public opinions, which was considered to serve as reference for policy making. While the results of the survey had been originally kept a secret from the public, they were somehow leaked during the Shanghai APEC Conference in September 2001. For more details of this survey, see CND (2001).

In short, the dominant results from our surveys echo the tenet of the earlier observations by other China analysts that people were discontented with the incumbent policies in most issue areas analyzed in this study. Based on these results, therefore, one can conclude that the level of specific support for the incumbent political authority was low among our respondents.

Summary and Conclusion

This chapter seeks to answer two important questions: How much popular support does the current communist regime enjoy? Which kind (or dimension) of political support does the regime rely on more? To answer these two questions, this chapter has accomplished several tasks.

First, I have established the measurement of both dimensions of political support: diffuse and specific support. The measurement consists of two multi-item, additive indexes for the two dimensions. The validity and reliability of each of the two indexes (i.e., the diffuse and specific support indexes) have been proved by the findings from earlier field observations and the empirical results from the analysis of the data collected in our three surveys. Both indexes not only have been used as indicators in this chapter to detect the extent of the two dimensions of popular political support in Beijing, but will serve as dependent variables in the analysis of the correlations between the two dimensions and various socioeconomic and sociopolitical factors in the chapters that follow.

Second, using the diffuse support index, I have examined the magnitude of diffuse support among our respondents. The results indicated that our respondents had quite strong diffuse support for the political regime in China: the mean scores of the diffuse support index in all three surveys were well above the midpoint of the index scale. More important, the respondents registered even stronger support for the items in the index, which are more closely related to the national government. The results from the initial analysis demonstrated that the respondents' strong nationalism and a preference for stability resulted in their stronger support for these items concerning the national government.

Third, utilizing the specific support index, I have also gauged the extent of specific support among respondents. In contrast to the level of diffuse support, the overall level of specific support was low among the respondents: the mean score of the specific support index remained well below the midpoint of the index scale in each of the three surveys. While the dominant picture of specific support in the Beijing surveys looked gloomy for the incumbent authority, the picture was not monochromatic: there were some variations among the items within the specific support index. Within the index, both the items about inflation control and welfare for the needy earned the highest average scores, while those about inequality and corruption had the lowest average scores. Except for the variation for the item about welfare for the needy, all these variations seemed to confirm the arguments and findings from the earlier studies of government policies in those issue areas.

From these findings about the levels of both diffuse and specific support, at least two important conclusions can be drawn. One is that the current political regime in China is still considered legitimate by respondents, because the respondents registered a high level of diffuse support. As mentioned above, this conclusion, based on the empirical findings from the three surveys, contradicts the dominant view among China observers that the regime has lost its legitimacy.

The other conclusion from the findings presented above is that the survival of the current political system in China apparently relies more on diffuse support than on specific support, since the level of diffuse support was much higher than that of specific support among respondents.[17] In other words, most people have so far considered the government as legitimate, even though they have been discontented with the policies made by the incumbent authority in most issue areas. These findings also seem to contradict those from some earlier studies that, because the current regime has lost its legitimacy with the population, it has survived based mainly on its policy performance in socioeconomic areas and coercive political control (Lieberthal 1995, 147; Chen and Deng 1995; Schoenhals 1999, 599; Wu 1999; Teiwes 2000). Why is there such a discrepancy? As mentioned in chapter 1, while specific support fluctuates abruptly, diffuse support tends to be relatively stable. Since our surveys covered only four years, the low level of specific support found in the surveys could be a temporary phenomenon. Therefore, if our surveys had covered a longer time period, the

17. This comparison is made based on the findings (presented earlier) that, in all three surveys, while the level of diffuse support was above the midpoint of the diffuse support index, that of specific support was below the midpoint of the specific support index.

average level of specific support over such a longer period could have been higher than the level found in this study. But in any case, only when we empirically prove the existence of such a distinction between the two dimensions of political support in their patterns of change or stability can we settle the disagreement between the arguments in the early studies and the findings in this study. The distinction in the patterns of change and stability will be examined in chapter 3.

Chapter 3

Relationship between Diffuse
and Specific Support

This chapter is devoted to an exploration of the differences and the complex relationship between diffuse support and specific support. Through the exploration of such differences and relationship, I attempt to answer several crucial theoretical and political questions. Which dimension of political support is more stable or volatile? Can the public's positive or negative evaluations of government performance (i.e., specific support) help, respectively, to build or erode their beliefs in the legitimacy of the government (i.e., diffuse support)? If they can, what can be said about the timing of the effects? The answers to these questions will help us to assess the overall trend and internal dynamics of popular support for CCP rule.

Differences between Diffuse and Specific Support

As discussed in chapter 1, there is a theoretical and conceptual distinction between diffuse and specific support. According to the theoretical hypothesis behind the distinction, diffuse support is more consequential for the stability of a political regime than specific support. Such a differentiation has been concisely summarized by Muller and Jukam (1977, 1563):

> If system affect [diffuse support] is negative among powerful or sizable segments of a polity, the threat to the stability of the prevailing regime will be great, even if affect for a particular incumbent administration [specific support] is positive; conversely, if system affect is positive among powerful or sizable segments of a polity, the threat to the stability of the

prevailing regime will be small, even if affect for a particular incumbent administration is negative.

Despite the utility of distinguishing between the two dimensions of political support, there has been little consensus within the literature on whether the distinction can be operationalized (Gibson and Caldeira 1992, 1127). Some analysts do not believe that it is possible to distinguish the two dimensions empirically, since separate indicators of them are often found to be highly correlated (Loewenberg 1971; Davidson and Parker 1972; Citrin 1974; Miller 1974a, 1974b). Others have argued that the distinction is real and has behavioral implications (Muller 1970b; Muller and Jukam 1977; Muller, Jukam, and Seligson 1982).

Given the theoretical and political importance of the distinction, I explore it empirically against the data from our three surveys. The purpose is to add to our empirical knowledge of the nature of the distinction and the sociopolitical implications in China. Following the Eastonian theoretical framework, I focus on two differences between diffuse and specific support: differences in their stability and their consistency.

Stability of the Two Dimensions of Political Support

According to the Eastonian theoretical framework, one of the most important differences between the two dimensions of political support is that diffuse support tends to be more stable than specific support (Macridis and Burg 1991, 9–10; Chen et al. 1997, 554). This is because, as mentioned in chapter 1, these two dimensions of political support are composed of two distinct sets of sociopsychological factors, which vary in stability and durability. Diffuse support is shaped mainly by prolonged sociopsychological forces, such as ongoing socializations and accumulated assessments of government performance. Once shaped, this support tends to be firm and stable (Finkel, Muller, and Seligson 1989; Gibson, Caldeira and Baird 1998). Thus, diffuse support is relatively stable and changes slowly (if it changes at all). As distinct from diffuse support, specific support is formed by spontaneous response to specific policies and performance of the incumbent authority. As Easton (1975, 439) has argued, "this kind of support varies with perceived benefits or satisfactions," and "when these decline or cease, support will do likewise." Thus, specific support is relatively volatile and changes swiftly. This theoretical proposition concerning the difference between the two dimensions of political support has been confirmed by several earlier studies of political support (Seligson and Muller 1987; Finkel, Muller, and Seligson 1989; Gibson and Caldeira 1992; Gibson, Caldeira, and Baird 1998).

But how could this proposition fare with the data from our surveys? To answer this question, I examine stability and change in diffuse and specific support separately against our data. To do so, I have taken two related, analytical steps. First, I have compared the mean score of each item in one survey with that in each of the other two surveys. Second, I have conducted T tests[1] to determine whether the differences among the three surveys for each item within diffuse and specific support indexes were significant or meaningful.

As for diffuse support, figure 3.1 demonstrates the mean scores and results from the T tests for all the items in the diffuse support index across the three years of the surveys. There are at least two salient trends one can extrapolate from figure 3.1. While the absolute mean scores for all the items within the diffuse support index had remained positive (that is, they were substantially above 2, a score referring to "disagreement" with the statement in the item), there were gradual decreases in the mean scores for all items from 1995 to 1999, except those for the item of "fair courts" that remained almost unchanged. The other important trend is that the differences in mean scores for all items between one survey and the next within a two-year span were not statistically significant (at the .05 level); differences between the first (1995) and last (1999) surveys within a roughly four-year span for some items (i.e., the items about obligation to the political system, protection of basic rights, and value congruence between the citizen and the regime) were statistically significant (at the .05 level). These two trends among the items within the diffuse support index indicate that diffuse support in Beijing in general had gradually eroded from 1995 to 1999, although, as mentioned in chapter 2, the absolute level of such support had still remained high or, at least, within the positive territory (that is, all mean scores were still away above 2).

To confirm these two trends among the individual items within the diffuse support index, I have also compared the mean scores for the entire

---

1. For statistic procedures and rationales of using T tests to compare means, see, for example, SPSS Application Guide (SPSS 1997, chapter 8).

Figure 3.1
Trends of Diffuse Support Items, 1995, 1997, and 1999

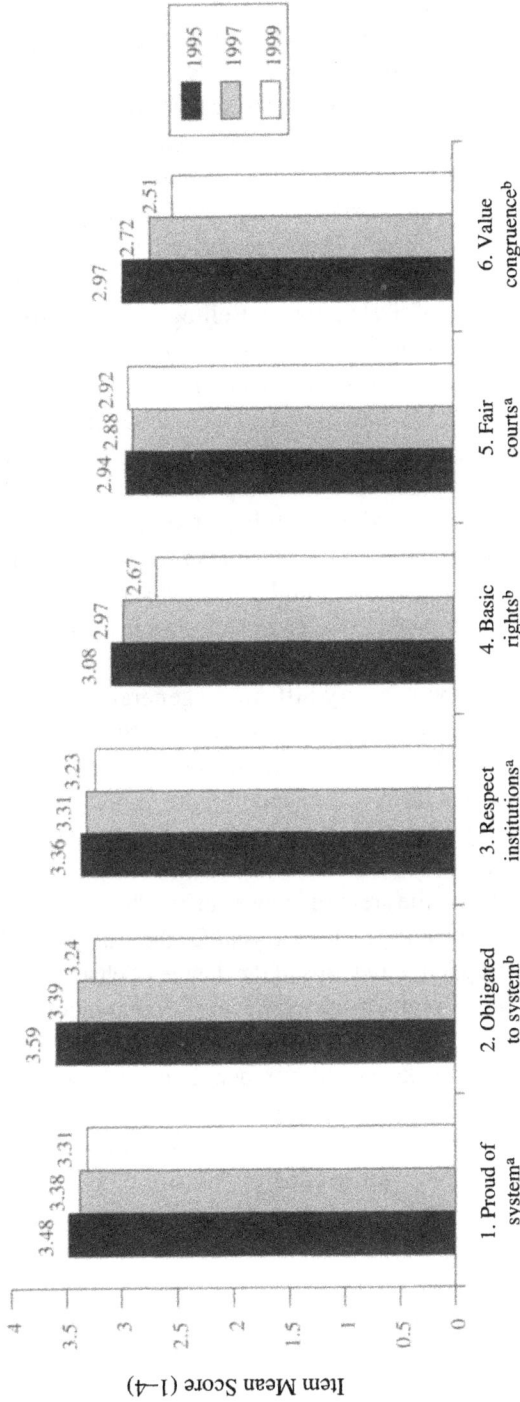

Legend:
- 1995
- 1997
- 1999

y-axis: Item Mean Score (1–4)

1. Proud of system[a]: 3.48, 3.38, 3.31
2. Obligated to system[b]: 3.59, 3.39, 3.24
3. Respect institutions[a]: 3.36, 3.31, 3.23
4. Basic rights[b]: 3.08, 2.97, 2.67
5. Fair courts[a]: 2.94, 2.88, 2.92
6. Value congruence[b]: 2.97, 2.72, 2.51

[a] The results from the T tests indicate that there were no statistically significant (at the .05 level) differences either between each survey and the next within a two-year span or between the first (in 1995) and last (1999) surveys within about a four-year span.

[b] The results from the T tests indicate that there were no statistically significant (at the .05 level) differences between each survey and the next within a two-year span, but there were statistically significant (at the .05 level) differences between the first (1995) and the last (1999) surveys within about a four-year span.

index as a whole across the three surveys.[2] Like the trends among the individual diffuse-support items, the mean scores for the index gradually declined from 1995 to 1999. Moreover, the results from the T tests indicate that the difference in mean scores between each survey and the next in a two-year span was not significant (at the .05 level), while such difference between the first (1995) and last (1999) surveys in a roughly four-year span was significant (at the .05 level). These results further confirm the two trends among the individual items within the index. Thus, one can conclude that diffuse support for the political regime in Beijing tended to be stable at least in the short term, and changes in this kind of support tended to be gradual over time. This finding supports the Eastonian theoretical proposition that diffuse support is relatively stable and changes slowly (if it changes at all).

Did specific support operate along the same patterns as seen in diffuse support? Following the same analytical steps as used for the analysis of diffuse support, I have examined the stability of specific support among our respondents. Figure 3.2 demonstrates the mean scores and results from the T tests for all the individual items in the specific support index across the three survey years. Compared to the patterns shown in figure 3.1 of the items in the diffuse support index, the predominant characteristic of figure 3.2 is irregularity or volatility: it is very difficult to generalize any trend among these items across the three survey years. Unlike the trends in the mean scores for the individual diffuse-support items that were homogeneous, the patterns of mean scores for specific support were highly heterogeneous. In terms of the direction of changes in the specific-support items from 1995, 1997, to 1999, there were at least three kinds: ascending (in the area of "inflation"), descending (in the areas of "job security," "inequality," "housing," and "pollution"), and peaking in the mid year (in the areas of "order," "medical care," and "corruption"). In terms of the degree of changes in these items across the three survey years, there were four different modes according to the results of T tests:

(1) Significant (at the .05 level) differences in mean scores between each survey and the next in a two-year span as well as between the first (1995) and last (1999) surveys in about a four-year span (in the areas of "inflation," "job security," "housing," "order," "pollution," and "corruption");

2. The mean scores for the entire index in the three surveys are shown in table 2.3.

Figure 3.2
Trends of Specific Items, 1995, 1997, and 1999

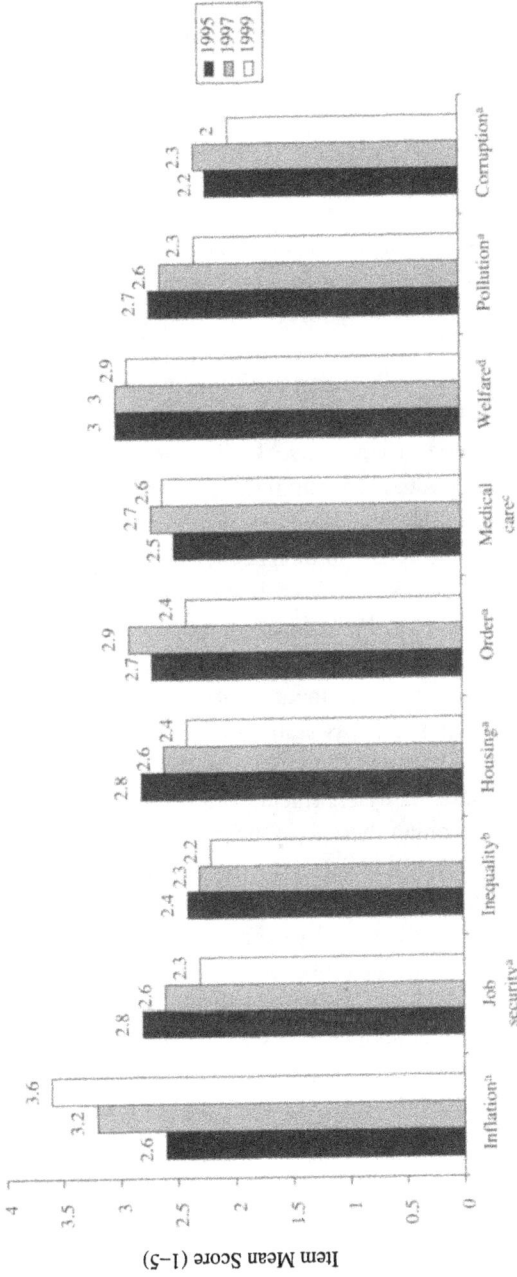

a Significant (at the .05 level) differences in mean scores between each survey and the next in a two-year span as well as between the first (1995) and last (1999) surveys in about a four-year span.

b Significant (at the .05 level) differences in mean scores only between the first (1995) and last (1999) surveys in about a four-year span, but not between each survey and the next in a two-year span.

c Significant (at the .05 level) differences in mean scores only between each survey and the next in a two-year span, but not between the first (1995) and last (1999) surveys in about a four-year span.

d No significant (at the .05 level) differences in mean scores either between each survey and the next in a two-year span or between the first (1995) and last (1999) surveys in about a four-year span.

(2) Significant (at the .05 level) differences in mean scores only between the first (1995) and last (1999) surveys in about a four-year span, but not between each survey and the next in a two-year span (in the area of "inequality");

(3) Significant (at the .05 level) differences in mean scores only between each survey and the next in a two-year span, but not between the first (1995) and last (1999) surveys in about a four-year span (in the area of "medical care");

(4) No significant (at the .05 level) differences in mean scores either between each survey and the next in a two-year span or between the first (1995) and the last (1999) surveys in about a four-year span (in the area of "welfare").

The volatility seen in figure 3.2 among the items in specific support was also mirrored in the distributions of the mean scores for the entire specific support index across the three survey years.[3] Unlike the trend of the diffuse-support index, which was gradually declining, the trend of the specific support index was abruptly fluctuating. First, the direction of changes in the specific support index was erratic. The mean score for the specific support index increased from 23.7 in 1995 to 24.5 in 1997, and then dove to the lowest level of the index, 22.8, in 1999. Second, the magnitude of changes in this index seemed to be huge in the short term. The results from the T tests indicate that the difference in mean scores between the 1997 and 1999 surveys in a two-year span was statistically significant (at the .05 level), while the difference between the 1995 and 1999 surveys in about a four-year span was not statistically significant (at the .05 level). All in all, the results confirm the Eastonian theoretical proposition that, compared to diffuse support, specific support is relatively volatile and changes swiftly.

The rationale behind the Eastonian theoretical proposition, as mentioned above, is that specific support is formed by spontaneous response to specific policies and performance of the incumbent authority, and hence it varies closely with changes in the policies and performance. Based on this rationale, one would expect that the fluctuation in specific support in our surveys should correspond with changes in the perceived policy performance of the incumbent authority. To confirm this expectation, I have examined the empirical link between respondents' evaluation of one of the most salient policy areas and the readily measurable consequence of policy performance in that

---

3. The distributions of the mean scores for the entire specific support index in the three survey years are presented in table 2.5.

policy area. The policy area in question is "inflation control." As the inflation rate declined substantially from 14.8 percent in 1995, to 0.8 percent in 1997, and −3 percent in 1999, the mean scores of respondents' evaluations of policy performance in inflation control significantly increased accordingly from 2.6 in 1995, to 3.2 in 1997, and 3.6 in 1999. These results strongly support the theory of a close relationship between the respondents' evaluation and policy performance. Therefore, it can be said that such a close relationship is the reason for the volatility of specific support.

Consistency of Diffuse Support and Specific Support

According to the Eastonian theoretical framework, another important difference between the two dimensions of political support is that diffuse support tends to be more consistent than specific support. This is due to the fact that these two dimensions of political support are shaped by two distinct sets of sociopsychological factors, and the different properties of these two sets result in the difference in the level of internal constraint or consistency between the two dimensions. Specifically, diffuse support is shaped mainly by such sociopsychological factors as ongoing socializations and accumulated assessments of government performance. All these factors are constructed through constant and systematic learning processes (for example, formal schooling) or continuous contemplation of sociopolitical reality. Thus, these factors determine a high level of internal consistency of diffuse support.

Unlike diffuse support, specific support is formed by spontaneous responses to specific policies and performance of the incumbent authority. Since these responses vary with a diverse assortment of specific policies and with ever changing results of the policies from time to time, they tend to be less systematic and more fragmented among themselves. Composed of such responses, therefore, specific support tends to be less consistent than diffuse support.

To test the theoretical proposition regarding the difference between the levels of consistency of diffuse support and specific support, I have computed the average inter-item correlation among the component items within each of the dimensions of political support for each survey.[4] The results are

---

4. The method of using average interitem correlation to detect the level of attitudinal consistency has been successfully employed in several earlier studies (Granberg and Holmberg 1988; Jennings 1992; Miller, Hesli, and Reisinger 1995; Chen 1999).

Figure 3.3

Levels of Consistency of Diffuse and Specific Support, 1995, 1997, and 1999

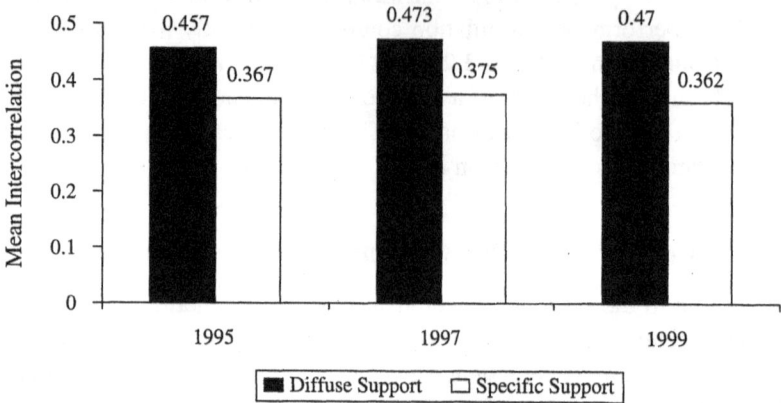

presented in figure 3.3. The empirical evidence presented in this figure indicates that the levels of consistency, measured by the mean scores of intercorrelation, for diffuse support were substantially higher than those for specific support in all three survey years. These results confirm the above-mentioned theoretical proposition that diffuse support tends to be more consistent than specific support and suggest that people construct their views on the political regime and incumbent performance quite differently.

In summary, the empirical evidence from our three Beijing surveys presented above has confirmed the two hypothesized differences between diffuse support and specific support. One is that diffuse support is more stable than specific support. Specifically, the results from our surveys suggest that, from 1995 to 1999, a steady descending trend could be seen for diffuse support among respondents, while there was an abrupt fluctuation in specific support. The other confirmed difference between the two dimensions of political support is that diffuse support tends to be more consistent than specific support. Specifically, I have found that the intercorrelation among the component items in the diffuse support index was much higher than that among the items in specific support.

These two confirmed differences in stability and consistency between two dimensions of political support may have at least two preliminary yet important implications for sociopolitical conditions in China, especially in today's urban China. First, the implication from the findings about the difference in stability is that people's support for the political regime (including its fundamental norms and values and institutions) does not necessarily coincide closely with their evaluations of the incumbent's specific policies and performance. If this can be understood to mean that there is no strong connection between government policy performance and people's support for the political system, then the incumbent authority in China could not boost its legitimacy by improving its policy performance, at least in the short term. But in China, especially urban China, how long does it take the incumbent authority to improve popular support for the political system substantially through its policy performance? Although this question cannot be answered definitively by our data for only about a four-year span, at least one possibility seems ruled out in this study. That is, within four years, the incumbent's continuous performance cannot change the level of people's support for the political regime substantially, since the results presented above demonstrate that while specific support ebbed and flowed, diffuse support changed by only 6 percent within the four years.[5]

Second, the important implication from the findings about the difference in consistency between the two dimensions of political support is that it is much more difficult for the incumbent authority in China to boost the legitimacy of the political regime than to gain some support for specific policies. This is because diffuse support or legitimacy for the regime is built upon a set of consistent values that entails not only a longer time period but a consistent ideology to cultivate. In contemporary China, however, such a consistent ideology has been wanting in the reform era. As mentioned earlier, on the one hand, the old official ideology—Marxism-Leninism-Mao Zedong Thought—has lost its appeal to the population especially since the onset of post–Mao reform. On the other hand, the current regime has failed to replace the old ideology with a new, consistent one, although it has fed the population with some pragmatic yet inconsistent principles (Rosen 1991; Link 1993; Chen 1995; Teiwes 2000). As an early study (J. Chen 1995, 28) points out,

> When the old ideology was shattered, Deng and his followers were unable to advance a new one. The functions of the old ideology were replaced with expedient slogans, such as "to get rich" by "practicing" any

---

5. Theoretically and practically, this downward trend of diffuse support may reverse with continuous improvement of specific support and enduring changes of other sociopolitical factors. But only over time can such a reversal take place.

pragmatic policies. However, when the reform brought about such hard-ship as high inflation and unemployment or did not move quickly enough to compensate people for their losses, there was no effective ideology or long-term vision to inspire the people to bear the suffering for a better future.

In short, unless the central authority can construct a set of consistent values to justify the long-term goals of the current regime and have the population believe in such values, the level of the legitimacy for the regime (or diffuse support) is likely to continue to decline.

The Relationship between the Two Dimensions of Political Support

Up to this point, the important differences in stability and consistency have been identified between diffuse and specific support, and from these differences some initial inferences have been made about the connection between the two dimensions of political support. Nonetheless, the precise relationship between diffuse and specific support has not been directly tested against our data from the three surveys.

Correlation between Diffuse and Specific Support

The above-mentioned findings about differences in stability and consistency should not lead to a conclusion that there is no relationship between diffuse and specific support. Rather, these findings can be understood to mean that, as the Eastonian theory suggests, some kind of weak relationship may exist between the two dimensions of political support. According to the Eastonian theory discussed in chapter 1, it is because of these differences that diffuse and specific support "should not bear a close relationship to one another" (Gibson and Caldeira 1992, 1127), and change in one type of support should not translate into change in the other in a one-to-one manner. Therefore, the relationship between the two dimensions of political support should not be strong.

Following these theoretical arguments, one can logically expect that those who already strongly support the regime are not likely to turn against the regime swiftly, if only for a short period of time they feel dissatisfied with some specific incumbent policies (Seligson and Muller 1987, 318–22). This is because, as mentioned above, diffuse support tends to be more stable and can be eroded only by a long term of performance deterioration.

Consequently, since the absolute levels of diffuse support for the regime among our respondents were high in all three surveys (table 2.1), I expect this weak relationship between the two dimensions of political support to take a form of corner correlation.[6] That is, high and middle levels of specific support tend to be associated with a high level of diffuse support, while a low level of specific support is a necessary but not sufficient condition for low-level diffuse support. To verify this expectation, I have run cross-tabulations between the two dimensions of political support for all three surveys.

Table 3.1 presents the results of the cross-tabulations. The overall results confirm the above-mentioned expectation of a weak relationship between diffuse and specific support. First, the results strongly support the hypothesized corner correlation between the two dimensions of political support: the dimensions are not associated in a one-to-one manner. As shown in table 3.1, in each of the three surveys, most cases are located on or above the diagonal. And only less than 30 percent of cases in the cells (boldfaced) above the diagonal: about 23 percent in 1995, and about 29 percent in 1997 and 1999.[7] As expected, in all three surveys, most of those who had a high level of specific support and around half of those who had a middle level of specific support registered a high level of diffuse support; more important, about a third of those who had a low level of specific support still retained a high level of diffuse support. This form of corner correlation between the two dimensions of political support has been also confirmed by the gamma coefficient that is almost twice as high as that of the tau_b for each of the three surveys, which is a clear indication of such a correlation.

Second, as expected earlier, the results in table 3.1 indicate that diffuse support and specific support were only weakly or moderately associated. Specifically, the values of Gamma and Tau_b for the relationship between the two dimensions of political support were not high in the three surveys.[8] Respondents' diffuse support and specific support were indeed related, albeit not strongly. Thus, it can be said that in the three surveys a relatively high level of diffuse support was weakly associated with mediocre specific support.

6. This term is adopted from the study by Seligson and Muller (1987) of the relationship between diffuse and specific support.

7. Each of these percentages is the sum of the boldfaced percentages for each year (table 3.1).

8. The Pearson correlations between the original diffuse and specific support indexes, presented in table 3.2, further confirmed the weak relationship between these dimensions of political support.

Table 3.1

Correlation between Diffuse and Specific Support, 1995, 1997, and 1999

Diffuse Support	1995 Specific Support			1997 Specific Support			1999 Specific Support		
	Low (%)	Medium (%)	High (%)	Low (%)	Medium (%)	High (%)	Low (%)	Medium (%)	High (%)
Low	11.9	**2.1**	**0.0**	18.4	**7.0**	**0.0**	16.2	**6.0**	**0.0**
Medium	54.1	42.4	**20.8**	53.3	49.1	**22.0**	50.3	47.1	**23.2**
High	34.0	55.6	79.2	28.3	43.9	78.0	33.5	46.9	76.8
Total	100	100	100	100	100	100	100	100	100
		gamma = .35* tau_b = .18*			gamma = .36* tau_b = .18*			gamma = .32* tau_b = .16*	

Note: Each of the original indexes of diffuse support and specific support is trichotomized into three categories: high, intermediate, and low levels. Percents in bold represent cases above the diagonal. * $P < .05$.

From this finding, a preliminary conclusion can be reached that citizens in Beijing considered the regime in general as legitimate, while they registered somewhat serious concerns over the government's performance in certain key policy areas. But what factors caused such a level of popular support for the current political regime, despite the mediocre evaluations of incumbent performance? This important question will be systematically addressed in chapter 4, where various sociopolitical factors are examined.

Impact of Sociodemographic Factors on the Correlation between Diffuse and Specific Support

Although I have established the existence of a weak or moderate relationship between diffuse support and specific support, an important question remains: Did this kind of relationship exist among our respondents who were from various sociodemographic categories? Or is the finding about the relationship between diffuse and specific support representative of the population across the major sociodemographic categories? If such a relationship were prevalent among people from only a certain sociodemographic group, then we would need to focus on this group when studying the interaction between diffuse and specific support. Conversely, if the relationship were equally evident across all major sociodemographic categories, we would consider this kind of relationship between the two dimensions of political support a universal one.

There is almost no study of the impact of sociodemographic attributes on the relationship between diffuse and specific support in China. Nonetheless, many early studies of political attitudes have argued that such principal sociodemographic attributes as sex, age, education, and income may significantly affect people's opinions of the political system and specific policies separately (Lock 1989; Rosen 1992; Zheng 1994; Yu and Liu 1994; Chan and Nesbitt-Larking 1995; Tang and Parish 2000). While these arguments do not deal directly with the relationship between the two dimensions of political support, it should not be too far-fetched to speculate from these arguments that such sociodemographic attributes may also affect the relationship. A potential reason for such a speculation could be that the nature of the relationship might be influenced by the components (i.e., support for the political system and evaluations of specific policies) of it, and these components may be affected by the sociodemographic factors.

To assess this speculation empirically, I have examined the correlations between the diffuse and specific support indexes in the three surveys, after

Table 3.2

The Relationship of Diffuse and Specific Support by Partial Correlation
Controlling for Sex, Age, Education, and Income, 1995, 1997, and 1999

	1995	1997	1999
(1) Correlation Coefficient (r)	.260*	.270*	.252*
(2) Partial Correlation Coefficient (r): Controlling for			
Sex	.261*	.269*	.248*
Age	.256*	.270*	.250*
Education	.262*	.271*	.254*
Income	.253*	.268*	.246*
All of the above	.250*	.273*	.251*

* $P < .05$.

controlling for the influence of respondents' sex, age, education, and income. Table 3.2 presents two kinds of correlations between diffuse and specific support: the correlations before and after controlling the sociodemographic variables. As can be seen in the table, there are virtually no substantial differences between these two kinds of correlations in all three surveys. Apparently, therefore, the key sociodemographic factors examined here exerted little meaningful influence, individually or collectively, on the relationship between the two dimensions of political support. Thus, one can conclude that the weak correlation between diffuse support and specific support, presented above, persisted across such major sociodemographic categories as age, income, education level, and sex in our samples.[9] This finding suggests that the durability of this relationship extends beyond the influence of demographic factors. In China, while sociodemographic factors may in fact influence respondents' evaluation of individual items captured in the diffuse and specific support indexes in this study and some issues identified in early studies, they do not seem to influence, in any meaningful way, the overall relationship of diffuse support and specific support.

9. This finding converges with the results from an earlier study of political support in Costa Rica and Germany (Finkel, Muller, and Seligson 1989, 345), which indicate weak impacts of similar demographic factors on the relationship between the two dimensions of political support.

Throughout this study, therefore, this weak relationship of the diffuse and specific support can be treated as a universal phenomenon across the major sociodemographic groups.

Implications of the Interaction between Diffuse and Specific Support for Political Stability

What implications could the interaction between diffuse and specific support have for political stability? This is a very important theoretical and political question. To address this question, Lipset has developed a four-fold theoretical typology (Lipset 1959, 90)[10] based on the theoretical assumption that support for the regime (diffuse support) is more powerful in influencing people's behavior and more stable than evaluation of incumbent performance (Muller and Jukam 1977). As illustrated in figure 3.4, this typology suggests four implications from four scenarios of relationship between the two dimensions of political support. First, when both diffuse support and specific support are high, political stability can be well maintained (cell *a*). Second, when both diffuse support and specific support are low, political stability will be seriously threatened and the breakdown of the political system will be imminent (cell *d*). Third, when diffuse support is high and specific support is low, the threat to the stability of the prevailing regime is small (cell *b*) at the time since diffuse still serves as a reservoir of popular support for the regime. But if this condition lasts too long, the diffuse support can be eroded by low-level specific support, and hence political stability will be seriously threatened. And fourth, when diffuse support is low and specific support is high, political stability is present yet fragile (cell *c*). For this last scenario, some analysts suggest that, although the stability of a regime is potentially threatened by the possibility of social turmoil, sustained "instrumental support [equivalent to specific support in this study] generated by positive regime performance can, with the help of ongoing socialization, be converted into affective support [equivalent to diffuse support]" (Macridis and Burg 1991, 9) and hence regime stability. This,

---

10. This typology has been also applied to other studies of political support in various social political settings (Muller and Jukam 1977; Muller and Williams 1980; Muller, Jukam, and Seligson 1982).

Figure 3.4

Implications of the Interaction between Diffuse Support and Specific Support

Specific Support

	High	Low
High (Diffuse Support)	Solid Stability (a)	Transitional Stability (b)
Low	Fragile Stability (c)	Instability (d)

according to Macridis and Burg, explains the survival of many nondemocratic regimes. This typology, with four hypothesized scenarios, suggests that diffuse support is "more consequential for the stability of a political regime" than specific support (Muller and Jukam 1977, 1563).

One of the early applications of this typology is Lipset's classic analysis of the political stability of several European countries during the Great Depression. In his analysis, Lipset (1959) argues that such societies as Germany, Austria, and Spain (which had low levels of legitimacy or diffuse support) experienced much higher rates of disruptive political protest and violence during the 1920s than did those countries presumed to have higher levels of legitimacy. The political implications of the interplay between diffuse support and specific support have also been demonstrated in several more recent empirical studies of political support in various societies (Muller and Jukam 1997; Muller, Jukam, and Seligson 1982; Burg and Berbaum 1989). These studies indicate that (1) diffuse support provides a thick emotional cushion upon which a regime can rely when its stability would otherwise be threatened by low specific support, and (2) specific support can buy stability, because it can be gradually converted into diffuse support. In summary, the theory and all the earlier empirical studies suggest

Table 3.3

Recast of the Correlation between Diffuse Support and Specific Support, 1995, 1997, and 1999

Diffuse Support	1995 Specific Support (%)		1997 Specific Support (%)		1999 Specific Support (%)	
	Not low	Low	Not low	Low	Not low	Low
Not low	70.5	25.3	65.8	28.6	63.2	30.4
Low	2.2	2.2	2.0	3.6	1.9	5.3

Note: The "not low" category in this table is the combination of the "high" and "medium" categories in table 3.1; the "low" category in this table is the same as the "low" category in table 3.1.

that both diffuse support and specific support are dynamically linked with consequences for the stability of any political regime.

To understand the implication of the interaction between diffuse support and specific support in contemporary China, we can recast the results from table 3.1 into two-by-two tables so as to relate directly to Lipset's theoretical typology illustrated in figure 3.4. Table 3.3 presents the results of such a recast. From these results, three trends emerge. A first trend is that while a majority (between 60 percent and 70 percent) of respondents in all three surveys were located in the upper-left cells (the combination of "not low" levels of both diffuse and specific support), there was a clear descending trend in the percentages in this cell from 70.5 percent in 1995 to 63.2 percent in 1999. This means that the number of people who felt somewhat positive about both the regime and the incumbent authority steadily declined over the years of our surveys.

A second important trend is that the percentages in the upper-right cells (the combination of "not low" diffuse support and "low" specific support) had steadily grown from 25.3 percent in 1995 to 30.4 percent in 1999. This indicates that although more people became less satisfied with the incumbent authority in about four years, they still remained somewhat supportive of the fundamental political system in China.

A third important trend that can be seen in table 3.3 is that the percentages in the lower-right cells (the combination of "low" diffuse support and "low" specific support) steadily increased from 2 percent in 1995 to 5.3 percent in 1999. This shows that an increasing number of people had become less supportive of both the political system and the incumbent authority over the four years, although the absolute proportion of this group in our samples was small.

In sum, the results presented in table 3.3 brought both good and bad news for the current CCP leadership. On the one hand, the good news was that a majority of the respondents (in the "not low" categories of both diffuse and specific support in table 3.3) were at least somewhat positive about both the political system and the incumbent authority. It was even better news that over a quarter of the respondents (in the "not-low" category of diffuse support and the "low" category of specific support) who were not very satisfied with the incumbent authority still at least moderately supported the political system. If we transplant these two proportions from the upper-left and upper-right cells for each survey in table 3.3 to cells *a* and *b* in figure 3.4, we may argue that, at least in the short run, political stability is likely to be maintained in China—especially in urban China—since an overwhelming majority of the respondents were in the categories of either "solid stability" or "transitional stability."

On the other hand, the bad news was that the percentage of those (in the "low" categories of both diffuse and specific support in table 3.3) who were least supportive of both the regime and the incumbent authority had constantly increased. If we transplant this percentage into cell *d* in figure 3.4, which stands for political "instability" in Lipset's typology, we may argue that the real threat to political stability had risen (though was not imminent) since the number of respondents in this cell had increased. Thus, this trend merits attention from China analysts as well as Chinese political leaders, although so far this group constituted a little over 5 percent of the respondents by 1999 (see the lower-right cell for 1999 in table 3.3).

Moreover, from the results presented in table 3.3, one can discern some interesting movements among the cells in each survey, which may further illuminate the important implications of the dynamic relationship between the diffuse and specific support for political stability in contemporary China. There were at least two important movements to which we need to pay attention. These major movements were the migrations of respondents from the upper-left cell (1) to the upper-right cell and (2) to the lower-right cell: that is, in the three surveys, while the percentages in the upper-left cell declined and those in the lower-left cell remained almost unchanged, the percentages in both upper-right and lower-right cells had grown. First, the migration from the upper-left cell to the upper-right cell suggests that in our samples, a low level of specific support did not immediately translate into a low level of diffuse support, and diffuse support eroded as specific support declined over time. However, this migration could be the first step toward the lower-right cell (which refers to the combination of both low diffuse and specific support), had the incumbent authority continued to fail to improve its policy performance over a longer period of time.

Second, therefore, the migration from the upper-left cell to the lower-right cell might have occurred through the upper-right cell in our samples. This could mean that, within the four years, some (if not many) of the respondents believed that they had already waited too long to see improvement in the incumbent performance and therefore became disappointed with the political system. In other words, the low or negative evaluations of incumbent performance could erode popular support for the political regime, while such erosion tends to be incremental. According to the Eastonian theoretical framework, however, if this trend continues, political stability will be seriously threatened, and the regime will eventually collapse (Seligson and Muller 1987; Finkel, Muller, and Seligson 1989).

Summary and Conclusion

This chapter sought to answer several critical theoretical and political questions: Which dimension of political support is more stable or volatile? Can the public's positive and negative evaluations of government performance (specific support) help, respectively, to build and erode their beliefs in the legitimacy of the government (diffuse support)? If they can, what can be said about the timing of the effects? These questions have been addressed through the examination of the differences and the dynamic relationship between diffuse and specific support against the data collected from the three Beijing surveys.

In terms of the differences between the two dimensions of political support, there are two important findings. One is that our respondents' support for the fundamental political system in contemporary China (diffuse support) was much more stable than their evaluations of the incumbent performance (specific support) within the four-year period of our surveys, although the former had steadily declined. This finding implies that in China, especially urban China, citizens' feelings about the political system, instead of their assessments of incumbent performance, still serve as a reliable popular base of CCP rule, although this base has gradually eroded. In addition, contradicting the conventional view among China scholars, this finding further confirms the argument made in chapter 2 that the survival of the current regime relies more on diffuse support than on specific support.

The other important finding on the difference between the two dimensions of support is that the respondents' attitudes toward the fundamental political system were much more consistent than their assessments of incumbent performance. This implies that although diffuse support is now a more stable base of CCP rule, to widen and deepen this base represents a very serious challenge for the CCP leadership. Due to the high degree of its consistency, diffuse support entails a set of cohesive values and principles to nurture. Nonetheless, such values and principles hardly exist in contemporary Chinese society.

As for the relationship between diffuse and specific support, I have found that there was a weak association between the respondents' evaluations of the incumbent authority and their support for the political regime, and this weak association prevailed across such major sociodemographic divides as sex, age, education, and income. The implication of these findings is that the public's positive and negative evaluations of government performance may help, respectively, to build or erode their beliefs in the legitimacy of the government. But this process of erosion is very likely to be incremental, especially in such an urban area as Beijing, where the base level of diffuse support is moderately high. Although we cannot determine the exact timing of the erosion, at least one possibility may be eliminated according to the findings on the relationship between the diffuse and specific support. That is, within a four-year period, the low evaluations of incumbent performance cannot substantially erode support for the political regime, *ceteris paribus.*

Moreover, in terms of the implication from the interplay of diffuse and specific support for political stability in contemporary China, I have found that the current CCP leadership may maintain stability now and in the near future, since the political regime still draws support from most of those who are satisfied and some of those who are dissatisfied with incumbent performance. Nonetheless, the threat to political stability has begun to grow, because there is an ongoing trend that more and more people who are unhappy with incumbent performance become upset with the entire political system in China.

Finally, it is worth noting that while the answers provided in this chapter to the questions regarding the interplay between diffuse and specific support and its implication for political stability have significantly advanced our understanding of political support in contemporary China, these answers are far from conclusive. Only until we understand the distinct sources and the behavioral consequences of each of the two dimensions of support can we gain more definitive answers to those questions. The distinct sources will be examined in chapters 4 and 5, and the behavioral consequences will be studied in chapter 6.

Chapter 4

Sources of Diffuse Support

The analysis in the previous chapters has not only depicted the magnitudes of diffuse support and specific support and the interaction between these two dimensions of support, but also revealed the differences between the two dimensions. Specifically, the differences have been found in stability and consistency between diffuse and specific support. These differences strongly suggest that respondents conceptualize the two dimensions of political support differently or that the formation of each dimension may be significantly influenced by a distinct combination of sociopolitical factors. Thus, to explain how people construct each type of support, such a distinct combination of sociopolitical factors should be examined separately for each of the two dimensions of political support. In this chapter, I will examine a set of sociopolitical factors that is expected to influence in various ways diffuse support, one of the two dimensions of political support. Through examination of these sociopolitical factors, two central questions will be addressed: Who is most likely to support the current political system in contemporary China? And why do people support this system?

In this study, I focus on the impacts of three categories of sociopolitical factors on people's feeling about the current Chinese political regime: sociodemographic attributes, high-politics orientations, and low-politics orientations. As discussed in chapter 1, theoretical arguments and empirical findings from earlier studies all suggest that while low-politics orientations should be weakly associated with diffuse support for the political regime, both sociodemographic attributes and high-politics orientations are supposed strongly to affect such support. In this chapter, I will first specify the relationship between variables in each of the three categories and diffuse support, and examine the relationship from both bivariate and multivariate perspectives against the data collected from the three Beijing surveys. Since, as discussed in chapter 1, the findings about such a relationship may be generalized beyond our samples, I will conclude this chapter with some general implications from the findings for the sources of diffuse support for the political regime in contemporary China.

The Impacts of Sociodemographic Factors on Diffuse Support

Within the category of sociodemographic attributes, I focus on age, sex, education, occupation, economic status, and the membership of the CCP. These attributes are expected to be strongly associated with diffuse support. As noted in chapter 1, sociodemographic attributes may capture some of the effects that family, peer groups, generations, social classes, and political membership have on political socialization processes; such socialization processes tend to have a strong and lasting impact on people's political values and beliefs, which then become the bases of diffuse support for the political system.

In earlier empirical studies of political development in democratic, nondemocratic, and transitional systems, there is a widespread theoretical consensus that such key sociodemographic factors as age, sex, education, economic status, and political membership may influence individuals' attitudes toward the political regime and political changes.[1] Particularly, several recent survey studies conducted in post–Mao China have provided empirical leads for the establishment of relationships between these key sociodemographic attributes and various political attitudes (Jennings 1996; Nathan and Shi 1993; Zheng 1994; Chan and Nesbitt-Larking 1995). In general, these empirical studies have strongly supported a general hypothesis that individuals' beliefs and values about politics are affected by various processes of political socialization, which are attributable to key sociodemographic factors.

1. For studies of democratic systems, see Almond and Verba (1963), Dahl (1971), Inglehart (1979), Barnes and Kaase et al. (1979), Jennings and Deth et al. (1990), and Gibson and Caldeira (1992). For studies of nondemocratic and transitional systems, see Bahry (1987), Silver (1987), Finifter and Mickiewicz (1992), Duch (1992), Gibson, Duch, and Tedin (1993), Rose and Mishler (1994), Miller, Hesli, and Reisinger (1994), Mason (1995), Miller, Reisinger, and Hesli (1996), and Finifter (1996).

Drawing upon these earlier studies, therefore, I expect that respondents with different sociodemographic characteristics vary in their attitudes toward the political regime. In this section, I will examine the bivariate relationship between each of the sociodemographic variables and diffuse support.

Age and Diffuse Support

Students of political attitudes and political participation emphasize the effect of the aging process on a person's sociopsychological orientation (Verba and Nie 1972, 139; Marsh and Kaase 1979). In general, they believe that younger people are naturally more active, more open to change, and more likely to be critical of the status quo. As Finifter and Mickiewicz (1992, 864) have noted, "virtually by definition, youth is part of the 'modern' sector of society, and youth groups are frequently among those active in movements for social and political change; conversely, the relationship between aging and resistance to change is a phenomenon widely observed." Such sociopsychological orientation of youth prevails across various sociopolitical settings (Almond and Verba 1963, 338–41; Marsh and Kaase 1979, 101; Shi 1997, 250). When studying political attitudes in the former Soviet Union, for example, Finifter and Mickiewicz (1992, 865) have found that "support for [political] change declines rather consistently with increasing age."

More important, this kind of relationship between aging and political attitude has also been confirmed by the evidence from some earlier surveys in China. Based on a nationwide survey conducted from 1986 to 1987, for instance, Chan and Nesbitt-Larking (1995, 308) found that the younger respondents tended to be more critical of the communist regime and were more likely to preserve their "private life" from government intervention than those who were older. Even more relevant to this study, based on the data from a sample survey in Beijing between late 1988 and early 1989, Shi (1997, 250) has also found that "age is negatively correlated with [civil or political] resistance in Beijing." To explain this finding, Shi argues that the youth tend to be more idealistic; therefore, "when realizing the huge gap between their own expectations about the performance of the political community created by the socialization efforts of the regime and the political realities in the society, young people grow to resent the existing political institutions. Naturally, they will challenge them" (Shi 1997, 250–1). In addition, he suggests that younger people are less likely to accept the norms and rules of the current regime in China, because they are influenced by "ideas of liberty and democracy" from the West in their formative age during the reform era (Shi 1997, 250).

The theory and empirical findings from earlier studies in Chinese and non-Chinese settings simply suggest that the younger a person, the more likely she or he is to challenge the current political system. In this study, then, I expect respondents' ages to be positively associated with their levels of diffuse support for the current political regime. That is, while older respondents are more likely to support the current political regime, younger ones are more likely to challenge the current regime and seek change. Here, I examine this expectation by running cross-tabulations between natural age groups and three levels of the diffuse support index.

As table 4.1 indicates, overall, respondents' ages were positively associated with their levels of diffuse support in the three surveys. Specifically, in

Table 4.1

Diffuse Support for Political Regime by Age, 1995, 1997, and 1999

Diffuse Support Index	Age					
	18–25 (%)	26–35 (%)	36–45 (%)	46–55 (%)	56–65 (%)	65–over (%)
			1995			
Low	34	19	16	4	0	0
Medium	41	48	43	43	42	35
High	25	33	41	53	58	65
Total	100	100	100	100	100	100
			gamma = .57*			
			1997			
Low	35	21	14	5	3	0
Medium	47	41	42	40	37	36
High	28	38	44	55	60	64
Total	100	100	100	100	100	100
			gamma = .55*			
			1999			
Low	30	21	11	7	3	4
Medium	44	42	47	42	43	33
High	26	37	42	51	54	63
Total	100	100	100	100	100	100
			gamma = .51*			

Note: The original diffuse support index is trichotomized into three categories: high, intermediate, and low levels. * $P < .05$.

the 1995 survey, while 65 percent of those at age 65 or older strongly supported the regime, only 25 percent of those at or under age 25 registered the
same level of support. Moreover, between these two age groups, the levels
of diffuse support grew consistently with increasing age. The same patterns
repeated in both the 1997 and the 1999 surveys. These results support the
earlier hypothesis about the effect of aging: Age is positively associated
with the level of diffuse support for the current political regime in China.

Sex and Diffuse Support

Scholars of Chinese politics seem to agree that there are some significant
differences between women and men in their political attitudes and behavior. They cite two kinds of reasons: (1) the distinct sociopolitical experiences
and statuses of these two groups, and (2) the Chinese traditions that hold
different expectations of women and men (Bauer et al. 1992; Lieberthal
1995, 309–10; Shi 1997; Jennings 1998; Louie 2001). Nonetheless, two
competing arguments can be discerned regarding the impact of gender on
people's attitudes toward the current political regime.

A first argument suggests that women tend to be more supportive of CCP
rule. Scholars of this argument have cited at least two main reasons for this
view. One reason is that women's political and socioeconomic conditions
have significantly improved under CCP rule since 1949 (Croll 1983; Li
1989; Lock 1989; Robinson and Parris 1990). Before the post-Mao reform,
the Party had made sincere and substantial efforts to promote gender equality as a part of orthodox Marxism-Leninism-Maoism by lifting women's
socioeconomic and political status. One famous sign of the Party's efforts
was the official slogan: "Women can hold up half the sky!" While socioeconomic parity between the sexes was by no means achieved, advocates of
this view believe that women advanced remarkably from their pre-1949 status in such areas as employment opportunity, pay, treatment at work place,
and sociopolitical status. Since the onset of post-Mao reform, as most employers and managers of both private and public enterprises alike have
been operating in favor of male over female employees (claiming economic efficiency and productivity), women have often seen the current
Party-state as the last resort of gaining sympathy and protection. This is because government at all levels in China is still, at least in theory, obligated
to make and implement regulations and laws to protect women's interests
as defined by the communist official ideology and out of nationalist concerns particularly in foreign-capital enterprises (Robinson and Parris 1990,

135–55). Thus, some recent studies even argue that, despite employers' gender discrimination, "women continue to gain on men in education, jobs, and, seemingly, bargaining power at home" under the post-Mao reform (Tang and Parish 2000, 315–6). In short, women in contemporary China have benefited from CCP rule since the establishment of the People's Republic of China (PRC).

The other reason for the argument that women tend to support the current political regime is related to traditional Chinese culture. This deeply rooted culture has strongly encouraged women to be passive and obedient subjects in all social units—from family to society. Therefore, Chinese women tend to be more compliant with any political authority, including the current communist regime, than their male counterparts (Robinson and Parris 1990; Shi 1997, 174).

A second argument derived from recent studies of Chinese politics implies that Chinese women are less supportive of the current regime. Unlike the first argument, which emphasizes the improvement of women's status since 1949, this argument is built upon the critical assessments of the gap between women and men in their social, economic, and political status (Andors 1983; Wolf 1985; Bauer et al. 1992), and the ongoing deterioration of women's conditions since the onset of post-Mao reform (Honig and Hershatter 1988; Lieberthal 1995, 309–10). In reference to the gap between women and men, Bauer and his associates (1992, 334), for example, argue that

> Four decades after the founding of the People's Republic, gender inequality persists in China. Women's lower position in the gender hierarchy is reflected in the continued preference for sons in most of China, in women's "double burden" of full-time paid work and major responsibilities for child care and housework, in the lack of representation of women in political affairs, in violence against women in the form of infanticide and wife battering, and attitudes about the proper qualities of husbands and wives.

Some analysts argue that women have become victims of the post-Mao reform as the authorities at almost all levels increasingly emphasize productivity and efficiency of the enterprises over gender equality (Yue and Li 1994, 170). They have been often discriminated against by both state- and privately owned firms in employment and pay. For example, the discrimination in employment against women has become so blatant that many job

Table 4.2

Diffuse Support for Political Regime by Gender, 1995, 1997, and 1999

Diffuse Support Index	1995		1997		1999	
	Female (%)	Male (%)	Female (%)	Male (%)	Female (%)	Male (%)
Low	8	2	12	4	9	5
Medium	50	40	49	43	48	43
High	42	58	39	53	43	52
Total	100	100	100	100	100	100

Note: The original diffuse support index is trichotomized into three categories: high, intermediate, and low levels.

ads often explicitly indicate the disqualification of women based on their sex (Yue and Li 1994, 170–1). Women have suffered higher unemployment than men in the reform era. In 1997, about 60 percent of the unemployed were female, although women were less than 40 percent of the urban work force (Bonin 2000, 155). As Lieberthal (1995, 310) concludes, therefore, "it appears that on balance women's positions in society have suffered under the reforms."

In sum, two competing propositions can be seen regarding the role of gender in influencing the attitudes toward the current CCP regime. While one proposition suggests women's tendency to support CCP rule, the other implies the opposite. To examine these two competing propositions, I ran cross-tabulations between respondents' sexes and their support for the regime in all three surveys. The results are shown in table 4.2.

As table 4.2 indicates, women in each sample were less supportive of the current political regime. In the three surveys, more female than male respondents scored "low" for the diffuse support index, while fewer female than male respondents scored "high" for the index. These results support one of the two competing propositions mentioned above that Chinese women are less supportive of the current regime.

Education and Diffuse Support

Education has been widely used by political scientists as a predictor of political attitudes. In their seminal work *The Civil Culture,* for example, Almond and Verba have argued that "educational attainment appears to have the most important demographic effect on political attitudes" (1963, 379).

But there is no consensus among scholars as to whether the level of education is positively or negatively associated with support for the political regime in such nondemocratic societies as communist ones.

There are at least two competing arguments about the effect of education on support for the political regime in a communist system. One suggests that people's level of educational attainment is positively related to their support for the regime (Fainsod 1961; Azrael 1965). That is, the higher a person's level of education, the more likely she or he supports the regime. According to this argument, the education system under communism indoctrinates the official ideology within the youth through a government-controlled curriculum and hence serves as an effective social mechanism to generate support for the regime (Azrael 1965, 267).

The other argument contends that education should be positively associated with the likelihood that one challenges the political regime in a communist society (Silver 1987). There are at least two major reasons for this argument. One is that given that most curriculums in any education system, including those in communist ones, are designed to train specialists in technical areas, education in general should encourage people to open their minds to new knowledge and ideas and to be critical of dogmatic and nondemocratic doctrines (Dobson 1980). The other reason is that, since those people with greater education are generally more interested in getting a wider range of information (Mickiewicz 1981, chapter 9), "they are likely to be more aware of alternatives to established practices" (Silver 1987, 102). Thus better-educated people are considered to be more likely to challenge the establishment, especially such a nondemocratic system as a communist regime.

Moreover, in their empirical studies, some scholars have also found evidence to support this theoretical argument. For example, in the former Soviet Union, the better-educated tended to be more critical of the current communist regime and supportive of democratic change (Silver 1987; Gibson, Duch, and Tedin 1992; Miller 1993; Miller, Hesli, and Reisinger 1994 and 1995). As Silver has noted, "advanced education is likely to be intellectually liberating and to induce a more critical stance toward official dogma" (1987, 101). More important, some China scholars have also argued that Chinese intellectuals tend to challenge authoritarian regimes, noting that intellectuals have always been the harbingers of liberal or democratic movements, such as the May Fourth Movement and the 1989 Democracy Movement, since the early twentieth century (Hamrin, 1987; Goldman 1994; Young 1995).

All in all, the two competing arguments leave us with two contradictory hypotheses. One expects education to be positively associated with support for the current regime; the other expects education to be negatively related to such support. To examine these competing hypotheses, I conducted a bivariate analysis of the relationship between the level of education and the index of support for the political regime.

The results from Figure 4.1 support one of the two competing hypotheses. That is, as the level of education increases, the level of support for the communist regime decreases. Specifically, as the respondents' education increased by each level of education, from "illiterate or elementary," "junior high," "senior high" to "college or higher,"[2] the mean scores for their diffuse support decreased accordingly. This pattern of association between education and diffuse support for the current political regime prevailed throughout the three surveys.

Occupation and Diffuse Support

Some earlier studies have found that a person's occupation influences his or her political attitudes, including attitudes toward the political system (Almond and Verba 1963; Klingemann 1979; Swafford 1987; Finifter and Mickiewicz 1992). For example, in their classic study of political cultures in five countries, Almond and Verba (1963, 105) have found that "persons in skilled and better-rewarded occupations" are more likely to be proud of their political systems. This is simply because those with certain occupations are considered to have benefited from the current political system in general.

Some recent studies in China have also indicated that people's occupations affect attitudes toward the government as well as their behavior in politics (Hook 1996; Liu 1996, chapters 2–4; Shi 1997; Jennings 1997, 1998). These studies reveal not only that the political orientations of people of different occupations may vary with the benefits they receive under the current regime but also that the different sociopolitical experiences associated with various occupations can make a difference in people's feelings about the

---

2. Some recent empirical studies of the sociopolitical impact of education in China have indicated that education, measured by the degree attained and level of study, has played an increasingly important role in determining a person's socioeconomic and political status, especially since the onset of the post Mao reform (Walder 1995; Walder 2000; Zhou 2000; Li and Walder 2001). Based on the measure used in these studies, I choose to use the degree attained to gauge the level of education among our respondents.

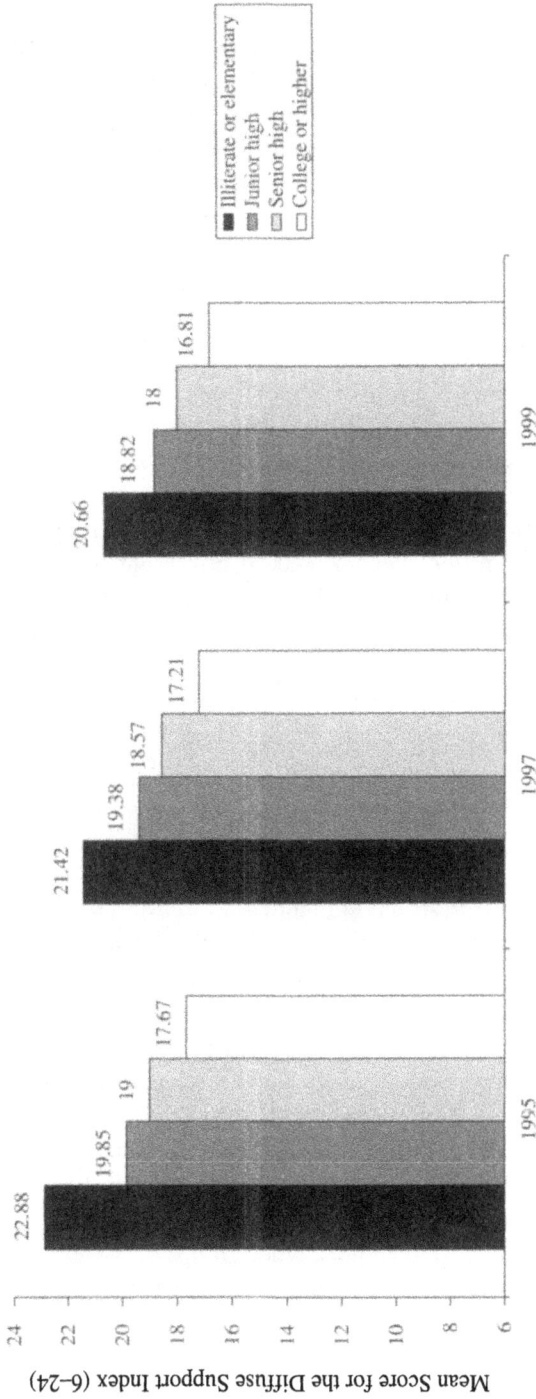

Figure 4.1
Diffuse Support by Education, 1995, 1997, and 1999

Legend:
- Illiterate or elementary
- Junior high
- Senior high
- College or higher

Mean Score for the Diffuse Support Index (6–24)

1995:
- 22.88
- 19.85
- 19
- 17.67

1997:
- 21.42
- 19.38
- 18.57
- 17.21

1999:
- 20.66
- 18.82
- 18
- 16.81

regime. For instance, some China scholars have analyzed the distinctive sociopolitical conditions and political orientations of one of the most politically dynamic occupational groups in urban areas—SOE workers. Based on their observations, these analysts conclude that SOE workers have become increasingly disgruntled with some negative effects of the central government's reforms in SOEs. Such effects include a serious threat of unemployment, deterioration of social welfare, rampant corruption by SOEs' leaders, and lack of protection of workers' rights (Walder 1996; Chan and Senser 1997; Croll 1999; Hu 2000). Workers' discontent with their current conditions and their belief in a bleak future have been dramatically reflected in a rise in labor unrest and demonstrations in many urban areas. According to a Hong Kong-based labor organization, the number of workers' demonstrations increased from about 60,000 in 1998 to 100,000 in 1999 (*Epoch Times* 2001, A3). Some China scholars have also identified distinct political orientations among other professional groups—such as college students (Rosen 1992; Goldman 2000); private entrepreneurs (Liu 1996, 230; Pearson 1997), bureaucrats (Tang and Parrish 2000, 168–73), and military personnel (Shambaugh 1996)—depending on their experiences with the current system.

All these studies indicate a structural impact of occupation on a person's political attitudes, particularly those toward the political regime. Thus, I expect that some major occupational divides may play an important role in determining respondents' feelings about the current political regime in China. To explore this expectation, I compare the mean scores for the diffuse support index among eight occupational categories. The results of the comparison are presented in Figure 4.2.

On the average, in all three surveys, college students had the lowest levels of support for the current political regime among the eight occupational groups. The mean scores of the students on the diffuse support index (a 6–24 scale) ranged from a low of 18 in 1995 to a high of 18.2 in 1997. Based on the findings presented above about the impact of age, one can attribute such a low level of diffuse support among the students to their young age that often results in critical attitudes toward the current nondemocratic system. Trailing the college students, SOE workers had the second-lowest scores, ranging from 18.68 in 1995 down to 18.08 in 1999. The SOE workers were less supportive than most other groups of the current regime, mainly because, as mentioned above, they gradually realized that they had become "sacrificial lambs" (Chan and Senser 1997, 116) for the regime's economic reform program. This combination of discontented workers and students,

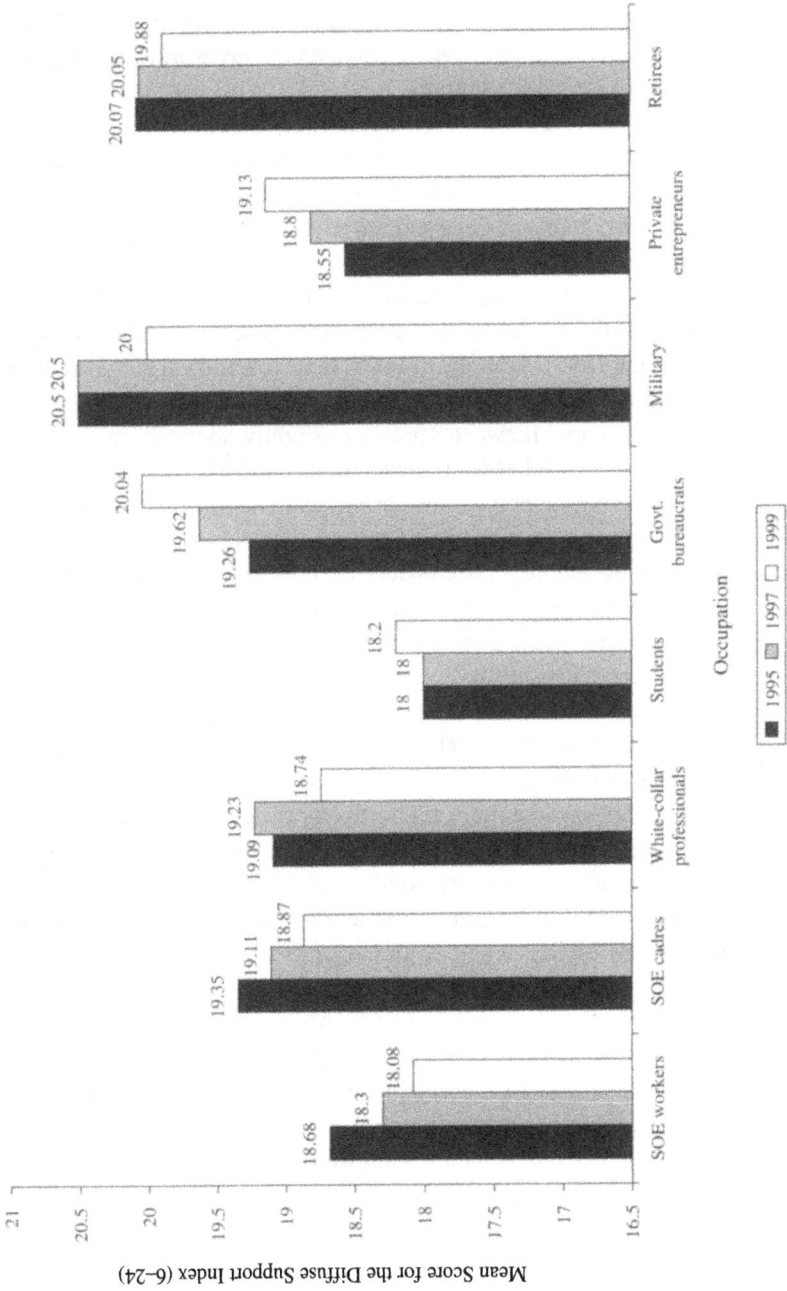

Figure 4.2
Diffuse Support by Occupation, 1995, 1997, and 1999

according to one scholar (Goldman 2000), presents a threat to political stability in contemporary China. For instance, during the 1989 Democracy Movement, students took the initiative and many workers responded with individual or organized support.

At the other end of the spectrum, military personnel were the most supportive of the current regime among all the occupational groups. In all three surveys, this group scored at or above 20 on the diffuse support index. This finding further confirms the argument advanced by some China scholars that the People's Liberation Army (PLA) has been the most thoroughly penetrated and the most tightly controlled by the Party and is the regime's most reliable political tool as compared to other groups in contemporary China (Shambaugh 1996). After the military, both government bureaucrats and retirees had the second highest levels of diffuse support. While government bureaucrats scored between 19.26 and slightly above 20 in the three surveys, retirees scored almost constantly around 20. The finding about the relatively strong support for the current political system by government bureaucrats apparently supports some earlier studies suggesting that bureaucrats have, by and large, been better off under the current political system, because such a system still provides them with the privileges and authority to harvest more social and economic benefits from the post–Mao reform, through such means as accepting fees and special accommodations from people who need services and regulatory permissions from the government (Zweig 1999, 64–7; Lu 2000). Yet, the finding on the relationship between retirement and the relatively high level of diffuse support might be spurious. The retirees were more supportive of the current regime, perhaps due to their age rather than to their retirement. This effect of aging on diffuse support has already been discussed.

Between the highest and lowest levels of diffuse support, four occupational groups—SOE cadres, white-collar professionals,[3] and private entrepreneurs—had mid-range levels. Overall, their scores for diffuse support lay between about 18.50 and mid 19.40. Among these three midrange groups, private entrepreneurs are of great interest for researchers. Why do the private entrepreneurs register a respectable level of support for the nondemocratic, communist regime in contemporary China?

Many studies have argued and showed that those who value free markets

---

3. This group includes researchers, schoolteachers, doctors, newspaper reporters, and artists.

are more likely to support a democratic system rather than a nondemocratic one (Hayek 1944; Dahl 1989; Duch 1993). From this argument, it seems to be logical to assume that compared to most other occupational groups, the private entrepreneurs who presumably value the free-market enterprise should be more likely to support a democratic political system and less likely to support a nondemocratic regime. But in contemporary China, this logic does not seem to be the case, because private entrepreneurs in China have been co-opted by the state into a kind of corporative arrangement led by the state (Wank 1995; Pearson 1997; Dickson 2000b). This corporative arrangement results also from the deeply rooted culture of clientelism and the incomplete market in contemporary China. Under this arrangement, entrepreneurs receive policy and regulatory assistance from the state, while in turn governments at various levels can have political control over the entrepreneurs and achieve economic benefits through the "rent" paid by the entrepreneurs. As Dickson (2000a, 45) has argued, therefore, the entrepreneurs have become "partners with the state in China, and are unlikely to be the source of political opposition." All in all, our finding about the relatively high level of diffuse supports for the current political regime among private entrepreneurs apparently is consistent with this argument.

Economic Status and Diffuse Support

Before examining the relationship between economic status and diffuse support for the political regime, I need to specify the measurement of economic status used in this study. There are mainly two kinds of indicators used by analysts to gauge people's economic status. One consists of so-called objective indicators, such as gross income and disposable income. The other is composed of so-called subjective indicators, such as subjective evaluation of one's economic position relative to others. Although these two kinds of indicators may be positively correlated, "the relationship is far from perfect" (Silver 1987, 124).[4] In this study, I have chosen to use a subjective indicator—the respondent's subjective evaluation of his or her economic position relative to others—to measure economic status.

There are two major reasons for this choice. One is that a subjective indicator is more relevant to diffuse support for the current political regime.

---

4. For more detailed discussions of this relationship, see works by Campbell, Converse and Rodgers (1976), Andrews and Withey (1976), and Marsh and Kaase (1979).

Only when people perceive themselves to be at a lower economic level compared to others do they feel deprived under the current system (Citrin et al. 1975, 15; Silver 1987, 123–4). Consequently, those who feel deprived might be more likely to be discontented with the political system. For this study, therefore, the subjective evaluation of relative economic position is the most suitable measure of economic status as a potential source of diffuse support for the current regime.

The other reason for choosing this subjective indicator is that it fits the unique socioeconomic conditions of contemporary China. In the current context of China's socioeconomic conditions, such objective indicators as personal income, savings, or personal net assets do not represent a person's real economic status. For example, most private entrepreneurs have much higher incomes than government bureaucrats. Nonetheless, monetary differences do not necessarily separate these two groups in terms of their de facto economic status. Members of both groups may enjoy very similar living standards (in many cases, bureaucrats may enjoy even higher living standards than average private entrepreneurs), such as spacious and well-decorated apartments, cars, frequent dining in fancy restaurants, and decent medical care. While the entrepreneurs usually use their monetary resources to maintain such living standards, the bureaucrats in general achieve these standards through their administrative power and government perks. In my field interviews, some government bureaucrats told me that they were driving cars that were either "borrowed" for as long as four years from their nongovernmental "clients" who needed assistance from the bureaucrats, or provided by their government agencies, in theory, for "job-related" use. Other government officials revealed that they were living in new apartments in coveted locations within the third beltway (*san huan lu nei*) in Beijing, which were all "purchased" from "generous" builders at prices unbelievably lower than market prices. Still, other officials bragged to me that they could dine in any fancy restaurants at any time, not worrying about costs, since there were always long lists of "friendly clients" who would feel honored to foot the bills. Thus, the difference between government bureaucrats and private entrepreneurs in income does not necessarily translate into a difference in economic status.

Such deceptive differences in income exist also among other groups. In my interviews, for instance, I have learned that retirees of national government agencies have pensions that are much lower than salaries made by many contract employees (e.g., white-collar workers), but the retirees enjoy much

Table 4.3
Distribution of Self-Assessed Economic Status, 1995, 1997, and 1999

	Lower (%)	Lower-middle (%)	Middle (%)	Upper-middle (%)	Upper (%)	Total (%)
1995	6	35	48	9	2	100
1997	8	33	50	8	1	100
1999	10	34	49	6	1	100

better benefits (e.g., free or low-cost medical care and subsidized housing) provided by their agencies, which carry enough value to offset the difference between their pensions and contract-worker salaries.

These anecdotes from my interviews are by no means isolated cases. Similar observations have been reported in other empirical studies (Shi 1997, 150). In short, such an objective indicator as income is misleading when used to gauge citizens' economic status in contemporary China. A subjective evaluation of economic position relative to others should serve the purpose of the analysis in this study, since such an evaluation, though not perfect, can more accurately reflect a respondent's de facto economic status.

Based on the above-mentioned reasons, therefore, I adopt the subjective evaluation of economic position[5] to measure the respondent's economic status. In the three Beijing surveys, I asked respondents to evaluate their economic positions relative to others on a 5-point scale (where 1 = lower level; 2 = lower-middle level; 3 = middle level; 4 = upper-middle level; and 5 = upper level). The results of this indicator are presented in table 4.3.

Overall, in the three surveys, about three-fourths of our respondents perceived themselves as members of the lower-middle and middle classes. While this overwhelming majority within the lower-middle and middle categories remained almost unchanged throughout the three surveys, there were some interesting shifts in both extremes of the scale. As the percentages in the lower economic-status category increased from 6 percent in 1995 to 10 percent in 1999, those in the upper-middle and upper categories combined decreased from 11 percent in 1995 to 7 percent in 1999. Although

---

5. Unlike spontaneous evaluation of specific government policy, the self-assessment of economic status comes from one's internalization of perceived economic position over a substantial period of time. Thus, once it is shaped, this internalized assessment tends to be stable.

the ranges of changes in these two extremes were not large, the changes might be indicative of a significant trend in the country's wealth distribution: as the size of the top economic group shrinks, that of the bottom economic group swells.

Do people's economic statuses influence their views on the current political system in contemporary China? It has been widely believed that economic status is associated with a person's attitudes toward the political system (Klingemann 1979; Citrin et al. 1975; Finkel, Muller, and Seligson 1989; Finifter and Mickiewicz 1992). This is simply because, as Marsh and Kaase (1979, 126) point out, "people located in different sectors of the social economy perceive and possess different interests" in politics. Specifically, the most common proposition regarding the impact of economic status suggests that people with lower economic status tend to be less supportive of the political system because they are more likely to feel deprived under the current system (Citrin et al. 1975, 15). To test this proposition, I examined the bivariate correlation between economic status and the level of diffuse support.

At least two important findings stand out from figure 4.3. First, in the three surveys, the level of diffuse support rose with economic status. This means that the higher the economic category to which people believe they belong, the more strongly they support the current political system. This finding is consistent with the economic deprivation proposition, mentioned above, that support for the predominant political system is positively correlated with economic status.

Second, the gaps among the mean scores of the five economic statuses for diffuse support shrank over the four-year period. This shrinkage resulted mainly from both the decreases in the mean scores of the upper, upper-middle and middle status categories, and the increase in those of the lower class. While the reasons for the decreases in the mean scores of the three higher statuses are not clear, the reason for the increase in the mean scores of the lowest status seems to be obvious. Since the mid 1990s, the central government—particularly the Ministry of Civil Affairs, the Ministry of Labor, and the Ministry of Personnel—has increased resources and initiated policies to alleviate the urban poverty. For example, under these policies, by 1997, most cities (including Beijing) had institutionalized safety-net systems for their urban poor, drawing on resources from two sources: local government finance and enterprise funds (UNDP 1999, 102). Thus, the urban poor could become supportive of the current regime due to the strengthening of the safety net.

Figure 4.3
Diffuse Support by Economic Status, 1995, 1997, and 1999

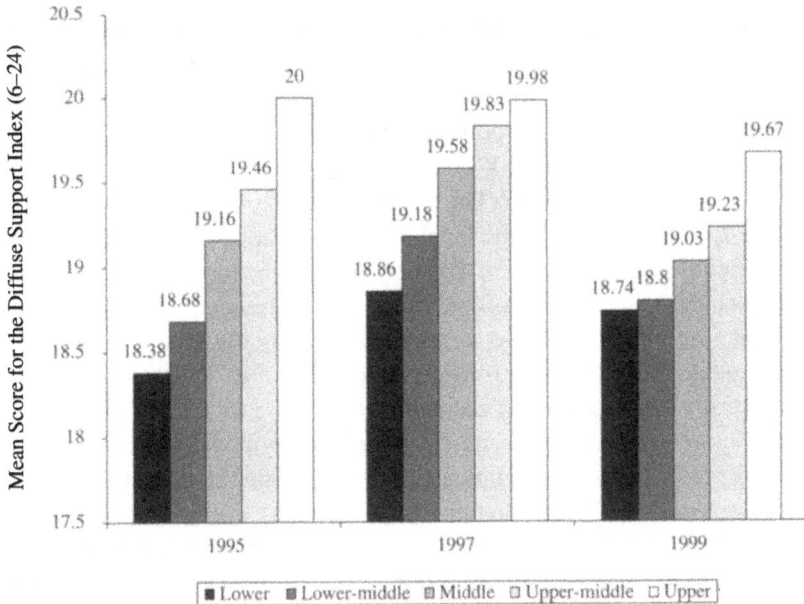

Party Membership and Diffuse Support

Among China observers, there has been a common proposition that members of the CCP should be more supportive of the political regime than nonmembers. This proposition is built upon two general arguments. One suggests that, because of the CCP's unchallengeable ruling position, its members still have many kinds of privileges that ordinary citizens lack (Jennings 1997, 267). Although the CCP's membership-recruitment strategy has changed from almost solely emphasizing political loyalty (or "redness") to giving more weight to educational qualifications and professional competence since the onset of post-Mao reforms, Party membership still carries career and material advantages (Walder 1986, 1995; Dickson and Rublee 2000; Li and Walder 2001). These advantages include "unusual access to information and influential individuals," more opportunities for "working the system" (Jennings 1997, 267), career promotion, the most prestigious jobs and higher income (Dickson and Rublee 2000). In other words, Party members are the greatest beneficiaries of the current political system, although their privileges have been reduced since the onset of post-Mao reforms.

The other argument supporting the proposition is that Party members are more likely than nonmembers to support the regime's norms and institutions, due to the political and ideological standards set for membership recruitment and continuous political education or organizational life (*zuzhi shenhuo*) within the Party. While, as many China observers (e.g., Chen 1995; Chen and Gong 1997; Pei 1998; Dickson 2000a) have pointed out, the Party organizations at the local levels have rapidly deteriorated since the onset of post-Mao reform, the Party still has the institutions of recruitment standards and organizational life in place. Although these two institutions are no longer as robust as they were during the Mao era, they still distinguish Party members from nonmembers in a systematic way. Specifically, the recruitment standards could serve as a minimal political yardstick to prevent those who are considered politically incorrect from joining the Party; the organizational life, though often sloppy, still provides the Party-state with opportunities to promote its norms and values. As Lieberthal (1995, 214) has noted, therefore, Party membership still "entails willingness to bend to Party discipline on issues on which the CCP leadership demands compliance." Moreover, the proposition about Party members' attitudes toward the political regime has been supported by empirical evidence from early survey studies of communist systems. For example, Bahry and Silver (1990, 838) found that Communist Party members and activists tended to be more supportive of the political values of the regime in the former Soviet Union. Also, an earlier study comparing elite and mass subjective orientations indicated that Party members and cadres in urban China were significantly more supportive of the current political regime than ordinary people (Chen 1999). All in all, as Bialer (1980, 191) has pointed out, Communist Party "membership develops a sense of having a stake in the system."

Is this proposition supported by the data from our surveys? The results presented in figure 4.4 provide a positive answer to this question. In all three surveys, CCP members were more supportive of the regime than non-CCP members were, while the mean scores for diffuse support within both groups declined over the four years. The pattern of the gap between CCP members and non-CCP members in their attitudes toward the current political regime was so robust that it sustained chronological changes in such attitudes within both groups. Thus, the results from our data support the

Figure 4.4

Comparison of Diffuse Support among CCP and Non-CCP Members, 1995, 1997, and 1999

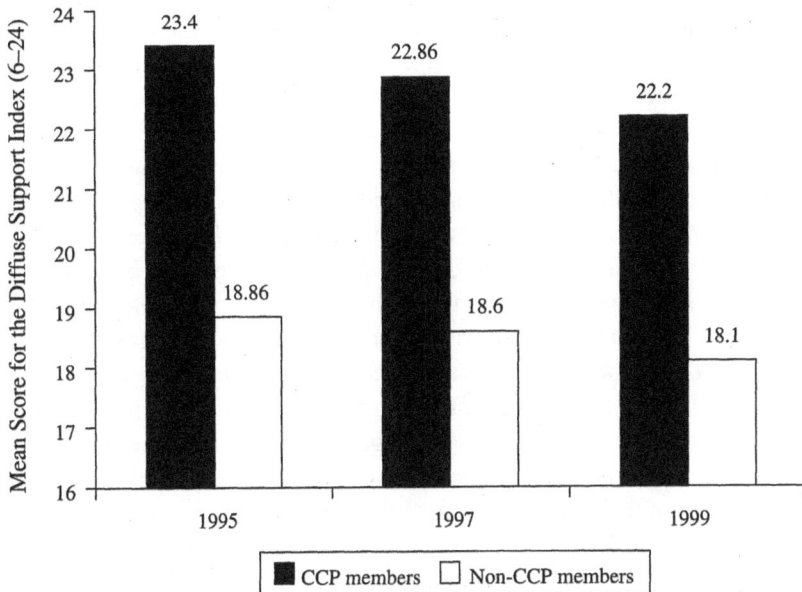

proposition developed in earlier studies about the attitudinal effect of Party membership.

Figure 4.4 reveals another interesting phenomenon that, in the four years of our surveys, the level of diffuse support among CCP members was falling apparently faster than that among non-CCP members. This finding supports earlier field observations that CCP members have become more skeptical about the communist ideology and less compliant to the party line since the onset of reform than they were during the Mao era, because of, for example, the drastic deterioration of Party organizations at the local levels in the reform era (Chen 1995; Chen and Gong 1997; Pei 1998; Dickson 2000a). The evidence from this study, however, is far from conclusive about the decline rate of diffuse support among CCP members in the long run and does not deal with the reasons for such a decline. More conclusive and indepth understandings of the decline rate and its causes still require a further study that focuses on those potential reasons.

The Impacts of High-Politics Orientations on Diffuse Support

Thus far, I have addressed the question mainly of who is most likely to support the current political regime. But the question of why people in China, especially today's urban China, support the regime remains unanswered. To answer this question, I will examine the effects of high-politics orientations in this section and those of low-politics orientations in the section that follows.

As defined in chapter 1, high-politics orientations are considered to be a set of citizens' attitudes toward issues and principles, which mainly involve politics at the national level and "the abstract ideas and language of politics" (Bialer 1980, 166). In this study, I include in the category of high-politics orientations such items as democratic values, interest in national politics, belief in the need for reform of the current political system, preference for political stability, and nationalist and patriotic sentiments. As discussed in chapter 1, I expect that high-politics orientations have strong impacts on diffuse support for the current political regime. Briefly, this is because high-politics orientations are a set of normative values and beliefs related closely to the nature of the political system or regime that is the main object of diffuse support. The impact of each high-politics orientation on diffuse support will be examined separately from a bivariate perspective in this section.

Democratic Beliefs and Diffuse Support

In this study, I have focused on three specific democratic beliefs that I believe are, among others, critical to a democratic system in China: (1) competitive elections of government officials with multiple candidates, (2) equal protection and rights for all regardless of political views, and (3) an independent media with freedom to expose and criticize government wrong-doings.[6] These beliefs concern high-politics, as they together involve fundamental preferences for a certain type of political system or regime, namely, democracy.

First, most scholars of democracy consider competitive, multicandidacy election to be imperative for a functioning democratic system (Schumpeter 1947; Dahl 1971; Huntington 1991; Gibson, Duch, and Tedin 1992; Duch

---

6. Because of the current political constraints in China, it was impossible to measure all the dimensions of democratic values addressed by previous studies, especially those deemed too politically sensitive, such as belief in the "multiparty system."

1993). They believe that only through such an institutionalized process can a government be established that is based on popular sovereignty and serves the common good. As Huntington (1991, 7) points out, a democratic system is the one in which "its most powerful collective decision makers are selected through fair, honest, and periodic elections in which candidates freely compete for votes and in which virtually all the adult population is eligible to vote." Therefore, the belief in competitive election has been considered an essential component of democratic values, which must be acquired in a transition from a nondemocratic regime to a democratic system (e.g., Gibson and Duch 1993; Finifter and Mickiewicz 1992).

Second, it has been argued that only when equal protection and rights are guaranteed by the law can individuals freely participate in the political process and democracy flourish (Macridis 1992, chapter 2; Macridis and Burg 1991, 14–15). According to John Locke (1967, chapter 4), freedom exists when the law protects all people and restrains rulers. In addition, the norm of equal protection and rights for all is associated with another underlying democratic principle: political tolerance. As some China scholars suggest, "the commitment to the equality of citizens and the protection of minority rights . . . requires tolerance for the viewpoints and political activities of opponents" (Nathan and Shi 1993, 111).

In China equal protection and rights are especially important and sensible indicators for democratic values, since China's traditional culture works against such democratic norms. Pye (1992, 67–84) suggests that Chinese traditional culture knows no equals, only superiors and inferiors, and that the Chinese perceive a sharp divide between friend and foe. Meanwhile, the Chinese communist regime has accumulated a notorious record of political intolerance since its establishment in 1949. Although "the large scale of class struggle" among the people, officially promoted by Mao during the Cultural Revolution, ended after Mao's death, political persecution and repression against dissidents have continued, as seen in the 1989 Tiananmen crackdown and the arrests of American-based Chinese scholars in 2001. Thus, the norm of equal protection and rights for all regardless of political views could be imperiled by political tradition and oppressive government policy.

Finally, there are at least two major theoretical reasons to consider belief in free and independent media as an important democratic norm to be included in this analysis. One is that for citizens to be able to evaluate their government and to hold it accountable, the media must have the freedom to criticize and comment on government policy and conduct (Gibson and Duch 1993, 80). The other reason is that independent and free media play a crucial role in facilitating the free flow of political opinions and information necessary for the emergence and maintenance of a democratic system (Remington 1993).

The sociopolitical setting in China also justifies treating this belief as an important democratic value. There has never been real freedom of the press in China, especially since the establishment of the communist regime in 1949. Moreover, the political culture of China does not advocate the idea of a free media. Traditional Chinese culture asserts that, since the national authority is assigned the responsibility of setting moral standards and deciding what is right and wrong for the people, the "wise and able" government ought to "govern every aspect of social life" including the media (Pye 1991, chapter 4). Valuing independent media, therefore, can be seen as another critical democratic norm that Chinese people must acquire for democratization.

From the discussion above, one can easily see that the current Chinese regime's norms and practices have thus far worked against all three democratic beliefs. While some democratic terms, such as "equal protection," "freedom of speech," and "freedom of association" appear in the Chinese constitution, these terms, as most Chinese democratic believers and China observers understand, do not mean what they mean in a democratic society. Even though the government's control over citizens' private lives has been drastically reduced since the onset of post-Mao reforms, the current regime led by the CCP has by no means given up one-party rule nor ceased its harsh oppression of political dissidents. Therefore, in this study I expect that those who strongly believe in democratic values tend to be less supportive of the current communist regime, since the regime is the antithesis of democratic values.

In all three surveys, I used the following statements to measure the respondent's beliefs in the three democratic norms:

1. Elections to governmental positions should be conducted in such a way that there is more than one candidate for each post.
2. Regardless of one's political beliefs, he or she is entitled to the same rights and protections as anyone else.
3. The media should be free to expose government wrongdoing, such as official corruption.

Agreement (including "agree" and "strongly agree") with any one of these statements is scored "1" (prodemocratic) whereas disagreement (including "disagree" and "strongly disagree") is scored "0" (nondemocratic). A summary variable for democratic beliefs is formed based on the respondent's sum (0–3) of the scores on all three items.[7] To test the expectation mentioned above, I ran cross-tabulations between the summary variable of democratic beliefs and the diffuse support index for the three Beijing samples. The results of the cross-tabulations are presented in table 4.4.

Overall, the pattern shown in table 4.4 strongly supports my hypothesis. That is, the level of diffuse support decreased as the level of democratic beliefs increased. For example, in the 1995 sample, while about 60 percent of those who had none or little support for democratic values scored "high" for support for the current political regime, only around 14 percent of those who strongly supported democratic values registered a "high" level of support for the regime. A similar pattern can be seen in the other two samples. In addition, the gammas for all three surveys have the negative signs, indicating a negative relationship between democratic beliefs and diffuse support for the current political regime.

Interest in Politics and Diffuse Support

Many studies of public opinion in the West link political awareness, which is presumably attributed to a person's interest in national politics, with support for the predominant regime's norms and values (Chong, McClosky, and Zaller 1985; Mueller 1973; Key 1961; McClosky and Brill 1983). As Geddes and Zaller (1989, 320) have noted, "the central idea in these . . . studies is that exposure to political communications—whether exposure is measured by . . . information about politics, or political involvement—tends to promote support for the 'mainstream' political norms embedded in those communications".[8] In other words, to a certain extent, those who are highly informed about politics are more likely to be susceptible to the influence of the prevalent political regime.

The important implication of these earlier studies for the analysis here is that interest in politics may also positively relate to support for the prevailing political regime. This is even more likely to be true in China where

7. The reliability analyses of this index yield reliability coefficients (alphas) of .76, .81, and .79 for the 1995, 1997, and 1999 surveys, respectively.

8. In their study of popular support for the Brazilian authoritarian regime, Geddes and Zaller (1989) also documented a dynamic relationship between political awareness and support for authoritarian norms.

Table 4.4

Correlations between Democratic Beliefs and Diffuse Support, 1995, 1997, and 1999

	Level of Democratic Beliefs								
	1995			**1997**			**1999**		
Level of Diffuse Support	None/Low (0–1) (%)	Medium (2) (%)	High (3) (%)	None/Low (0–1) (%)	Medium (2) (%)	High (3) (%)	None/Low (0–1) (%)	Medium (2) (%)	High (3) (%)
Low	7.9	20.4	47.4	6.5	18.0	48.2	10.1	22.3	47.1
Medium	34.0	48.1	38.3	39.4	44.5	35.2	33.6	46.9	38.1
High	58.1	31.5	14.3	54.1	37.5	16.6	56.3	30.8	14.8
Total	100	100	100	100	100	100	100	100	100
	gamma = −.68*			gamma = −.65*			gamma = −.64*		

Note: The original diffuse support index is trichotomized into three categories: high, intermediate, and low levels. * $P < .05$.

almost all the news media and political communications are still controlled by the government. Thus, I expect that respondents who are highly interested in politics at the national level tend to be more likely to support the current political regime.

Drawing upon Almond and Verba's (1963, 88) indicators for political interest, I used the following three questions to measure the degree of interest in politics among our respondents:

1. How much are you interested in politics?
2. How much do you care about national affairs?
3. How often do you talk about politics with friends and family members?

Questions 1 and 2 concern the degree of respondents' interest in high politics: politics in general and major national issues. Given an assumption that the frequency of conversation about politics with intimates reflects the level of political interest (Inglehart 1997, 309), question 3 is designed to supplement the first two questions. For each of the first two questions, the respondents were asked to assess their levels of political interest on a 4-point scale, where "1" indicates no interest (or total apathy) and "4" stands for high interest. For question 3, respondents were asked to rate their frequency of talking about politics with their acquaintances also on a 4-point scale, where "1" refers to "never talk" and "4" indicates "always talk." These three items were combined to form an additive index.[9] To test my hypothesis that those who are highly interested in politics at the national level tend to be more likely to support the current political regime, I examined the bivariate correlation between this index and the diffuse support index for the three surveys. The results are shown in table 4.5.

In all three samples, as expected, the more interested respondents are in politics, the more supportive they are of the current political regime. For instance, in all three surveys, while only around 10 percent of those who had little interest in politics were in the "high" category of diffuse support, more than 55 percent of the highly interested were in that category. Again, the gammas for the three surveys have positive signs, showing that interest in politics was positively associated with diffuse support.

---

9. The reliability analyses of these three items yield reliability coefficients (alphas) of .78, .81, and .80 for the 1995, 1997, and 1999 surveys, respectively.

Table 4.5

Correlations between Interest in Politics and Diffuse Support, 1995, 1997, and 1999

	Level of Interest in Politics								
	1995			1997			1999		
Level of Diffuse Support	None/Low (%)	Medium (%)	High (%)	None/Low (%)	Medium (%)	High (%)	None/Low (%)	Medium (%)	High (%)
Low	53.3	20.1	4.7	32.6	18.8	6.3	39.1	15.3	5.2
Medium	38.7	34.2	36.8	55.2	36.7	38.8	49.8	35.5	36.1
High	8.0	45.7	58.5	12.2	44.5	55.0	11.1	49.2	58.8
TOTAL	100	100	100	100	100	100	100	100	100
	gamma = .58*			gamma = .47*			gamma = .57*		

Note: The original indexes of diffuse support and interest in politics are both trichotomized into three categories: high, intermediate, and low levels. * *P* < .05.

Perceived Need for Further Political Reform and Diffuse Support

It is erroneous to say either that China has never engaged in political reform during the post-Mao era or that the country's fundamental, nondemocratic political system has changed during this period. Rather, limited political reform in China, with its ebbs and flows, has lasted for more than two decades since it was initiated by Deng Xiaoping in the late 1970s.[10] This reform has so far aimed at the improvement of the CCP's legitimacy, sociopolitical stability, and administrative efficiency rather than the establishment of a true democratic system (Burns 1999). The reform consists of such important policy and regulatory initiatives as local elections in both urban and rural areas,[11] separation of Party and government functions, abolition of the life tenure system for Party and government leaders, and legalizations in both economic and social domains.[12] While these initiatives have played roles in improving the educational and technical quality of Party-government leaders and bureaucrats and the efficiency of government agencies, none of them is designed to, or will in the near future, change the political and ideological foundations of the current system.

Thus, any deepening of such limited reform will naturally require changes in the current regime's ideological norms and fundamental political structures (the one-party rule). Consequently, people who perceive the need for a further political reform should be more likely to challenge and oppose the current political regime's norms and structures. In this study, therefore, I hypothesize that the perceived need for a further political reform should be negatively associated with diffuse support for the current regime.

Moreover, in the current Chinese setting there is good reason to examine the role of attitudes toward political reform in influencing a person's support for the regime. Since the 1989 Tiananmen crackdown and the demise of communist regimes in Eastern Europe and the former Soviet Union, the regime led by the CCP has become even more cautious about political liberalization and democratization. The CCP leaders have become more vigorous in stressing the need for political stability and economic advancement,

---

10. One of the detailed descriptions and in-depth analyses of the process of the post–Mao political reform can be found in the work by Baum (1994).

11. While the local elections in urban areas are applicable only to deputies to local People's Congresses, those in the rural areas are instituted for the selections of both deputies to local People's Congresses and members of Village Committees.

12. For a summary of major policy and regulatory initiatives in the post-Mao political reform, see the work by Burns (1999).

instead of political reform, as primary national goals (Chen and Zhong 1998, 37). Thus, the examination of the effect of the perceived need for further political reform should shed some light on the public's attitudes toward the national goals set by the regime's leadership as well as the fundamental political system.

In the three Beijing surveys, I measured the perceived need for further political reform by asking respondents to assess a straightforward statement: "today, what our country needs the most is a further political reform." To test my hypothesis regarding the relationship between such perceived need and diffuse support, I examine the correlation between respondents' assessments of the statement and their scores for the diffuse support index.

The results of the correlation analysis (table 4.6) show that, in all three surveys, those who perceived no need for a further political reform were more supportive than those who perceived the need. For example, in the three samples, between 50 percent and 60 percent of those seeing no need for a further political reform strongly supported the current political regime, while only less than 18 percent of those believing in such need strongly supported the regime. Thus, the empirical evidence from our data supports our hypothesis.

Strong Preference for Stability and Nationalist Sentiments and Diffuse Support

In chapter 2, I examined the unique effects of the strong preference for sociopolitical stability and nationalist sentiments on certain individual items in the diffuse support index, which mainly pertain to the national government. Here, I will examine the effects of these two high-politics variables on the entire index of diffuse support. Since, as shown in chapter 2, these two high-politics variables are closely related, as they both strongly imply the important role of the national government, I explore their effects on diffuse support together.

Strong Preference for Sociopolitical Stability

As mentioned in chapter 2, in today's China, most people have a strong preference for sociopolitical stability. For instance, in our three samples over 80 percent of the respondents preferred a stable and orderly society to a freer society that could be prone to social disruption. This finding is consistent with another study that found acute fear of the consequences of social chaos

Table 4.6

Correlations between Need for Political Reform and Diffuse Support, 1995, 1997, and 1999

Level of Diffuse Support[b]	Perceived Need for Further Political Reform[a]					
	1995		1997		1999	
	No Need (0) (%)	Need (1) (%)	No Need (0) (%)	Need (1) (%)	No Need (0) (%)	Need (1) (%)
Low	4.9	37.7	4.0	42.0	8.5	38.1
Medium	35.0	44.1	40.8	40.5	41.9	45.2
High	60.1	18.2	55.2	17.5	49.6	16.7
Total	100	100	100	100	100	100
	gamma = −.54*		gamma = −.52*		gamma = −.51*	

[a] Agreement (including "agree" and "strongly agree") with statement is coded "1"; disagreement (including "disagree" and "strongly disagree") is coded "0."

[b] The original diffuse support index is trichotomized into three categories: high, intermediate, and low levels. * $P < .05$.

among most Chinese people (Qiao and Chen 1994, iii–v). Such an over-whelming preference results from at least two major sources. One is government propaganda. Using references to the breakdown of sociopolitical order in former Soviet republics and East European countries after the fall of communist regimes, the CCP leadership has made relentless efforts to stress political stability as a prerequisite for national economic growth and individuals' well-being (Zhong 1996). The CCP leadership has used the government-controlled media and exploited the Chinese people's fear of chaos (*luan*). The other cause of the strong preference for stability is Chinese traditional culture, which gives social harmony a top priority. As Pye (1992, 123) has pointed out, most Chinese "accept completely the need for order."

Even more importantly, government propaganda and traditional culture also make people believe that only a strong, centralized authority can provide needed sociopolitical tranquility. This connection between strong central authority and stability has been manifested best in a school of political thought in China, "new authoritarianism" (*xing quanwei zhuyi*), which gained currency in the wake of the 1989 Tiananmen crackdown. This school of thought argues that only the centralized state, under a strong leadership, best fits Chinese society and can maintain political stability while promoting economic development (Link 1992; Soutman 1992; Baum 1994, 238–9; Fewsmith 2001a, part 2). By default, therefore, the current CCP regime becomes a strong "authority" that is supposed to provide needed sociopolitical stability and order. As one China scholar suggests, this sociopsychological connection between the current regime and stability has led many people "both old and young, to conclude that China needs an authoritarian regime for fast and stable economic growth" (Zheng 1994, 235). As a result, when considering the current regime as a whole, which includes both the national government and a set of norms promoted by the government, those who strongly prefer stability should be more supportive of the regime, broadly defined.

Nationalist Sentiment

Beliefs and expectations about what kind of role China should play in regional and world affairs are "part of a generic Chinese nationalism rooted in a sense of Chinese national identity that developed historically over a very long period and that acquired its current characteristics in the course of the past century and a half" (Levine 1995, 43). In today's China, as mentioned in chapter 2, this kind of nationalist sentiment has increasingly gained currency within the population. Such a strong sentiment was evident in our Beijing surveys: over 80 percent of the respondents believed that China should play an important role in Asia and the world, and should be a stronger world power in the next century.[13] Strong nationalism among the Chinese people, as some recent studies (Downs and Saunders 1998; Zheng 1999; Chen 2001; Fewsmith 2001a) point out, results mainly from two sources: the government's continuous promotion of it for the purpose of strengthening its legitimacy and the public's yearning for a strong national identity under a perceived foreign threat.

Nationalism in today's China not only explicitly stresses loyalty and obligation to the national government, but accords with the values and norms promoted by the government. Since the early 1990s, the national government has made more efforts in its education campaign to promote what some China scholars (e.g., Zhao 1998) call "state-led" nationalism. In this kind of campaign, the government not only equates the "nation" (*guo*) to "state" (*zhenfu*), but emphasizes the government-defined "Chinese characteristics" that encompass such core norms of the regime as the necessity of one-party rule, the absolute priority of stability/order over individual freedom, and the necessity of "gradual" (if any at all) democratization in China (Zhao 1998, 2000).

In other words, Chinese people have been repeatedly bombarded through the ongoing campaign with the message that being patriotic and nationalistic means to support the national government as well as the norms and values promoted by the government. As a result, many Chinese people, including intellectuals and college students, have "accepted the themes of the patriotic education campaign" (Zhao 2000, 21). Evidence includes the emergence or revival of such conservative schools of thought as the new authoritarianism or neoconservatism, which advocate principles very similar to those of the government, such as a strong, centralized state and political stability

13. As explained in chapter 2, I measured the nationalist sentiment using two statements: (1) "China should play more important a role in Asia and the world," and (2) "China should and will be a stronger power in the world in the next century." Respondents were asked to rate each of the two statements on a 4-point scale where "1" indicates strong disagreement with a statement, and "4" refers to strong agreement. These two items are combined to form an additive index for nationalist sentiment in each survey.

Table 4.7

Correlations between Preference for Stability and Nationalist Sentiment and Diffuse Support, 1995, 1997, and 1999

	Diffuse Support		
	1995	1997	1999
Preference for Stability	.44*	.51*	.50*
Nationalist Sentiment	.46*	.50*	.48*

Note: Diffuse support is the original additive index. All entries are Pearson correlations (r). * $P < .05$.

(instead of democratization) as prerequisites for a stronger China.[14] Thus, I expect that, in our samples, those who have strong nationalist sentiment should score high on the entire index of diffuse support, which concerns both the government and norms promoted by it.

All in all, I have hypothesized that the preference for sociopolitical stability and nationalist sentiment is more likely to be positively associated with the diffuse support index. To test this hypothesis, I examined the bivariate correlations between these two high-politics orientations, on the one hand, and the diffuse support index, on the other. As table 4.7 shows, both preference for sociopolitical stability and nationalist sentiment were highly correlated with the diffuse support index in the three samples. Pearson correlations ranged from a low of .44 to a high of .51, which indicates strong associations.

The Impacts of Low-Politics Orientations on Diffuse Support

As defined in chapter 1, low-politics orientations refer to a set of attitudes toward issues that directly touch citizens' daily life, communal matters, and the conditions of the work place (Bialer 1980, 166). In this study, accordingly, I include in the category of low-politics orientation such items as satisfaction (or dissatisfaction) with personal living conditions, interest in local issues, and assessment of local-government policy dealing with cer-

14. For detailed and in-depth discussions on these schools of thought, see works by Zheng (1999), Zhao (2000), and Fewsmith (2001a, chapter 3).

tain local issues. As discussed in chapter 1, I expect that there may be associations between these low-politics orientations and diffuse support, but such associations should be weak, or at least weaker than those between high-politics orientations and diffuse support. In this section, I explore these associations from a bivariate perspective.

Satisfaction with One's Material and Social Life and Diffuse Support

It has been argued that individuals' satisfaction with or positive assessment of their socioeconomic conditions contributes to their support for democratic systems and hence to the stability of established democracies (Inglehart 1977; Barnes, Farah, and Heunks 1979; Thomassen 1989). As Inglehart has noted in his empirical study of forty-three societies, "if, in the long run, people feel that life has been good under a given regime, it enhances feelings of diffuse support for that regime" (Inglehart 1997, 176). Analysts who tested this proposition in the former Soviet Union during the late 1980s have found that satisfaction with material life is also positively associated with support for the established nondemocratic political order or with reduced interest in changing the political status quo (Silver 1987; Finifter and Mickiewicz 1992). Based on his findings from a survey of emigrants from the Soviet Union in the early 1980s, Silver (1987, 126) concludes that "increases in material satisfaction are associated with greater support for regime norms."

Nonetheless, while all these earlier studies find a positive connection between personal material satisfaction and support for the current political regime, the magnitude of such a connection has varied in these studies. Some of the studies find a strong correlation between satisfaction and support for the regime, others present mixed or weak correlations. Such differences in the magnitude of the relationship between satisfaction and regime support may result from different measures of satisfaction used in these studies. It seems evident that, as measures of satisfaction used in these studies become more general or broader, the correlation between satisfaction and regime support turns out stronger. For example, when Inglehart (1997, 176) used such a broad measure as *"satisfaction with one's life as whole,"*[15] he found a strong connection; when Silver (1987) adopted much

---

15. The italics are in the original.

narrower measures, he detected weak and mixed effects on support for
regime norms.

Drawing upon the lessons and insights from the earlier studies, I adopt two
principles to design my measurement of satisfaction with socioeconomic
conditions among our respondents in order to gauge satisfaction more
accurately. First, I choose a midrange measure to detect respondents' satisfaction with their socioeconomic conditions. This is because a midrange
measure can strike a good balance between an overly broad or abstract
measurement, which could not distinguish from the respondent's feeling
about the entire political system, and a very narrow measurement, which
might be limited to certain specific issues while missing the overall picture.

Second, I focus on the subjective dimension of satisfaction when designing the measure. In some previous studies of popular support for the
political regime, personal life satisfaction has been defined as individuals'
"subjective perceptions" of their life improvement or fulfillment, which are
more likely to have behavioral consequences (Barnes, Farah, and Heunks
1979; Millar and Clayton 1987; Silver 1987; Thomassen 1990). As Silver
puts it, "rather than objective measures of material welfare, subjective measures of material satisfaction seem more appropriate, for it is the satisfaction
of people's perceived wants, not merely the objective improvement of their
material condition, that is said to generate support for the regime" (1987,
123–4). Thus, individuals' satisfaction is measured here as subjective perception of their socioeconomic condition improvement since the onset of
post-Mao reforms.

Following these two principles, I tap into two subjective aspects of satisfaction: satisfaction with material life and satisfaction with social life. To
measure material satisfaction, I asked respondents how satisfied they were
with their "living conditions (including housing, income, food, clothing, etc.)
since the reform." For satisfaction with social life, I asked them how
satisfied they were with their "social status (including job prestige, respect
from others, power to influence, etc.) since the reform." For both questions,
respondents were asked to register their levels of satisfaction on a 4-point
scale, where "1" stands for "very dissatisfied" and "4" stands for "very
satisfied." An additive index of satisfaction is formed based on a respondent's sum of scores for these two questions. This bi-item indicator meets
the two principles mentioned above: it is subjective and mid-ranged (neither too narrow nor too broad). I expect to find a positive and moderate relationship in our samples between satisfaction with one's living conditions
and diffuse support for the regime.

The results of the bivariate analysis presented in table 4.8 shows that, as expected, the levels of satisfactions with economic life and social life were positively associated with that of diffuse support for the current political regime. For example, in all three samples, about 50 percent of those who were very satisfied with their economic and social lives strongly supported the regime, while around a quarter of those who were least satisfied did so. Moreover, it should be noted that, as the gammas in the three surveys indicate, the relationship between satisfaction and diffuse support was moderate by conventional standards. The strength of such a relationship relative to that of other relationships will be further explored in the multivariate analysis that follows.

Interest in Local Issues and Assessment of Local Policy and Diffuse Support

Some analysts have argued that ordinary citizens in communist societies tend to be more interested in low-politics issues that are closely related to their personal lives and hence are self-motivated to participate in low-politics or political activities at the local and communal levels (Bialer 1980; Bahry and Silver 1990; Shi 1997). This is because, as Shi (1997) points out in his study of political participation in Beijing, while people are discouraged by the political system from trying to influence and participate in decision-making processes at the national level (high-politics), they are offered opportunities by the system to affect decision implementations at the local level and in their work units (*danwei*), which all involve their everyday lives.

Although these earlier studies do not directly deal with the connection between interest in local and communal issues (or low-politics issues) and assessment of local government policies, on the one hand, and diffuse support for the current political regime at the national level, on the other, they seem to imply that there should not be a strong connection between these two sides. For example, Bialer (1980, 167) argues that, in the communist system, low politics and high politics hardly intersect. What Bialer means by "high" politics includes the fundamental political system and predominant ideology, both of which are similar, if not equivalent, to the concept of diffuse support in this analysis. From Bialer's argument one may extrapolate a hypothesis that interest in local issues and assessment of local policy should not be strongly associated with the level of their diffuse support. To test this hypothesis, I conducted a bivariate analysis of the relationships

Table 4.8

Satisfaction with One's Life and Diffuse Support

	Level of Satisfaction								
Level of Diffuse Support	1995			1997			1999		
	Low (%)	Medium (%)	High (%)	Low (%)	Medium (%)	High (%)	Low (%)	Medium (%)	High (%)
Low	34.2	20.4	15.8	37.1	21.4	14.5	36.6	25.8	17.9
Medium	39.2	48.8	40.0	38.6	47.6	40.0	38.1	42.0	33.0
High	26.6	30.8	48.2	24.3	31.0	45.5	25.3	32.2	49.1
Total	100	100	100	100	100	100	100	100	100
	gamma = .24*			gamma = .26*			gamma = .25*		

Note: Both indexes of original diffuse support and satisfaction are trichotomized into three categories: high, intermediate, and low levels. All entries are percentages, except those for gamma. * $P < .05$.

Table 4.9

Correlations between Interest in Issues and Assessment of Local Policy and Diffuse Support, 1995, 1997, and 1999

	Diffuse Support[a]		
	1995	1997	1999
Interest in local issue[b]	.114*	.113*	.157*
Assessment of local policy[c]	.025	.030	.018

Note: All the entries are Pearson correlations (r). * $P < .05$
[a] Diffuse Support is the original diffuse support index.
[b] The question for interest in local issues reads: "How much are you interested in issues in your neighborhood and/or your work unit?"
[c] The question for assessment of local policy reads: "Overall, how would you rate the municipal government in terms of its policies dealing with local issues with which you are most concerned (e.g., community's order, traffic, hygiene, etc.)?"

between these two low-politics variables and the diffuse support index. The results of the analysis are presented in table 4.9.

The results indicate that in all three surveys, the correlations between both interest in local issues and assessment of local policy and diffuse support were very weak, although the relationship between interest in local issues and diffuse support was statistically significant. These findings suggest that people in China seem to separate more or less their interest and assessment of local affairs from their diffuse feelings about the political system as a whole. In addition, the findings apparently support the hypothesis that, in communist society, interest and involvement in low-politics or local affairs do not, at least strongly, relate to "high" politics. But it should be briefly noted that a more conclusive judgment of the relative strength of the correlations between these low-politics variables and diffuse support should be made based on the multivariate analysis that follows in the next section.

Multivariate Analysis

I have thus far examined the bivariate correlations between demographic attributes and high- and low-politics orientations, on the one hand, and diffuse support, on the other hand. In order to determine the independent effects of those explanatory variables and the relative weights of these effects on diffuse support, however, we need to employ a multivariate analysis that incorporates all the above-specified, explanatory variables (i.e., sociodemographic attributes, high-politics orientations, and low-politics orientations). The results of this multivariate analysis are shown in table 4.10.

All together, sociodemographic attributes, high-politics orientations, and low-politics orientations explain 25 percent, 30 percent, and 27 percent of variance in diffuse support, respectively, in the 1995, 1997, and 1999 samples. With a few minor exceptions, the results from these three multiple regression models (ordinary least squares) confirm the hypotheses and the results of bivariate analyses, which were presented earlier in this chapter.

First, these results provide strong evidence for the argument made throughout this chapter that people's demographic attributes and high-politics orientations play significant roles in shaping their diffuse support for the current political regime. In terms of the effects of sociodemographic attributes, the results indicated that age, sex, education, economic status, some occupational groups, and CCP membership, all of which were expected to have significant effects, did have the expected signs and did have independent impacts on diffuse support. Specifically, these results show that those who were older, who were men, and who were less educated but had higher self-evaluations of economic status, and who were CCP members tend to be more supportive of the regime. Moreover, among the eight occupational groups analyzed here, SOE cadres, white-collar professionals, and government officials were all more supportive of the regime than ordinary SOE workers, with government officials being the most supportive group.

In terms of the impacts of high-politics orientations, the results from the three multiple regression models reveal that, as expected earlier, democratic values, interest in politics, perceived need for political reform, preference for sociopolitical stability, and nationalist sentiment all had significant effects (with expected signs) on diffuse support for the current political regime. Specifically, on the one hand, beliefs in democratic values and in the need for reform were negatively associated with the level of diffuse support. On the other hand, interest in politics, preference for stability, and nationalist sentiment were positively related to diffuse support. In other words, while those who strongly believed in democratic values and keenly perceived the need for fundamental political reform tended to be less supportive of the regime, those who were more interested in politics in general and had strong preferences for sociopolitical stability and strong nationalist mentalities were more supportive of the regime.

Second, the results in table 4.10 show that, after controlling for the effects of the sociodemographic attributes and high-politics orientations, such low-politics orientations as interest in and assessment of local affairs and satisfaction with one's economic and social conditions did not exert a statistically significant impact on diffuse support. In other words, when sociodemographic attributes and high-politics orientations are taken into account, whether people are interested in local affairs, how they evaluate local issues, and how much they are satisfied with personal economic and social conditions do not meaningfully affect their feelings about the regime in each survey.

Third, the empirical evidence in table 4.10 also indicates a sharp contrast in the magnitudes of effects on diffuse support between both sociodemographic attributes and high-politics orientations, on the one hand, and low-politics orientations, on the other. In all three surveys, while most of the sociodemographic attributes and all of the high-politics orientations had statistically significant impacts on diffuse support, none of the low-politics orientations had such an impact. In short, the effects of both sociodemographic attributes and high-politics orientations on diffuse support are so robust that these effects persisted in all three surveys even after controlling for low-politics orientations, whereas the effects of low-politics seemed to pale. Thus, this evidence, along with the other results mentioned above, supports one of the most important general hypotheses postulated in chapter 1: that is, since both sociodemographic attributes and high-politics orientations are directly associated with diffuse support, they are more powerful in influencing diffuse support than the low-politics orientations that are presumably indirectly associated with diffuse support.

Fourth, it is worth noting the relative strengths of the variables within each of the categories of sociodemographic and high-politics categories. From the statistics of standardized coefficients (beta) in the three regression models, one can easily identify several variables in each of the two categories that have distinctly powerful influences on diffuse support. In the category of sociodemographic attributes, self-assessed economic status and age seemed to be more powerful than other variables in that category in influencing diffuse support; the variable of self-assessed economic status exerted the strongest influence. In the category of high-politics orientations, beliefs in democratic values and in need for political reform, and preference for stability had stronger impacts than other variables in the category on diffuse support; the variable of belief in need for political reform had the strongest impact. In other words, of all the explanatory variables included in the multiple regression analysis, economic status and a belief in the need for political reform seemed to be the best predictors of diffuse support for the current political regime.

Table 4.10

Multiple Regression (OLS) of Diffuse Support by Sociodemographic Attributes, High-Politics Orientations, and Low-Politics Orientations, 1995, 1997, and 1999

Independent Variables	Diffuse Support								
	1995			1997			1999		
	b	s.e.	beta	b	s.e.	beta	b	s.e.	beta
Age	.05*	.01	.15	.04*	.01	.17	.05*	.00	.20
Sex[a]	-.36*	.11	-.9	-.38*	.16	-.10	-.38*	.20	-.10
Education[b]	-.29*	.11	-.11	-.56*	.16	-.16	-.48*	.17	-.12
Economic status[c]	.94*	.08	.34	.70*	.10	.23	.86*	.16	.27
Occupations[d]									
SOE cadres	.31*	.15	.06	.70*	.37	.07	.62*	.37	.06
White-collars	.34*	.12	.06	.56*	.35	.06	.33*	.18	.07
Govt. bureaucrats	.65*	.15	.10	.89*	.34	.09	.92*	.40	.08
Military	.56	.47	.03	.60	.49	.05	.11	.68	.01
Students	-.23	.61	-.01	.22	.79	.01	-.00	.14	-.00
Private entrepreneurs	.30	.42	.02	.31	.57	.02	.52	.45	.02
Retirees	.59	.50	.06	.46	.47	.02	.37	.44	.04
CCP members[e]	.73*	.31	.10	.86*	.29	.12	.82*	.28	.11
Democratic values	-.65*	.22	-.11	-.70*	.20	-.12	-.67*	.21	-.11
Interest in politics	.30*	.16	.08	.44*	.15	.10	.47*	.25	.08
Need for reform	-.94*	.08	-.31	-.87*	.28	-.28	-.81*	.09	-.26
Preference for stability	.56*	.16	.13	.51*	.15	.12	.61*	.15	.11
Nationalism	.19*	.04	.11	.20*	.06	.10	.28*	.15	.11
Satisfaction	.21	.16	.04	.07	.13	.02	.19	.16	.09
Interest in local fairs	.20	.23	.04	.16	.23	.02	.10	.22	.01
Assessing local policies	.40	.30	.03	.23	.15	.04	.32	.19	.05

	b	s.e.	b	s.e.	b	s.e.
Constant	10.8	1.61	10.2	1.56	10.1	1.06
R^2	.29		.33		.312	
Adjusted R^2	.25		.30		.27	
N	638		646		652	

Note: b refers to unstandardized coefficient, whereas beta stands for standardized coefficient. s.e. = standardized error. * $P < .05$.

[a] Male = 1; female = 2.

[b] Illiterate or elementary = 1; junior high = 2; senior high = 3; college or higher = 4.

[c] Lower level = 1; lower-middle level = 2; middle level = 3; upper-middle level = 4; upper level = 5.

[d] The "SOE workers" is used as the reference category (reflected in the intercept) for occupations.

[e] Non-CCP member = 1; CCP member = 2.

Finally, among the results presented in table 4.10, there are some exceptions to my earlier expectations about the impacts of several occupations. Although I had anticipated the significant impacts of being military personnel, a college student, private entrepreneur, and retiree on diffuse support, these variables did not exert such impacts in all three regression models. A possible reason for the lack of independent effects of military-personnel and private-entrepreneur variables could be that each of these variables had too few respondents in our surveys to have stable estimates in such a multiple regression analysis. Thus, if there were more respondents for each of these variables, the coefficient of each variable could be significant. On the other hand, a potential explanation for the absence of independent impacts of college-student and retiree variables is that the impacts of both variables could be muted by the variable of age that is closely related to, and much more powerful than, being student and being retiree. In other words, college students and retirees are, respectively, less and more supportive of the regime, probably due mainly to their age.

Summary and Conclusion

Throughout this chapter, I have attempted to address two central questions: Who is most likely to support the current political system in China? And why do people support the system? These two questions have been answered through the examination of different effects of three categories of sociopolitical factors—sociodemographic attributes, high-politics orientations, and low-politics orientations—on the level of diffuse support against the data collected in the three Beijing surveys. The empirical findings from both bivariate and multivariate analyses presented in this chapter have provided support for the hypotheses—postulated in the first chapter and earlier in this chapter—about the different types of relationships between the three categories of sociopolitical factors, on the one hand, and diffuse support, on the other hand. These empirical findings can be highlighted through my answers to the two central questions that were raised in the beginning of the chapter.

First, who is more or less likely to support the current political regime in China? From the data collected in Beijing, I have found that older persons, males, less educated individuals, those claiming higher self-evaluations of economic status, and CCP members tend to be more supportive of the regime. Not surprisingly, I have also found that, among all professions tackled in this study, government officials are most supportive of the regime.

Second, why do people support the current political regime led by the CCP or why do they choose not to support the regime? Based on the findings from the Beijing surveys, one may conclude that some people are more likely to support the regime because they strongly prefer sociopolitical stability, because they have stronger nationalist feeling, or because they have a stronger interest in politics in general. Also, one can conclude that some people are less likely to support the regime mainly because they strongly believe in democratic values or the need for fundamental political reform.

From these empirical findings, one can easily discern the sharp contrasts between the regime's opponents and proponents in terms of their sociodemographic, sociopolitical, and socioeconomic characteristics. From sociodemographic and sociopolitical perspectives, it is evident that most potent opponents come mainly from the more energetic and modern sectors of the population: they tend to be young and better educated, and believe in democratic values and see the need for fundamental political change.[16] On the other hand, the current regime apparently can find its most reliable proponents among the less resilient and more traditional or conservative sectors of the population: they tend to be older and less educated, and have a strong preference for the political status quo.

Although the current political regime still enjoys a moderately high level of support (as indicated in chapter 2), the sociodemographic and sociopolitical characteristics of the opponents predicate a serious political challenge to the regime's relentless effort to buttress its legitimacy. A modified modernization theory (Inglehart 1997) stresses the close interaction between economic development or modernization and value changes. As Inglehart (1997, 15) suggests, "economic development, cultural change, and political change are linked in coherent and even, to some extent, predictable patterns." According to this theory, one could argue that if the ongoing trend of economic modernization and growth continues in China more people will join the ranks of the modern sector of the population who are better educated and more inclined to support fundamental political change. Since this sector, as our findings indicated above, tends to be less supportive of the

16. According to some modernization theorists, the modern citizen tends to be well-educated, open-minded, and democratic (Lerner 1958; Inkeles and Smith 1974; Inkeles and Diamond 1980; Inglehart 1990).

current CCP rule, it is more likely the regime will gain more opponents than proponents from the ongoing processes of economic development.

From a socioeconomic perspective, one can tell that the regime's opponents may come from some groups that are considered to be socially and economically "deprived" or "disadvantaged"[17] under the current political system (especially during the reform era). These deprived groups include women, SOE workers, and those who believe themselves to be at lower levels of economic status. On the other hand, the regime's proponents come from some groups who have usually been considered socially and economically "advantaged" under the current system. These groups include government officials, Party members, and those who believe themselves to be at higher levels of economic status.

These sharp socioeconomic contrasts between opponents and proponents also pose a potential political challenge to the current political regime. It seems to be very difficult, if not impossible, for the regime to narrow socioeconomic gaps between the opponents and proponents. Narrowing such gaps not only takes time but entails fundamental reforms in economic and political structures. Yet such reforms will bring about more political risks for the regime. These potential risks and their political implications will be explored in chapter 7.

17. Citrin and his associates (Citrin et al. 1975) used these terms to describe those who believed themselves to be at lower levels of economic status or "have nots."

Chapter 5

Sources of Specific Support

The theoretical assumption developed in the previous chapters suggests that the formation of each of the two dimensions of political support—diffuse and specific—is significantly influenced by a distinct combination of sociopolitical factors. Based on this assumption, I examined the effects of the three categories of sociopolitical variables—sociodemographic, high-politics, and low-politics categories—on diffuse support in chapter 4. In this chapter, I explore the impacts of these sociopolitical variables on specific support with the anticipation that these sociopolitical variables influence specific support differently from the way they affect diffuse support. By examining the effects of those sociopolitical variables, I intend to answer two important questions: Who is most likely to support the incumbent authorities (as opposed to the political regime) in contemporary China? And why do some, but not all, people support the authorities?

Drawing upon theoretical arguments from earlier studies, as discussed in chapter 1, one may hypothesize that low-politics orientations should be strongly associated with specific support, while both sociodemographic attributes and high-politics orientations are supposed to be weakly or indirectly related to such support. To test this general hypothesis, I will examine the relationship between each of the three categories of sociopolitical variables and specific support from both bivariate and multivariate perspectives. Some general implications for the sources of specific support in contemporary China will be drawn from the findings about such a relationship.

The Impacts of Sociodemographic Attributes on Specific Support

To answer the first research question of who is more likely to have strong support for the incumbent authorities, I examine in this section the impacts of sociodemographic attributes on the level of specific support. For the purpose of comparison, I focus on the same sociodemographic variables as those tackled in chapter 4. These sociodemographic variables include age, sex, education, occupation, economic status, and membership in the Chinese Communist Party.

It has been assumed in this study that these sociodemographic variables are not associated with specific support as closely as they are with diffuse support. This is because there is a discrepancy at least in stability between sociodemographic variables and specific support. That is, as mentioned in chapter 1, while the sociodemographic attributes remain stable or unchanged over a short period of time, specific support shifts swiftly with changes in people's responses to specific government policies and performance. Such a discrepancy, in effect, should be even more evident in contemporary China because the country has been undergoing remarkable socioeconomic changes (for example, changes in housing, medical care, job security, environment, and social order), which have been initiated mainly by government policies.

Nonetheless, this theoretical assumption does not suggest that sociodemographic variables are completely unrelated to specific support. Rather, it allows us to speculate that specific support may be associated to a certain extent with the sociodemographic attributes since some of the government's policies and its performance can benefit people in one sociodemographic grouping or another at any given point in time. Thus, some sociodemographic variables should have meaningful impacts on specific support at one moment, although such impacts may not be as strong as those sociodemographic variables exert on diffuse support. Such meaningful impacts on specific support have been found in both nondemocratic societies (Millar and Clayton 1987) and democratic societies (Campbell 1981; Davis, Fine-Davis, and Meehan 1982; Shanks and Miller 1990, 1991).

Age and Specific Support

Does the incumbent government enjoy more support from the young or the old? Fortunately, a recent study (Tang and Parish 2000, chapter 5) of Chinese urban residents' political attitudes has established some empirical and theoretical baselines for us to answer this question. Based on the data collected in Chinese cities during the late 1980s and the early 1990s, Tang and Parish (2000, 115–23) reported that younger people tended to have lower evaluations of government's policy "outputs." According to Tang and Parish, this is because young people have higher expectations for post-Mao reforms in various socioeconomic areas, and hence they tend to be less content with current government performance in those areas. This perspective is consistent with the observation made by another China scholar that the youth tend to be more idealistic; they are more likely to perceive the "huge gap" between their own expectations of government performance and the real results of government policies, and in turn they tend to challenge authorities due to such a perceived gap (Shi 1997, 250–1). Drawing upon these early studies of urban China, therefore, I expect the relationship between age and specific support to be positive: younger respondents in our samples may have lower specific support as measured by their evaluations of the authorities' performance in major policy areas.

Although those earlier studies help us develop a hypothesis about the direction of the relationship between age and specific support, they cannot assist us in determining the strength of the relationship because they do not differentiate magnitudes of such a relationship. Thus, our expectation about the strength of this relationship is mainly derived from the theoretical argument developed earlier in this study, suggesting that age should moderately or weakly relate to specific support. To explore both the expected direction and the strength of this relationship, I examined the bivariate correlation between various age groups, on the one hand, and the level of specific support, on the other. The results are presented in table 5.1.

There are two important findings that can be discerned from the results summarized in table 5.1. First, the respondent's age seemed to be positively associated with the level of specific support. That is, in all three samples, the younger the respondent, the lower was his or her evaluation of the government performance. This finding apparently confirms the empirical evidence and theoretical arguments in the earlier studies mentioned above.

Second, however, the positive relationship between age and specific support was not very strong; nor was it stable across our three surveys. Although the relationship was statistically significant in the 1995 and 1999 surveys, it was quite weak: the gammas were only .14 and .11 for the two surveys, respectively. Furthermore, the relationship, as the gamma indicates, was not statistically significant in the 1997 survey. These results on the magnitude and consistence of the relationship suggest that, while sociodemographic attributes did have some meaningful impact on specific support,

124

Sources of Specific Support

Table 5.1

Specific Support by Age, 1995, 1997, and 1999

Specific Support Index	Age					
	18–25 (%)	26–35 (%)	36–45 (%)	46–55 (%)	56–65 (%)	65–over (%)
			1995			
Low	30	25	21	18	19	16
Medium	64	70	72	75	73	69
High	6	5	7	7	8	15
Total	100	100	100	100	100	100
			gamma = .14*			
			1997			
Low	22	23	24	22	20	19
Medium	72	67	68	71	67	67
High	6	8	8	7	13	14
Total	100	100	100	100	100	100
			gamma = .07			
			1999			
Low	48	45	44	43	40	34
Medium	43	42	40	41	40	48
High	9	13	16	16	20	18
Total	100	100	100	100	100	100
			gamma = .11*			

Note: The specific support index is trichotomized into three categories: high, intermediate, and low levels. * $P < .05$.

such an impact did not seem to be strong and consistent over time. These results seem to confirm our own theoretical hypothesis that such a demographic attribute as age tends to be weakly associated with specific support.

Sex and Specific Support

There are two competing arguments regarding women's attitudes toward government policies and performance in some major socioeconomic areas since the beginning of post-Mao reforms. One suggests that women tend to have a higher evaluation of the incumbent government policies and performance. This is because governments at all levels in China are still, in theory, obligated to make and implement regulations and laws in various

Table 5.2

Specific Support by Gender, 1995, 1997, and 1999

Specific Support Index	1995		1997		1999	
	Female (%)	Male (%)	Female (%)	Male (%)	Female (%)	Male (%)
Low	32	20	27	22	28	23
Medium	62	68	67	62	64	63
High	6	12	6	16	8	14
Total	100	100	100	100	100	100
	gamma = −.14*		gamma = −.11*		gamma = −.10*	

Note: The original specific support index is trichotomized into three categories: high, intermediate, and low levels. Male = 1; Female = 2. * $P < .05$.

socioeconomic areas to protect women's interests (Robinson and Parris 1990). Moreover, some proponents of this argument believe that despite the remnants of discrimination against women, Chinese women have been better off in social and economic life since the post-Mao reform began. As Tang and Parish (2000, 231) have pointed out in their recent study of socio-economic transition in post-Mao China, "overall, Chinese urban women are faring quite well during this transition to market economy."

But the other argument suggests that women are less supportive than men of the current leaderships in the reform era. This is because women have become victims of government policies that explicitly or implicitly emphasize productivity and economic efficiency over gender equality (Yue and Li 1994, 170). For example, as the central government deepened the so-called SOE reform in the late 1990s to improve the efficiency of SOEs, women suffered higher unemployment rates than men. As mentioned in the previous chapter, in 1997, about 60 percent of the unemployed were female, although women accounted for less than 40 percent of urban employees (Bonin 2000, 155).[1]

To explore these two competing arguments against the data from the three Beijing surveys, I examined the bivariate correlations between the sexes and the level of specific support. The results, shown in table 5.2, reveal

1. The data from our three surveys apparently echo this aggregate information: women's evaluation of incumbent policy performance in the area of "protecting job security" was lower than men's.

that gender difference was significantly associated with the level of specific support in all three surveys. In each survey, women's evaluation of government policy performance tended to be lower than men's. This finding apparently supports one of the two contending arguments: Women are more likely than men to perceive themselves as the victims of government policies in the reform era. The gammas (table 5.2), however, were quite low in all three surveys, confirming the hypothesized moderate relationship between these two variables.

Education and Specific Support

Previous studies in various sociopolitical settings have found different impacts of education on respondents' evaluation of government performance. But the most relevant to this analysis are some empirical findings and theoretical arguments from the studies for such nondemocratic societies as China and the former Soviet Union. Based on data collected in Chinese urban areas from 1987 to 1991, Tang and Parish (2000, 108–19) have found that the better educated tend to have lower evaluations of incumbent policy performance in such areas as inflation control, housing, medical care, and so on, which are similar to the areas covered in our specific support index. This finding was also confirmed in a more recent empirical study based on the data collected in six Chinese cities in 1999 (Tang 2001). Similarly, in their study of Soviet mass attitudes, Millar and Clayton (1987, 53–5) have found that the well-educated (i.e., college-educated) tend to have the lowest evaluations of government policies in various socioeconomic areas.

There are at least two reasons for a low evaluation of government policy performance by the better educated under the communist system. First, the better educated tend to believe that their talents are constrained by government policies, and they "could do much better under a . . . more openly competitive system" (Tang and Parish 2000, 117). Second, as advanced education even under the communist system can be "intellectually liberating" (Silver 1987, 101–2), the better educated are more likely to characterize communist government policies as being arbitrary. Thus, the better educated tend to be more critical of incumbent policies and performance. Based on these explanations and the above-mentioned empirical findings, I expect that, in our samples, there should be a negative association between the level of education and the level of specific support.

As table 5.3 shows, there was a negative relationship between education and specific support within each of the three samples: the better educated

Table 5.3

Specific Support by Education, 1995, 1997, and 1999

Specific Support Index	Education			
	Elementary (%)	Junior high (%)	Senior high (%)	College (%)
		1995		
Low	16	21	25	28
Medium	75	73	70	67
High	8	6	6	4
Total	100	100	100	100
		gamma = −.12*		
		1997		
Low	20	22	24	27
Medium	70	70	68	69
High	10	8	8	4
Total	100	100	100	100
		gamma = −.10*		
		1999		
Low	16	25	22	29
Medium	77	70	73	67
High	6	5	5	4
Total	100	100	100	100
		gamma = −.09		

Note: The specific support index is trichotomized into three categories: high, intermediate, and low levels. * $P < .05$.

had lower evaluations of incumbent policy performance. For example, in the 1995 survey, while 16 percent of those with an elementary education registered a low level of evaluation of government policy performance, about 30 percent of those with a college education gave the same evaluation. Similar patterns held true in the other two surveys. Overall, these results are consistent with the findings from the previously mentioned empirical studies for contemporary China and the former Soviet Union. Yet such a negative relationship did not seem to be strong and stable over time: the correlations (measured by gammas) between education and specific support were quite weak for all three samples; such correlations were statistically significant for the 1995 and 1997 samples, but not for the 1999 sample.

Occupation and Specific Support

Some earlier studies of public attitudes toward post-Mao reforms have argued that people with different occupations may have quite different views
of the government's policies and its performance, as well as the political
regime (Hook 1996; Liu 1996; Tang and Parish 2000; Tang 2001). According to these earlier studies, the most obvious and important reason for the
existence of the occupational effect is that people of various occupational
groups may benefit or lose from incumbent policies in some socioeconomic
areas at any given time. Perhaps, the most salient case in point, which has
been often cited in studies of contemporary urban China, is that most SOE
workers have become increasingly discontented with the serious negative
effects of incumbent policies to deepen reforms in the state-owned enterprises
(Walder 1996; Croll 1999; Hu 2000; Wang and Hu 2000). These negative
policy effects include the imminent threat of unemployment, a drastic decline in social welfare, and a lack of genuine protection of workers' basic
rights. As Tang (2001) has found (based on a survey of six Chinese cities in
1999), SOE workers are most likely to have a low evaluation of incumbent
policy performance in such areas as housing, health, and job security (areas
of which are also tackled in our specific support index). Similarly, other
studies have also found that different attitudes toward incumbent policy performance may also result from other occupational identities, such as being
a college student (Goldman 2000), a private entrepreneur (Pearson 1997),
a bureaucrat (Lu 2000), and a member of the military (Shambaugh 1996).

In general, these earlier studies suggest the existence of a structural impact of occupation on people's evaluations of incumbent policy performance. Such a structural impact is a function of socioeconomic gains or losses
from incumbent policies that affect various occupations. Nonetheless, few
of the earlier studies have explored the persistence or strength of occupational impact on the evaluation of incumbent policy and performance. It has
been assumed in this study, as explained earlier in the book, that the connection between sociodemographic attributes and specific support may exist but that such a connection is likely weak or moderate. Specifically, the
moderateness of the connection may be reflected in the form of marked variations in the strength or patterns of the connection over a short period of time.
Thus, I expect that there should be connections between occupations and
specific support measured by the evaluations of incumbent policy performance, while the patterns of the connections may not persist over time in our
three samples.

Figure 5.1 summarizes the bivariate relationships between eight occupations, on the one hand, and the level of specific support, on the other hand. By looking at the overall occupational impacts in all three surveys together, one can discern at least three groups of occupations that had distinct levels of specific support. There were two groups at the two extremes, which had the lowest and highest levels of specific support, respectively, and there was a group in the middle, which had a medium level of such support. First, at the one extreme, SOE workers had the lowest mean scores for specific support among the eight occupational groups in all three surveys, which were on an average about 18.8 on a 9–45 summary scale. This result seems to confirm findings and arguments in the earlier studies mentioned above, suggesting that SOE workers had become increasingly discontented with the serious negative effects of incumbent policies to deepen reforms in SOEs during the late 1990s. Closely trailing SOE workers, college students and intellectuals, or white-collar professionals, had the second lowest scores for specific support, which were on an average around 19–20. This finding apparently supports the age-effect and educational-impact hypotheses mentioned above, indicating that the younger and better educated tend to have lower evaluations of government policy performance (see also Tang and Parish 2000, 108–19; Tang 2001).

Second, at the other end of the spectrum, government bureaucrats and the military personnel registered the highest level of specific support. On the average, mean scores for specific support given by these two groups were about 28 on the 9–45 scale. These results support the argument in some earlier studies that both government officials (Lu 2000) and the military (Shambaugh 1996) in general had benefited from incumbent policies in the 1990s.

Finally, between those two extremes, the respondents in the remaining three occupations—SOE cadres, private entrepreneurs, and retirees—had expressed middle-range levels of specific support over the time span of the three surveys. Overall, the average of their mean scores for specific support was around 23–24. The SOE cadres were more supportive of the incumbent policies than the ordinary SOE workers, perhaps because the former were generally in a much better position to protect themselves from serious negative effects (for example, layoff) of the SOE reforms. Although the benefits for retirees had declined in the reform era, retirees in our samples seemed to be more supportive than the SOE workers of incumbent performance in the major policy areas. Possible reasons behind this result could be that the retirees did not face such devastating, imminent socioeconomic threats as being laid off or sudden reductions of income, and that the central government

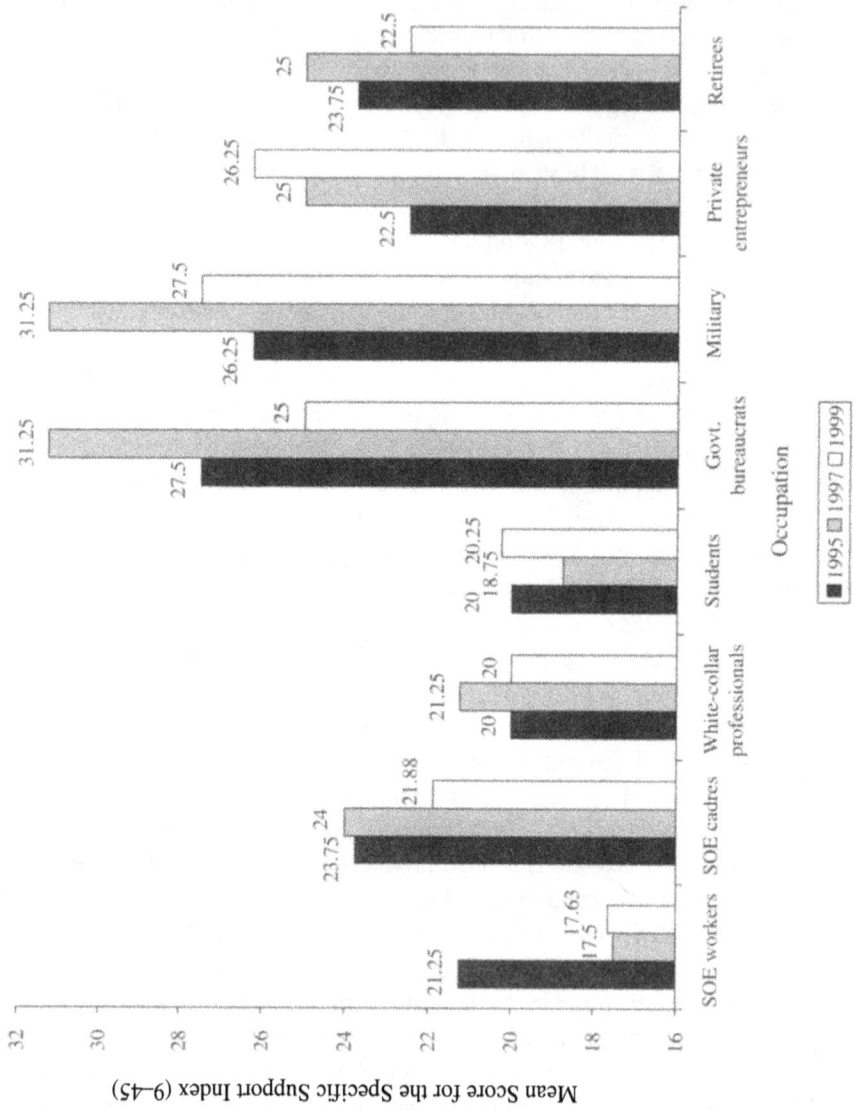

Figure 5.1
Occupation and Specific Support

had stressed retirement support in its social welfare reform plan since the mid 1990s (Croll 1999, 692–3). Private entrepreneurs also joined this mid-range group, registering a respectable level of specific support. This seems to contradict the finding from a recent survey study (Tang 2001) that the private sector had the lowest evaluations of incumbent performance. Nonetheless, our result apparently is consistent with the argument in some other studies suggesting that Chinese private entrepreneurs have benefited from incumbent policies, and they have been co-opted by the state into a kind of corporative arrangement (Pearson 1997; Dickson 2000b).

In short, it can be said that there were differences among occupations in the level of specific support when the aggregate results from all three surveys are taken into account. The pattern of the differences, however, was not necessarily the same in each survey. For example, although the average of SOE workers' mean scores for all the surveys was the lowest among all the occupations, the SOE workers' mean score in 1995 was not the lowest. The likely reason for such a drastic change was that after 1995 the central government began to implement fully the Labor Law and the Ninth Five-Year (economic development) Plan, both of which legitimated laying off employees by SOEs that operated at a loss (Solinger 1999). As a result, after 1995, SOE workers began to feel the imminent threat to their job security, and hence became more disgruntled with incumbent policies.

While it suffices to cite SOE workers' attitudinal change over time for present purposes, a similar case may hold true for other occupations included in this study. In short, the occupational impacts on specific support may vary drastically over a short period of time: in the case of this study, every two or four years between our three surveys. Such variations apparently support one of our general theoretical hypotheses mentioned above: the pattern of the relationship between such a sociodemographic variable as occupation and the level of specific support may not persist over time, because the incumbent policies and their effects change more frequently than people's occupations.

Economic Status and Specific Support

In chapter 4, I specified the so-called subjective indicator as the measure of economic status in this study. This subjective indicator is the self-assessment of one's economic level relative to others' on a 5-point scale (where 1 = "lower level"; 2 = "lower-middle level"; 3 = "middle level"; 4 = "upper-middle level"; and 5 = "upper level"). This subjective indicator has been chosen because, as mentioned earlier, it is more likely to impact political support (Citrin et al. 1975, 15; Silver 1987, 123–4), and it fits the unique form of socioeconomic stratification in contemporary China (Shi 1997, 50). It has been argued in some earlier studies that those who perceive themselves to be in the lower economic positions relative to others tend to be less supportive of incumbent policy performance, since they are likely to feel deprived economically by incumbent policies (Citrin et al. 1975; Farah, Barnes, and Heunks 1979). Based on this argument, I expect a positive relationship between economic status and the level of specific support for incumbent policy performance in our samples.

Figure 5.2 shows the overall picture of the relationship between self-assessed economic status and the level of specific support in the three surveys. The overall results from the three surveys reveal that the relationship was a curvilinear one, rather than the linear one suggested in some earlier studies for non-Chinese settings (Citrin et al. 1975; Farah, Barnes, and Heunks 1979). The peak of the curve for the curvilinear relationship, however, was located differently in our three surveys. While in both 1995 and 1997 surveys specific support reached its highest level (the peak) among those who were at the middle level of self-assessed economic status, in the 1999 survey the highest level of such support was among those who were at the lower-middle level. As figure 5.2 shows, in both 1995 and 1997, specific support started at a low level among those who regarded themselves as members of the lower class, gradually peaked among members of the middle class, and then declined to a low level among the upper class; in the 1999 survey, starting at a low level within the lower class, specific support leaped right away to its peak within the lower-middle class and then gradually declined as economic status increased.

These results have two important implications. First, they suggest that in general incumbent policies in the major socioeconomic areas might have increasingly benefited the lower-middle and middle classes rather than the upper class at least by the late 1990s. As an overwhelming majority of respondents in our samples identified themselves with the lower-middle and middle classes (table 4.3), it could be speculated that the incumbent authorities drew support (if any support at all) more from a majority than from a small portion of the population in other economic classes. Second, the change in the location of the peak for the curvilinear relationship within a rather short time span (between 1997 and 1999) suggests that the level of specific support may shift swiftly over time among those of the five self-assessed economic classes. Such a shift results from spontaneous responses

Figure 5.2
Economic Status and Specific Support

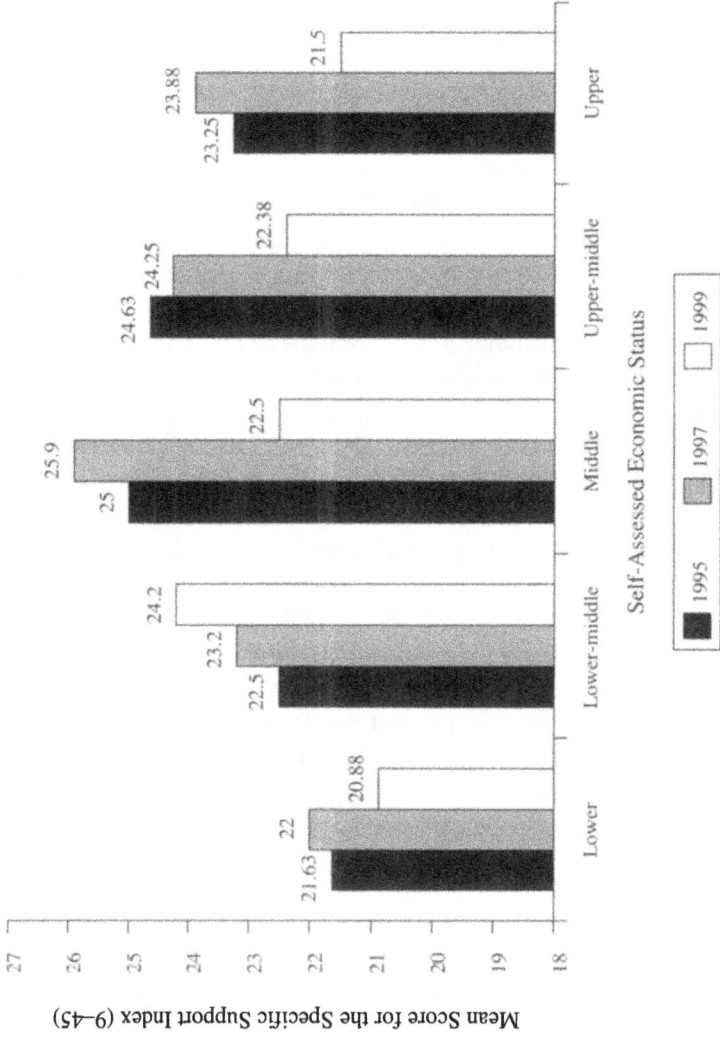

from members of these classes to changes in incumbent policies. Consequently, one should not take the pattern of the relationship at one point in time for granted.

Party Membership and Specific Support

In chapter 4, we found that CCP members tend to have much stronger diffuse support for the current political regime than do non-CCP members and that the strong and positive relationship between Party membership and diffuse support persists across all three surveys. But should one also expect a strong and positive relationship between Party membership and specific support to be present in our samples? To answer this question, one should first assess whether Party members as a group benefited more than non-Party members from incumbent policies in the reform era.

It has been widely argued in studies of contemporary Chinese politics that even though post-Mao reforms have caused some "temporary dislocations and new kinds of stresses" (Jennings 1997, 367), Party members have quickly adapted themselves to the reforms and have become as a class the greatest beneficiary of reform policies due to their advantageous sociopolitical positions (Brugger and Reglar 1994; Pei 1994, chapter 3; Lieberthal 1995; 258–9). For example, survey data led Dickson and Rublee (2000, 109) to conclude that "Party members do enjoy material advantages compared with the rest of the populations; specifically, they earn more money and have easier access to the most prestigious jobs." According to these observations, therefore, I expect that Party members should be more supportive of the incumbent authorities than nonmembers, since Party members tend to gain more from incumbent policies.

The empirical evidence from our three surveys, presented in figure 5.3, supports the expectation. That is, overall, Party members were more supportive than non-Party members of the incumbent authorities in all three surveys. While the mean scores of Party members for incumbent policy performance were between a low 30 and a high 32 in a 9–45 scale in the three samples, those of non-Party members ranged from a low 22 to a high 24. More important, the difference between the mean scores of Party members and non-Party members was statistically significant (at the .05 level) in each survey. This finding is consistent with that from an earlier study, revealing that "Party members were more satisfied with reform" (Tang 2001, 896).

Thus far, I have examined bivariate relationships between various sociodemographic attributes, on the one hand, and specific support, on the other

Figure 5.3

Party Membership and Specific Support

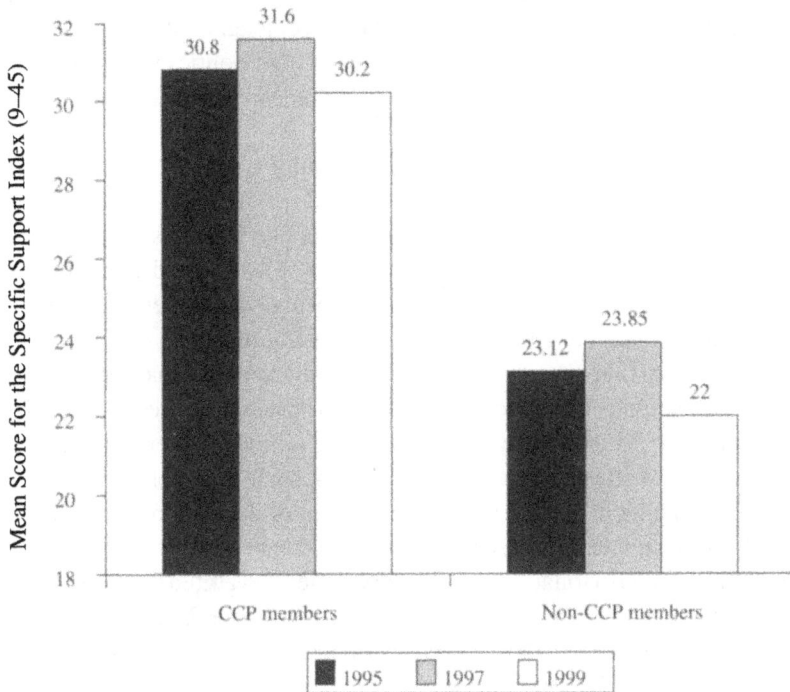

hand, against the data collected in the three Beijing surveys. All in all, the results presented above have indicated that those who were older, who were male, who were less educated, who were mainly in the middle-economic class, and who were Party members tended to have higher levels of specific support. In addition, among the eight occupational groups included in this study, government bureaucrats and military personnel tended to have the strongest support for the incumbent authorities, whereas SOE cadres, private entrepreneurs, and retirees, on the one hand, and SOE workers, college students, and intellectuals, on the other hand, were more likely to have an intermediate level and the lowest level, respectively, of specific support. Yet, the independent impact of each sociodemographic factor on specific support and the relative strength of the impact will be more conclusively examined through the multivariate analysis that follows in this chapter.

The Impacts of High-Politics Orientations on Specific Support

The second research question raised in this chapter is: Why do the incumbent authorities receive support from some people and not others? To answer this question, I will explore the effects of high-politics orientations on specific support in this section and then those of low-politics orientations on such support in the next section.

It is assumed here that high-politics orientations, defined as a set of attitudes toward politics at the national level and the "abstract ideas and language of politics" (Bialer 1980, 166), should not be very closely associated with specific support. Briefly, this is because, as discussed in chapter 1, specific support is derived primarily from positive assessments of specific government policies and performance of the authorities.

In communist societies, such assessments are based mainly on cost-benefit calculations of the policies and performance that directly affect individual daily life and local community's conditions, rather than on attitudes toward abstract normative values about such high-politics issues as the type of political system and the procedure of decision making. Bialer (1980), for example, has observed that the disconnection between the calculation of daily personal and community issues and attitudes toward high-politics issues appears more robust in the former Soviet Union. According to a China scholar (Shi 1997, 6–8), a disconnection of this sort results in large part from the lack of such political institutions as meaningful elections and public interest groups, institutions that should serve as links between daily life and high politics. In other words, people in China cannot influence incumbent policies concerning their daily lives by changing national leaders, decision-making procedures, or one-party rule, all of which are part of high politics. Therefore, like their counterparts in the former Soviet Union, Chinese people have been socialized with a political structure that discourages, if not totally disallows, a connection between incumbent policies and high politics, and hence the people are more likely to separate their assessments of incumbent policies and high-politics issues.

But there is a competing approach suggesting that abstract values might affect people's assessment of incumbent policies and performance in any kind of society. Some scholars of Western public values have posited that "it is the value orientations of people that are the major determinants of policy dissatisfaction [or satisfaction]" (Farah, Barnes, and Heunks 1979, 424). For example, based on empirical data collected from Western societies,

Inglehart (1977, 1979, 1990) has long argued that as industrialized societies reach a high level of material affluence, people's normative values experience a significant shift from those emphasizing the fulfillment of basic material needs to those (known as postmaterialist values) stressing social equality and justice, quality of life, and aesthetic needs. In turn, such a significant shift in normative values leads to a change in people's views on government-specific policies dealing with various socioeconomic issues. Specifically, those who believe in postmaterialist values contend that government policies should be made to "improve the quality of life of all citizens" (Farah, Barnes, and Heunks 1979, 424) rather than only to meet material needs of certain social classes. In short, this approach suggests that abstract normative values about such high-politics issues as the norms and orientations of political system do affect people's assessment of incumbent policies and performance; when the values and value priorities change, so do people's views about government policies and performance.

Based on the two different theoretical approaches mentioned above, we now have two competing hypotheses: the disconnection hypothesis, derived mainly from earlier studies of communist societies; and the connection hypothesis, based mainly on studies of Western societies. The disconnection hypothesis suggests that people's high-politics orientations should not be closely associated with their evaluation of incumbent policy performance in contemporary China. The connection hypothesis indicates that high-politics orientations might be significantly associated with the assessment of incumbent policy performance.

To test these two hypotheses, I conducted a limited multiple regression analysis examining the effects of high-politics orientations on specific support, holding constant the impacts of sociodemographic variables. The same high-politics orientations as those examined as the predictors of diffuse support (in chapter 4) are included in this analysis: interest in politics, democratic values, perceived need for further political reform, preference for stability, and nationalist sentiment. The results are presented in table 5.4.

Table 5.4 reveals a mixed picture of the effects of high-politics orientations. When such typical demographic variables as age, sex, education, and economic status are controlled, only interest in politics and a perceived need for further political reform have significant impacts on specific support. This pattern was consistent in all three surveys. These results provide limited support for both the disconnection hypothesis and the connection hypothesis.

Table 5.4

Multiple Regression (OLS) of Specific Support by High-Politics Orientations, 1995, 1997, and 1999

	Specific Support								
	1995			1997			1999		
Independent Variables	b	s.e.	beta	b	s.e.	beta	b	s.e.	beta
High-politics orientations									
Interest in politics	.69*	.21	.16	.57*	.20	.12	.96*	.42	.12
Democratic values	.49	.48	.05	.26	.45	.01	.63	.41	.06
Need for reform	-.64*	.35	-.09	-.79*	.33	-.12	-.83*	.27	-.19
Preference for stability	-.31	.39	.04	-.39	.37	-.05	-.46	.32	-.05
Nationalism	.21	.23	.06	.18	.19	.04	.17	.13	.05
Control variables									
Age	.01	.02	.04	.02	.02	.01	.00	.02	.01
Sex[a]	-.08	.48	-.01	-.04	.14	-.00	-.28	.44	-.03
Education[b]	-.35	.29	-.06	-.58*	.28	-.09	-.28	.31	-.04
Status[c]	.00	.00	.08	.00	.10	.02	.00	.00	.01
Constant	13.33			20.2			15.14		
R^2	.05			.04			.06		
Adjusted R^2	.03			.02			.05		
N	631			646			652		

Note: b refers to unstandardized coefficient, whereas beta stands for standardized coefficient. s.e. = standardized error. * $P < .05$.

[a] Male = 1; Female = 2.

[b] Illiterate or elementary = 1; junior high = 2; senior high = 3; college or higher = 4.

[c] Lower level = 1; lower-middle level = 2; middle level = 3; upper-middle level = 4; upper level = 5.

On the one hand, the disconnection hypothesis is in part substantiated by the finding that three of the five high-politics orientations—democratic values, preference for stability, and nationalist sentiment—were not statistically significantly associated with specific support. On the other hand, the connection hypothesis is partially supported by the finding that the remaining two of five high-politics orientations—interest in politics and a perceived need for further political reform—did play a significant role in shaping people's specific support.

Why do some high-politics orientations play an important role in influencing specific support among our respondents, while others do not? I do not have a full answer to this question due to the lack of empirical data in our surveys. Nonetheless, I do want to offer some indicative elements of an answer that will explain the mixed findings about the roles of high-politics orientations.

In general, I speculate that both the disconnection argument and the connection argument, mentioned above, may hold true in a transitional society such as China's. This is because, in this transitional society, there are sociopolitical and sociopsychological factors conducive to both connection and disconnection between people's high-politics orientations and their evaluation of incumbent performance. People still cannot link most of their normative values with incumbent policies, due to the lack of institutional channels (meaningful elections at the national level) and hence, in some cases, the lack of conceptual connections in people's minds to link them. Yet they may connect some normative values with the evaluation of incumbent policies because of the significant liberation of private life and individual thinking in the post-Mao era and in some cases, government propaganda intended to rally public support for its public policies, which in effect facilitate the links between some high-politics orientations and incumbent policy performance. Based on this general speculation, I intend to explore some possible reasons for the mixed findings about the effects of high-politics orientations.

First, that interest in politics was significantly positively associated with specific support might be explained by the effect of the official propaganda through the mainstream media, which are tightly controlled by the government. As discussed in chapter 4, those who are highly interested in public affairs at the national level and in politics in general are more likely to acquire information and ideas from such mainstream media. And since the media in China have served as one of the major outlets of official views on various policy issues, those who are interested in politics and hence frequently access the media are more likely to agree with government justifications of and views on incumbent policies and performance.

Second, there is at least one possible reason for those who supported further political reform to be more critical of incumbent policy performance. As personal thinking becomes more liberalized in the reform era, more people consciously or unconsciously compare China with other societies (especially advanced industrialized societies). Through such comparisons, people have been increasingly aware that different political systems may lead to quite different public policies. Thus, although there is virtually no obvious institutional connection between incumbent policies and the political system in China, people may still mentally link these two entities together. As a result, those who perceive the need for change in the current political system (for whatever reasons) are more likely to pay attention to the shortcomings of incumbent policy performance, since a defective system tends to produce faulted policies.

Finally, that the remaining three high-politics orientations—democratic values, preference for stability, and nationalist sentiment—failed to have significant impacts on the evaluation of incumbent policy performance may be explained simply by the argument made in the aforementioned studies of communist systems. That is, sociopolitical constraints prevent people from connecting some of the high-politics orientations with specific support. People tend to separate their democratic values from their evaluation of incumbent policy performance, probably because the political system in China has hardly allowed people to influence incumbent policies through democratic participation in politics at the national level or at any level in the urban setting. Moreover, both a strong preference for stability and a nationalist sentiment, as discussed in chapter 4, have been encouraged by the government as it has sought to enhance allegiance to the political regime rather than affect for specific public policies.

In sum, as to the effects of high-politics orientations on specific support, I have found that while respondents' interest in politics and belief in the need for further political reform had significant impacts on specific support measured as incumbent policy performance, their belief in democratic values, preference for sociopolitical stability, and nationalist sentiment did not exert such impacts. More specifically, in terms of the two orientations that had significant effects, interest in politics was positively associated with specific support, whereas the perceived need for further political reform was negatively related to such support.

The Impacts of Low-Politics Orientations on Specific Support

To continue to answer the second research question raised in this chapter of why people do or do not support the incumbent authorities in contemporary China, I now explore the effects of low-politics orientations on specific support. Low-politics orientations, as defined throughout this study, refer to a set of attitudes toward issues that directly touch peoples' daily lives and communal matters. Accordingly, I focus on the effects of such low-politics orientations as satisfaction with personal living conditions, interest in local issues, and assessment of local government policies, which have been examined as explanatory variables for diffuse support in chapter 4.

As discussed in chapter 1, it has been assumed that such low-politics orientations should be closely associated with specific support as measured by people's evaluation of incumbent policy performance. There are, as mentioned earlier, at least two major reasons for this assumption. One is that both specific support and low-politics orientations deal with concrete socioeconomic issues rather than abstract values, and they do so only from different angles. While specific support taps into incumbent policies in concrete issue areas, low-politics orientations stress the socioeconomic consequences of these policies at the individual and communal levels. The other reason is that since the central authorities in China still have almost unlimited political prerogatives to influence and control local affairs and individual life, their policies are even more likely to have a direct impact on individuals' lives and communal conditions. As a result, citizens' assessment of incumbent policies in China, especially urban China, should be closely linked to the evaluation of their living conditions and local affairs.

Satisfaction with One's Material and Social Life and Specific Support

In order to theorize the relationship between satisfaction with one's material and social life and specific support, it is useful to reiterate briefly what these two categories of variables actually measure. On the one hand, specific support measures respondents' assessment of incumbent performance in such policy areas as controlling inflation, combating official corruption, providing job security, minimizing socioeconomic inequality, improving housing conditions, maintaining order in society, providing adequate medical care, providing social welfare services to the needy, and combating pollution. These policy areas not only collectively capture the respondents' support for the incumbent authorities but also tackle their feelings about various important aspects of socioeconomic life.

On the other hand, satisfaction with one's material and social life tap into respondents' subjective assessment of two major aspects of their personal life: general living conditions and general social status since the reform. This variable stresses a discrepancy between the individuals' perception of the quality of the two aspects of life they feel they are entitled to and what they perceive they are getting: the more satisfied they are, the smaller the discrepancy.

I expect that respondents' satisfaction with their personal lives in these two aspects should be strongly and positively associated with the level of their specific support. Based on what these two categories of variables actually measure, one can infer at least two reasons for the presence of such a correlation between them. First, the two aspects of personal life—material conditions and social status—dealt with by the life-satisfaction variable may be constantly affected by incumbent performance in policy areas mentioned above, such as inflation control, housing improvement, providing medical care, minimizing inequality, etc. Thus, individuals' assessment of incumbent policy performance should be significantly affected by their satisfaction or dissatisfaction with material and social life. Second, since the satisfaction variable emphasizes the discrepancy between what respondents actually have and what they believe they deserve, those who perceive a larger discrepancy should be more likely to give a low evaluation of incumbent policies that are considered to perpetuate the discrepancy (Farah, Barnes, and Heunks 1979).

To explore this hypothesized relationship between satisfaction with one's material and social life and specific support, I ran cross-tabulations between these two variables for the three Beijing surveys. The results presented in table 5.5 confirm the hypothesized relationship. In all three surveys, those who were more satisfied with their material and social life tended to have stronger specific support. For example, in the three samples, over 50 percent of those who were most (shown as "high" in table 5.5) satisfied with their material and social life also had the highest ("high") level of specific support, whereas about the same percentage (over 50 percent) of those who were least ("low") satisfied also had the lowest ("low") level of specific support. It should be noted moreover, that, as the gammas (table 5.5) indicate, the association between satisfaction with one's material and social life and specific support was quite strong, ranging from .52 in 1999, to .58 in 1995, and .61 in 1997. I expect such a strong correlation to sustain the multivariate analysis that follows.

Table 5.5

Specific Support by Satisfaction with One's Material and Social Life, 1995, 1997, and 1999

	Satisfaction with One's Material and Social Life								
	1995			1997			1999		
Specific Support	Low (%)	Medium (%)	High (%)	Low (%)	Medium (%)	High (%)	Low (%)	Medium (%)	High (%)
Low	54.2	32.4	10.8	57.1	30.4	4.5	63.9	45.2	14.2
Medium	38.2	40.8	30.9	38.6	48.6	30.0	35.2	33.1	35.1
High	7.6	26.8	58.3	4.3	21.0	65.5	2.9	21.7	50.8
Total	100	100	100	100	100	100	100	100	100
	gamma = .58*			gamma = .61*			gamma = .52*		

Note: Both indexes of original specific support and satisfaction are trichotomized into three categories: high, intermediate, and low levels. * $P < .05$.

Interest in Local Issues and Assessment of Local Policies and Specific Support

Interest in local issues and assessment of local policies are two related yet separate low-politics orientations, both of which were examined as explanatory variables for diffuse support in chapter 4. In general, it is a person's interest in local issues that leads to his or her attention to and assessment of local public policies. In turn, a person's assessment of local public policies should affect one's specific support for the incumbent authorities. In other words, interest in local issues indirectly influences specific support through assessment of local policies, whereas assessment of local policies directly affects specific support. These two sequential relationships are explored separately as follows.

The Relationship between Interest in Local Issues and Assessment of Local Public Policies

Are people in China interested in local issues? If so, why are they interested? As I discussed in chapter 4, some important studies of mass political attitudes and behavior in such communist societies as the former Soviet Union and China have found that most people in those societies tend to be highly interested in local issues that are closely related to their personal life and are self-motivated to participate in local affairs (Bialer 1980; Bahry and Silver 1990; Shi 1997). The data from the three Beijing surveys confirm these findings: over 85 percent of our respondents were either interested or very interested in issues in their neighborhood and/or their workplace.

There are two important reasons for such strong mass interest in local affairs. First, as Shi (1997) explained in his study of political participation in Beijing, although the communist system does not allow the public to influence and participate in decision-making processes at the national level, the system does offer people opportunities or, in some cases, encourages them to participate in and hence affect decision implementations concerning issues (or low-politics issues) at the local level and in their work units (*danwei*). Thus, one can say that the political system encourages people in China to be interested in issues at the local level. The other reason is more obvious: participation in local decision making may bring people in communist society more concrete incentives (for example, obtaining better housing, improved work conditions, and higher income) by influencing local institutions and officials, since people cannot achieve their personal goals by influencing decision making at the higher level (Bialer 1980). This argument, therefore, can be understood to mean that concrete incentives also prompt people to become interested in local issues as well as to participate in local decision making.

It is clear that people are highly interested in local issues, because they can improve their own everyday life through influencing local issues. And since local issues that are closely related to people's everyday life are constantly affected by local public policies, people's interest in these issues naturally leads to their assessment of those policies. In short, although it is difficult to anticipate the direction of the relationship between interest in local issues and assessment of local public policies, the existence of such a relationship is expected among our respondents.

To explore this relationship, I have examined the Pearson correlations between interest in local issues and assessment of local policies among respondents in the three surveys. The results indicate that interest in local issues and assessment were highly and positively correlated. These correlations were .44, .47, and .45 in the 1995, 1997, and 1999 surveys, respectively. On the one hand, these results support the above-mentioned expectation that the people's interest in local issues and their assessment of local public policies are directly or strongly related. On the other hand, the results reveal that the relationship between these two variables is positively correlated. This means that the higher a person's interest in local issues, the more likely he or she is to have positive views about local policies.

The Relationship between Assessment of Local Public Policies and Specific Support

Specific support measured by the evaluation of incumbent policy performance at the national level should be closely associated with people's evaluation of local public policies. This is because, as mentioned above, the central authorities in China still have almost unlimited political and administrative prerogatives to influence and control local public policies dealing with important local issues. For example, the central authorities' policies in urban housing reform and calls for nationwide anticrime campaigns have all been implemented by local government agencies (including neighborhood organizations), and have significant impacts on the everyday lives of people, especially urban residents. Although local leaders may have some discretion in implementing the policies made by national authorities, they cannot substantively alter the direction and essence of national policies.

Because national and local policies are so highly correlated in reality, therefore, citizens' assessment of local public policies is expected to be strongly
and positively associated with their specific support for the national incumbent authorities, which is measured by the evaluation of incumbent policies
at the national level.

This expected relationship is confirmed by the empirical evidence from
the three Beijing surveys. The Pearson correlations between the assessment
of local policies and the evaluation of incumbent policy performance at
the national level were .44, .47, .49 in the 1995, 1997, and 1999 samples,
respectively. These results suggest that those who were more supportive of
local policies tended to have a higher evaluation of incumbent policy performance at the national level. From a policy perspective, moreover, the
results reinforce the argument mentioned above that, in China, national and
local public policies are closely associated.

I have thus far examined separately the relationships between interest in
local affairs and assessment of local policies, and between assessment of
local policies and support for incumbent policy performance (specific support). In order to obtain a more cohesive picture of the interactions among
these variables, I conducted a partial correlation analysis of the relationships among them. The results are presented in figure 5.4. These results are
similar across the three surveys: despite the fairly strong intercorrelations
between assessment of local public policies and interest in local issues, their
relationships with specific support were different. The correlation between
interest in local issues and specific support was weak when assessment of
local public policies was controlled for. But the association between assessment of local policies and specific support was strong, even when interest
in local issues was controlled for. These results suggest that interest in local
issues might indirectly influence specific support for the incumbent authorities at the national level through assessment of local public policies,
whereas assessment of local policies directly affects specific support.

In sum, through bivariate analyses of the roles of low-politics orientations, we have found that both satisfaction with one's material and social
life and assessment of local public policies were strongly associated with
specific support for the incumbent authorities, whereas interest in local affairs was indirectly related to such support through assessment of local public policies. Moreover, the results from the bivariate analyses indicate that
both satisfaction with one's material and social life and assessment of local
public policies were positively associated with specific support, suggesting
that those who felt satisfied with personal life and those who had a high

Figure 5.4

Relationships among Interest in Local Issues, Assessment of Local Public
Policies, and Specific Support

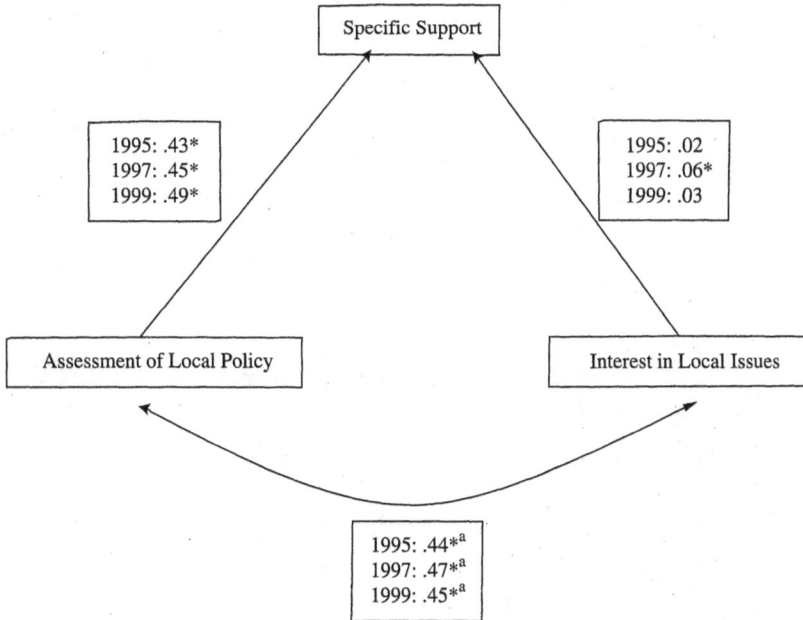

Note: The similar statistical scheme has been employed in the work by Muller, Jukam,
and Seligson (1982, 254–5). * $P < .05$.
[a]Zero-order correlation.

evaluation of local public policies were more supportive of the incumbent
authorities.

Multivariate Analysis

Thus far, results from the bivariate and limited multivariate analyses have
demonstrated different kinds of correlations between specific support, on
the one hand, and such explanatory factors as sociodemographic attributes,
high-politics orientations, and low-politics orientations, on the other hand.
Yet, since these explanatory factors are potentially interrelated, each relationship revealed above in the bivariate and limited multivariate analyses
may be a spurious reflection of some other factor. In order to detect the

Table 5.6

Multiple Regression (OLS) of Specific Support by Sociodemographic Attributes, High-Politics Orientations, and Low-Politics Orientations, 1995, 1997, and 1999

Independent Variables	Specific Support								
	1995			1997			1999		
	b	s.e.	beta	b	s.e.	beta	b	s.e.	beta
Age	.00	.02	.03	.00	.03	.01	.01	.02	.02
Sex[a]	-.31	.30	-.04	-.75	.50	-.05	-.57	.44	-.05
Education[b]	-.18	.22	-.04	-.44	.36	-.05	-.24	.32	-.03
Economic status[c]									
Lower-middle	.07	.16	.01	.00	.03	.00	.23*	.10	.07
Middle	.30*	.10	.07	.65*	.33	.08	.55*	.30	.08
Upper-middle	.28	.24	.04	.24	.30	.03	.19	.21	.02
Upper	.18	.20	.03	.24	.29	.04	.10	.15	.02
Occupations[d]									
SOE cadres	.68	.50	.06	1.07	.84	.05	.99	.73	.05
Intellectuals	-.38	.57	-.03	.76	.96	.03	.61	.85	.03
Govt. bureaucrats	2.03*	.95	.09	1.26*	.79	.07	2.52*	1.40	.08
Military	.72	.60	.05	2.62	1.80	.06	1.08	.87	.05
Students	-1.29	1.08	-.04	.22	.19	.04	.56	.59	.03
Private entrepreneurs	.32	.74	.02	.56	1.24	.02	.51	.45	.05
Retirees	1.05	.85	.05	1.10	.92	.06	1.04	.81	.06
CCP members[e]	.06	.04	.02	.10	.67	.01	.09	.59	.01
Democratic values	.30	.27	.04	.43	.47	.04	.37	.41	.04
Interest in politics	.64*	.35	.08	1.27*	.60	.10	.93*	.52	.09
Need for reform	-.72*	.38	-.12	-.89*	.38	-.17	-.79*	.26	-.15
Preference for stability	-.29	.21	-.04	-.37	.35	-.04	-.35	.31	-.04

	b	beta	s.e.	b	beta	s.e.	b	beta	s.e.
Nationalism	.08	.09	.04	.15	.15	.04	.17	.13	.05
Satisfaction	1.82*	.21	.30	1.40*	.19	.31	1.22*	.16	.30
Interest in local fairs	.33	.15	.05	.28	.25	.03	.16	.18	.02
Assessing local policies	1.20*	.31	.25	1.30*	.36	.26	1.02*	.17	.28
Constant	7.71		2.03	13.12		3.42	11.74		3.01
R^2	.172			.186			.175		
Adjusted R^2	.153			.160			.149		
N	621			618			651		

Note: b refers to unstandardized coefficient, whereas beta stands for standardized coefficient. s.e. = standardized error. * $P < .05$.

[a] Male = 1; female = 2.

[b] Illiterate or elementary = 1; junior high = 2; senior high = 3; college or higher = 4.

[c] The "lower class" is used as the reference category (reflected in the intercept) for economic status.

[d] The "SOE workers" is used as the reference category (reflected in the intercept) for occupation.

[e] Non-CCP member = 1; CCP member = 2.

independent impact of each explanatory variable on specific support and the relative strength of such impact, I have conducted a multiple regression analysis that includes simultaneously all three groups of explanatory factors examined above: sociodemographic attributes, high-politics orientations, and low-politics orientations. The results of this analysis are presented in table 5.6.

Overall, the results from the regression analysis presented in table 5.6 confirm most of the results from the bivariate and limited multivariate analyses above. They support the underlying hypothesis developed throughout this study that in general low-politics orientations play a more powerful role than do sociodemographic attributes and high-politics orientations in shaping people's specific support for the incumbent authorities.

First of all, while the coefficients of all the sociodemographic attributes had expected signs, only those of belonging to two economic classes and being a bureaucrat were statistically significant. Specifically, compared with people in the lower class, those in the middle class were more supportive of the incumbent authorities in all three surveys, while those in the lower-middle class became more supportive only in the 1999 survey. These results confirm the finding from the bivariate analysis that there was a curvilinear relationship between economic status and specific support. Moreover, in all three surveys, government bureaucrats were much more supportive of the incumbent authorities than the SOE workers (as the reference group in the occupational category). Age, sex, education, Party membership, and most occupations, however, could not independently influence specific support, even though they have the potential to affect specific support along the expected directions. It is also important to note that while economic status and being a bureaucrat had independent impacts on support for the incumbent authorities, the magnitudes of such impacts were much weaker than those of some low-politics orientations.

It is also worth noting that among all sociodemographic attributes, self-perceived economic status and being a bureaucrat seemed to be more powerful in explaining the evaluation of incumbent performance than such factors as CCP membership, education level, age, and sex, all of which are normally considered to be important variables (Tang 2001). While our findings do not necessarily dismiss the importance of any sociodemographic attributes, they do indicate that some of the attributes may be more powerful than others in explaining specific support, especially in urban China. It seems to be the case that in today's China being a government bureaucrat and belonging to some economic classes play more important roles in determining people's attitudes toward the incumbent authorities than other sociodemographic variables.

Second, among the high-politics orientations, only interest in politics and belief in the need for a further political reform had independent impacts on specific support. Specifically, those who were interested in politics were more supportive of the incumbent authorities, while those who believe in the need for a further political reform tended to be less supportive of the authorities. Such a pattern was consistent across the three surveys. And these findings from the comprehensive multiple regression analysis accord with the results from the limited multivariate analysis presented earlier. It should be also noted that although these two high-politics orientations—interest in politics and belief in the need for a further political reform—exerted independent effects on specific support, the strength of these two variables still failed to match that of low-politics orientations.

Finally, among the low-politics orientations, satisfaction with personal life and assessment of local public policies were significantly and positively associated with support for the incumbent authorities, while interest in local affairs had little independent and direct impact on such support. These results suggest that those who were more satisfied with their personal material and social lives and who were more positive about local public policies tended to show stronger support for the incumbent authorities, while interest in local affairs could indirectly influence people's views about the authorities (through assessment of local public policies, as the bivariate analysis has shown). Moreover, the impact of two low-politics orientations—personal-life satisfaction and local-policy assessment—on specific support was the strongest among those of all explanatory variables included in this multiple regression analysis (table 5.6). This pattern of the relationships was evident in all three surveys.

Summary and Conclusion

Who is most likely to support the incumbent authorities (as opposed to the political regime) in contemporary China? Why do or do not some people support the authorities? Throughout this chapter, these two key questions have been answered through the examination of the various effects of three categories of sociopolitical factors—sociodemographic attributes, high-politics orientations, and low-politics orientations—on specific support. The answers to the two questions and the important implications from these answers are highlighted as follows.

First, who is most likely to support the incumbent? Based on the data from our three Beijing surveys, I have found that those who perceive themselves to belong to the middle class and who are government bureaucrats are more likely to support the incumbent authorities. On the other hand, although other sociodemographic identities—such as Party membership, age, and education—may also play some roles in shaping specific support, they are by no means as influential as self-perceived economic status and being a bureaucrat. These findings imply that although incumbent policy performance has distinguished people economically and to a certain extent occupationally, it has not differentiated people along the divides of sex, education, and political status (Party membership).

Second, why do or do not some people support the incumbent authorities? The empirical findings presented in this chapter suggest that some people support the incumbent authorities mainly because they are satisfied with their personal social and material lives and feel positive about local policies and, to a less extent, because they have a strong interest in politics (which makes them susceptible to the influence of the government-controlled media). On the other hand, people express little or no support for the incumbent authorities when they believe that the fundamental political system needs to be changed. Moreover, among all subjective factors that have been examined in this study, personal-life satisfaction and a high evaluation of local public policies are the most powerful motivations for people's support for the incumbent authorities.

Finally, the overall empirical evidence shown in this chapter confirms the underlying hypothesis regarding the sociopolitical correlates of specific support, namely that low-politics orientations (such as personal life satisfaction and evaluation of local public policies) are strongly associated with specific support, while both sociodemographic attributes and high-politics orientations are weakly or indirectly related to such support. This confirmation has at least two important implications. One is that the incumbent leaders may boost their support by effectively addressing low-politics issues that directly touch people's daily lives and communal matters. Thus, a technocratic type of leader will be more likely to draw strong support from the citizens, since this leader is usually more practical and skillful in coping with people's concrete concerns in their everyday lives and communities.

The other implication is that specific support for the incumbent authorities may change frequently (as demonstrated in chapter 3), in large part because the major sources—satisfaction with personal social and material life and assessment of local issues—of specific support shift swiftly with ebbs and flows of personal and communal conditions. Thus, popular support for any incumbent leaders may fade away[2] when their policies become ineffective in solving most salient problems in people's everyday lives. This is especially the case in contemporary China, where many social and economic problems—such as a surge in urban unemployment and a decline in social welfare—may evolve quickly to a level of crisis, as economic and political developments rapidly unfold.

2. For example, Premier Zhu Rongji enjoyed overwhelming popularity among the ordinary people when he took office in 1998; by late 2000, he had lost it due mainly to the perceived failure of his policies in coping with the mounting problems of SOEs (CND 2001, December 3; Pan and Pomfret 2002).

Chapter 6

The Behavioral Consequences
of Political Support

Thus far, analysis has been focused on two attitudinal dimensions of political support, both of which are referred to by Easton (1965, 159) as "covert [i.e., attitudinal] support." Yet, can such covert support or alienation transform into what Easton calls "overt [i.e., behavioral] support" or overt alienation in post-Mao China? In other words, do people's attitudes toward the political system (diffuse support) and assessment of the incumbent authorities (specific support) significantly influence their political behavior or political participation? If so, how? The answers to these questions should have direct implications for the stability and viability of both the incumbent government and the political system.

In this chapter, I attempt to address these critical questions by examining the major forms and intensity of mass political participation in Beijing during the second half of the 1990s, and exploring the differing impacts of the two dimensions (diffuse and specific) of political support on mass political participation. As discussed in chapter 1, while the descriptive results from the surveys about mass participation in Beijing may not be generalized directly to other parts of China, the findings about the relationship between political support and mass participation will yield some general implications for the behavioral consequences of such support in China, especially urban China. These implications will be discussed at the end of the chapter.

Mass Political Participation

Since the outset of post-Mao economic and political reforms in the late 1970s, more and more ordinary citizens have been reportedly participating

154

in public affairs and politics in both urban and rural areas of China (Shi 1997; Jennings 1997; Manion 1996, Chen 2000; Tang and Parish 2000; Chen and Zhong 2002), even though China's political system has never been democratic—especially by Western standards. In order to assess the impacts of the two dimensions of political support on people's political behavior, we need first to have an adequate understanding of the major forms and extent of mass political participation in contemporary China. This is because the forms and extent of participation serve as the primary institutional and socio-political conditions under which covert (attitudinal) support or alienation turns into overt (behavioral) support or alienation.

The Major Forms of Mass Political Participation in Urban China

In order to grasp the major trends of mass political participation in urban China, we fashioned four questions to measure four specific political acts: (1) voting for deputies to local People's Congresses, (2) complaining to leaders at various levels, (3) voicing concerns to local people's deputies, and (4) writing letters to the authorities at any level.[1] These four political acts can be classified into two major conceptual categories: voting behavior that consists of item 1 itself, and contacting behavior that includes items 2–4.[2]

1. Other forms of political participation, such as protest, demonstration, and petition, are politically risky and are very likely to lead to persecution and severe punishment. We did not include these highly risk-laden acts in our surveys due to two reasons. One is that most citizens do not consider these acts to be options for the pursuit of their goals because of the risks. For instance, only 1 percent of respondents in each of two earlier surveys of urban residents in China in the late 1980s would resort to protest when dissatisfied (Shi 1997; Tang and Parish 2000). As a result, these risky acts would merit the support of so few participants in any survey that a reliable multivariate analysis could not be done. The other reason is that since the government has demonstrated its intolerance of such political acts, respondents would be more likely to give untruthful responses to any questions concerning these acts. Therefore, survey researchers in Chinese politics correctly focus on the most common and legal activities when studying political participation (Manion 1996; Shi 1997; Jennings 1997; Tang and Parish 2000).

2. These two conceptual categories were confirmed by the results from an exploratory factor analysis. From the analysis, two factors emerged for each sample: voting behavior was composed of voting in local People's Congress elections, and contacting behavior consisted of complaining to leaders at various levels, voicing concerns to local people's deputies, and writing letters to the authority at any level. These two factors together explained 58 percent, 49 percent, and 52 percent of the variance among the four political acts for the 1995, 1997, and 1999 samples, respectively.

There were two major reasons for us to choose these two categories of mass political participation. One was that although these forms of participation did not exhaust all political acts conducted by citizens, they were the most common political acts in China (Manion 1996; Shi 1997; Jennings 1997; Tang and Parish 2000). Thus, they were most likely to represent the fundamental trends of mass political participation. The other reason was that, as a China scholar noted, these acts were "legitimate in China, at least in theory" (though not all risk-free), so that questions about these acts were "unlikely to make respondents give interviewers false answers" (Shi 1997, 27). Consequently, the responses to these questions were expected to be reliable. Following is an examination of the sociopolitical background and characteristics of each of these two major categories.

Voting Behavior

In the late 1970s and the early 1980s, the CCP under Deng Xiaoping amended the electoral law for the elections of People's Congresses—Chinese "legislatures"—at various levels. Specifically, the new law introduced direct elections for local People's Congresses.[3] According to this law, in theory, voters could nominate candidates and have a choice among multiple candidates for each contested seat. Of all four major forms of mass political participation examined in this chapter, voting in these elections has been the most common political act of urban citizens. Thus, we need to pay closer attention to this type of political behavior by examining both the political and structural constraints on and citizens' choices in these elections and the political role of the local People's Congresses.

First, let us look at the political and structural constraints on the elections, which have been mainly determined by the CCP. The fundamental motive of the CCP leadership to introduce and maintain the new electoral law has been mainly twofold. First and foremost, the CCP leadership intended to regain and reinforce the legitimacy of its one-party rule through liberalized yet limited local elections (O'Brien 1990, 126; McCormick 1996, 31). By allowing people to elect deputies directly to the lowest level of People's Congresses, the post-Mao leaders expected to create an image of the

---

3. Article 97 of the 1982 Constitution of the People's Republic China provides that "deputies to the People's Congresses of counties, cities not divided into districts, municipal districts, townships, nationality townships and towns are elected directly by their constituencies" (National People's Congress 1982).

government's "representativeness" among the citizens (McCormick 1996). Secondly, these electoral reforms were also intended to heighten the efficiency of the government (O'Brien 1990, 126), ideally as the "popularly" elected deputies act on behalf of their constituencies to advocate sensible policies and stop unpopular governmental decisions at various legislative levels. Whether and how well this second objective has been achieved through local elections remains questionable. But it must be noted that since the outset of the electoral reforms, the CCP leaders have always linked this objective to their ultimate political goal: strengthening the legitimacy of the "Party leadership" (*dang de lingdao*) (Archive Research Office of the Central Committee of the Chinese Communist Party 1994, chapter 10). In short, these limited electoral reforms were mainly intended by the CCP to strengthen its own legitimacy by improving its own governability rather than to initiate democratic competition across political and ideological divides.

Out of this fundamental motive, the CCP leaderships—from Deng Xiaoping to Jiang Zemin—have firmly imposed at least two formidable constraints on the local People's Congress elections. One is political. In order to prevent any organized and individual opposition from challenging its position of absolute rule, the CCP has directly or indirectly controlled virtually the entire process of local People's Congress elections: from the nomination of candidates, electorate deliberation, to the determination of final candidates on the ballot (Halpern 1991, 38; Burns 1999, 591). Such political control has been done mainly through the Party-dominated, local election committees (Shi and Lei 1999, 21–3). These committees also control the final results of the elections via the so-called three ups and three downs procedure[4] in which the local Party leaderships eventually get the voters' "consent" for the final candidates placed on the ballot—most of whom are either Party members or at least obedient to the party line (McCormick 1996). Furthermore, no opposition parties or organizations are allowed in these elections, although the so-called democratic parties that have long been co-opted by the CCP may participate in the elections, serving only as window dressing of "democracy with the Chinese characteristics." As a result, with few exceptions,[5] "People's Congress deputies are mainly politically reliable

4. In this procedure, the initial lists of nominees generated from electorate deliberations are submitted to the local election committees, considered, and returned back to the electors, who further deliberated, passing the list back up to the election committees and so forth for "three ups and three downs" (McCormick 1996, 40).

5. In his recent works, Shi has noted these exceptions by citing two "famous cases" of two princelings, Chen Yuan and Chen Haosu, who lost in their local elections (Shi

cadres, intellectuals, workers, peasants, and minority representatives who
accept the contour of the regime" (O'Brien 1994, 85). Actually, the great
majority (about 75 percent to 80 percent) of the winning candidates are
members of the CCP (McCormick 1996, 39; Wang 1998, 190).[6] Thus, under the CCP's tight political control, these elections "rarely challenge Party
power or government decisions" (O'Brien 1994, 85).

The other constraint imposed by the CCP in these elections is an ideological one. The CCP has implemented a list of measures to prevent the local
People's Congress elections from becoming a forum spreading what it calls
bourgeois liberal thoughts or political views contrary to the official ideology.
The Party prohibits any large-scale or publicized electoral campaigning
that it considers part of "bourgeois democracy" (as opposed to "socialist
democracy"), and it requires that all electoral activities and deliberations
be carried out within a limited scope (for example, work unit or *danwei*) under firm control by the Party-dominated election committee (Wang 1998; Shi
and Lei 1999, 23 and 28–30). By doing so, the CCP has almost eliminated
any effective channels for potential dissidents to articulate their opinions in
local elections. Consequently, as McCormick observed, "with the exception
of a few isolated cases, . . . candidates [could not] campaign in the usual
sense of that word," and they could typically give only a few-minutes-long
self-introduction stating mainly that they were "the sort of persons recom-
mended in the official guidelines" (McCormick 1996, 41).

Not only has the CCP severely limited the scope and format of electoral
activities and deliberations, but it has made relentless efforts to control the
substance of the activities and deliberations in order to make sure that no
political view contrary to the CCP's "four cardinal principles"[7] sneak into
the local elections. Especially since the inconvenient appearances of a few
non-Marxist candidates (who strongly advocated some radical political views
deviating from the party line) in the 1980 local elections (Halpern 1991, 46;

1997, 36; Shi 1999, 1120). But, as other China analysts argue (O'Brien 1994, 85; Mc-
Cormick 1996, 39; Nathan 1997, 235), these exceptions still remain exceptions after all
and have not yet led to a fundamental (or qualitative) change in the political orientation
of winning candidates as a whole.

   6. For example, the results of the local People's Congress elections in 1993 indicated
that over 80 percent of the winning candidates were CCP members (Wang 1998, 190).

   7. The four cardinal principles include: (1) supporting the CCP's leadership, (2) adhering to socialism, (3) upholding Marxism-Leninism-Mao Zedong Thought, and
(4) maintaining the proletarian dictatorship (Wang 1999, 57).

O'Brien 1990, 129),[8] the CCP has instructed all electoral committees to watch and prevent any speeches "threatening the Party's leadership" or the nation's "stability and unity" (Wang 1998, 279).

In short, "with scattered exceptions in 1979–1980," as Nathan (1997, 235) rightly concludes, local People's Congress elections so far "have not turned into competitive campaigns owing to tight Party control." Thus, as mentioned above, the overwhelming net outcomes of these elections have been very much in accordance with the CCP's expectations. Politically, most of the winning candidates are Party members, none of them comes from organized oppositions, and very few of them are independent candidates who operate without the Party's support or approval. Ideologically, very few of the winning candidates advocate political views different from the party line, although some of them made "constructive suggestions" on some specific local policy issues.

Second, in order to have a better understanding of voting in local people's congress elections as a form of political participation, we also need to ascertain what choices are available to voters in such elections. Despite the aforementioned political and ideological constraints, the current electoral system still offers voters two kinds of choices in local people's congress elections. One is that, as mentioned above, voters can have alternative candidates (but within the political and ideological constraints set by the CCP). In other words, while voters cannot find or vote for any candidates who challenge the fundamental norms and institutions of the political regime in most cases, they can choose better or the least worst candidates on the CCP-sanitized ballots. More important, most final candidates on the ballots differ only in degree rather than in kind: they might be slightly different in their opinions only on some specific local policy issues or in their popularity among the voters.

The other choice available to voters is to abstain from the elections without penalty. While in prereform elections the people were coerced by the regime to vote (see Townsend 1967; Chen 2000, 649), in today's partially reformed or semicompetitive elections, they are given a choice between voting and nonvoting. In other words, today's voters have freedom of nonvoting in the current elections. With this freedom, those who dislike the

8. For example, in 1980 at Beijing University and Hunan Normal University, some candidates advocated radical ideas in so-called publicized electoral campaigns in local People's Congress elections (Nathan 1985, 193—23; McCormick 1996, 40—1).

fundamental political and ideological orientations sanctioned by the Party may choose nonvoting as a protest. Conversely, those who support (or at least are indifferent about) those political and ideological orientations tend to participate in these local elections by choice.

Third, an adequate assessment of the role that deputies to local People's Congresses can play may also prepare us to analyze the subjective motivation for voting. According to the PRC constitution, the local People's Congresses should play an important role in representing citizens' interests and supervising governments and their officials in their respective areas.[9] In reality, however, the congresses and their deputies have by no means met such constitutional expectations. Based on extensive field observation, for example, McCormick (1996, 42) has vividly described the local People's Congress's lack of means and power to exercise constitutionally prescribed functions, as follows:

> Once elected, deputies . . . tend to disappear. The overwhelming majority of deputies whom I interviewed did not receive time off work other than to attend annual meetings and for one or two inspection tours per year. Nor did most deputies have any means for regular communication with their constituents. . . . Deputies are generally not allowed to speak from the floor to the whole congress. Nearly all of the time the whole house is in session is dominated by the local leadership reading lengthy work reports. The major work of most sessions of People's Congresses is to approve these reports. . . . Deputies are encouraged to forward requests from their constituents to the government but these are also filtered through the leadership prior to reaching their targets.

In short, systemic political factors have prevented the local People's Congresses and their deputies from playing a true representative and legislative role. The local People's Congresses therefore become more or less a facade of democracy, which simply gives "substance to the Party's claim to have established a democracy" (McCormick 1996, 41).

An overall picture of local People's Congress elections seems to be quite clear from what has been discussed above. On the one hand, local People's Congress elections operate under the two severe constraints—political and

9. See chapter 1 of the General Principles of the 1982 Constitution of the People's Republic (National People's Congress 1982).

ideological. On the other hand, these elections offer the electorate mainly two limited choices: a choice of multiple candidates (within the Party limit) for each position and a choice of abstaining from voting. These constraints and choices in the elections so far, I believe, have constituted fundamental rules of the game in the local People's Congress elections. Furthermore, apparently, local People's Congresses and their deputies derived from the local elections have fallen short of representing constituents' interests and overseeing the government. The limits of the elected congresses and deputies have also served as important factors influencing voters' attitudes toward the elections themselves. Under these circumstances, how does political support as a set of attitudes affect people's voting behavior? This question will be addressed in the analysis that follows.

Contacting Behavior

As mentioned above, this category of political participation consists of three specific political acts: complaining to leaders at various levels, voicing concerns to local people's deputies, and writing letters to the authority at any level. Since the goals of these acts tend to be particularistic and participation in them is individualistic (as I will explain later), I group them into one category for analytical purposes. In order to have a better understanding of this form of participation, I attempt to address several important questions that concern the nature and structural setting of this category of political act.

First, about what do people in China want to contact government officials at various levels? This category of political act can be regarded as "particularistic" political activities in urban China (Tang and Parish 2000, 187–99). By engaging in such acts, people express their concerns about and interests in concrete personal and, sometimes, community issues, such as employment, wages, housing, welfare, education, medical care, community order, and the local environment. The issues dealt with in this category of political act are the so-called low-politics issues, which do not directly relate to the fundamental norms and structures of the political system (Shi 1997, chapter 2).

Second, why do people in China need to contact leaders at various levels through different channels to fulfill their everyday needs? In their recent survey-based study of urban China, Tang and Parish (2000, 189) have argued that "the government still controls resource allocation and provides extensive social services in urban areas, such as employment, income, housing, education, and health care." Although such government controls have gradually declined since post-Mao reform, most ordinary people still depend on the government for a large part of their everyday needs. In this kind of structural setting, therefore, people who are not satisfied with the existing allocation of resources or services by the government may still feel the need to contact work unit leaders or government officials at various levels to seek desired changes in policies and regulations.

Third, how do people contact and voice their concerns to leaders at various levels? To achieve their personal and communal goals, people in urban areas may contact and voice their opinions to leaders in many ways. Based on his field observation, Shi (1997, 45) has summarized the various options used by ordinary people in urban areas:

> Some people choose to contact officials at the work unit level; others go to higher government organizations. Participants use various strategies when contacting government officials. Some people contact government officials in a conciliatory manner, to persuade government officials to make beneficiary decisions; others choose a confrontational style, to put pressure on the officials to induce desired changes. Still others contact government officials through patron-client ties, to turn the relationship from a hierarchical one into an exchange.

Choosing how to contact leaders usually depends on one's resources and purposes. In most cases, contact is made individually (as opposed to within-organization).

Compared to voting in the elections for local People's Congresses, however, this kind of political act requires more initiative, time, and communication skill. In addition, these acts are not totally risk-free, as some officials and agencies involved in complaints may retaliate against complainers. Not everyone is willing and can afford to take such risks. In short, contacting officials and voicing concerns to them at various levels are certainly more demanding and riskier than voting in local elections. Thus, I expect that in our samples the number of the respondents who engaged in these acts should be much lower than that of those who voted in elections for local People's Congresses.

Finally, how does the government see this form of mass participation? As mentioned above, the typical concerns and opinions voiced by citizens who contact leaders at various levels usually involve the so-called low-politics issues. Since these low-politics issues, in general, do not directly relate to such high-politics issues as the fundamental norms of CCP rule, the government usually does not consider such acts as a political threat to the regime (unless this kind of act turns out to be an organized movement). In most cases, therefore, the Party not only allows but encourages citizens to participate in these direct, personalized activities of contacting various leaders and officials to improve its own image among the people (Shi 1997, 45). For instance, the government has set up institutions at various levels to receive complaining individuals and letters. Typically, these institutions include Letters and Visits Offices (*xinfang bangongshi*) at the district and county levels, Letters and Visits Departments (*xinfang chu*) at the provincial and centrally controlled municipal levels, and the Letters and Visits Bureau (*xinfang ju*) of the State Council at the national level. The major functions of these institutions are to accept complaints from individual visitors and letters about problems with policies and regulations and wrongdoings of officials at lower levels, and to pass these complaints to responsible or higher government agencies (Wang 1998). Also, the government-sanctioned media have often publicized and praised officials and agencies that promptly and properly responded to complaints from citizens.

To summarize, there are distinctions as well as similarities between these two major categories of mass political participation, both of which have important implications for our analysis of the role of political support in shaping political behavior. One of the critical distinctions between these two categories is in the potential results from participation. On the one hand, voting (or nonvoting) may result in spiritual gains[10] of voters, since elected congresses and deputies generally do not deliver concrete policy initiatives. Thus, this type of political behavior is more likely to be associated with one's beliefs and values about the political system. On the other hand, contacting leaders at various levels to complain about specific policies and regulations and officials and agencies could lead to particular material benefits for individuals. Thus, this type of political behavior is likely to be "unrelated to a person's beliefs about the larger political system" (Bahry and Silver 1990, 826); rather, it tends to be correlated with one's evaluation of incumbent policies.

Also, an important commonality between these two categories of political acts is that both categories are legitimate and, to a certain extent, encouraged by the government, although none of them is totally risk-free. Consequently,

10. The "spiritual gains" here refer to the individual's satisfaction from expression of values through voting or nonvoting.

people may exercise their free will to determine whether they should participate in each of political activities within the two major categories. Thus, these activities may provide a reliable test of the relationship between political support as a set of attitudes and political behaviors.

The Intensity of Mass Political Participation in Beijing

How many people participate in each activity within the two major categories of political actions in Beijing? And how many people are involved in any political activity or activities at all? The answers to these two questions will help us assess the magnitude of the behavioral consequences of political support in urban China.

The Frequency of Each Political Act

Table 6.1 shows the frequencies of the four specific political acts within the two major categories of participation in our samples. As expected, of the four political acts, voting was most commonly engaged in by our respondents in all three samples. About 63 percent, 50 percent, and 51 percent of eligible voters in our samples voted, respectively, in the 1993, 1996, and 1999 local People's Congress elections. These results have at least two important implications. One is that voting in today's China is by no means as

Table 6.1
Frequency of Political Acts, 1995, 1997, and 1999

Political Act	1995 (%)	1997 (%)	1999 (%)
Voting Behavior:			
Have you voted in the most recent district or county election?[a]	63.1	49.6	51.3
Contacting Behavior:			
In the past year, have you ever voiced your concerns or opinions to leaders at any level?	12.3	15.8	19.6
In the past year, have you ever contacted a deputy to any levels of People's Congress for your complaints?	6.8	3.2	2.4
In the past year, have you ever written a letter to the authority at any level to express your concerns?	1.8	1.4	4.1

Note: All percentages represent positive (yes) responses.
[a] The most recent local elections here refer to those held in 1993, 1996, and 1999. Thus, eligible voters in the 1995, 1997, and 1999 samples presumably had a chance to vote, respectively, in the 1993, 1996, and 1999 elections.

universal as described in some early studies of pre-reform communist systems (Townsend 1969; Gilison 1968). This is mainly because, as mentioned above, the government no longer coerces citizens to vote, and the citizens can choose voting or nonvoting. The other implication is that enthusiasm among citizens for voting in local elections has in general declined,[11] as the falling of voter-turnout rates in our surveys indicate. The general decline may have resulted from the political and ideological controls that have been increasingly tightened by the Party since the first local elections in the early 1980s (when some candidates were criticized by the government for spreading bourgeoisie liberal thoughts), which in effect discouraged many of those who long for more meaningful elections.

Among contacting acts, voicing concerns or opinions to leaders at any level was the most common political act (which was less common than voting) in our samples. The percentages of the respondents who voiced concerns or opinions were 12 percent, 16 percent, and 20 percent in the 1995, 1997, and 1998 samples, respectively.[12] The remaining two political acts within this category—contacting deputies and writing to authorities—were much less common than contacting leaders (and least common among all four political acts). Within the past year, 7 percent, 3 percent, and 2 percent of the respondents in the 1995, 1997, and 1999 samples, respectively, had contacted local People's Congress deputies, while only 2 percent, 1 percent, and 4 percent in each of the three surveys, respectively, had ever written a letter to authorites at any level. These results confirm our earlier expectation that these three political acts in the category of contacting behavior are less commonly performed than voting, in part because they require more initiative and skills for participants than voting does.

More importantly, the results of the three contacting acts also reveal some interesting trends within the category. The percentages of the respondents who voiced their concerns or opinions and who had written a letter to an authority climbed during the three surveys, while the rate of those who had contacted local People's Congress deputies declined in the same period.

11. This decline becomes even clearer when the turnout rates found in our surveys are compared with the turnout rate of 72 percent in 1988 presented in an early survey study in Beijing (Shi 1997, 143).

12. Apparently, the frequencies of this political act in our survey were much lower than the frequency (42 percent) of that act in a survey conducted in 1989 (Shi 1997, 94). The discrepancy could be caused by different time limits imposed in our surveys and the earlier survey: while our surveys used a one-year limit ("in the past year"), the earlier survey had a five-year limit ("during the past five years").

These two opposite trends within the contacting category suggest that the role of local People's Congress deputy has become less relevant to people's pursuit of particularistic interests than that of government leaders and authority at any level. A possible reason for such trends could be that both the perceived and the real power of the local People's Congresses and their deputies have gradually eroded at least in such an urban area as Beijing. These important trends require a separate study focusing on the local People's Congresses.

The Spread of Political Participation

How many people in Beijing engaged in any one of the political acts included in this study? Or are these political acts confined only to a proportion of the population? And how actively do those participants engage in political acts within the two categories of political behavior? These questions have a lot to do with the total magnitude of the sociopolitical impact of mass political participation. To answer these questions, I have composed an additive index for each survey to show the spread of political participation among the respondents. The results of each index are shown in table 6.2.

On the one hand, less than half, though quite a substantial proportion, of the respondents in each survey did not engage in any of the four political acts within the two major categories of participation. That is, those who were totally inactive (according to our participation measures) accounted for 38 percent, 43 percent, and 47 percent of the 1995, 1997, and 1999 samples, respectively. On the other hand, more than half of the respondents in each sample reported having engaged in at least one of the four political acts. Over 40 percent of each sample had performed one of the four acts, while a little over 10 percent and less than 2 percent of each sample had conducted two acts and three-to-four acts, respectively.

Table 6.2

The Spread of Political Participation, 1995, 1997, and 1999

Additive Participation Index	1995 (%)	1997 (%)	1999 (%)
Engaging in NONE of the four activities	38.1	43.1	47
Engaging in ONE of the four activities	46.2	43.1	41.4
Engaging in TWO of the four activities	14	13.1	11.2
Engaging in THREE to FOUR activities	1.7	0.7	0.4
Total	100	100	100

The results presented in table 6.2 also indicate that during the time span of our three surveys, the number of participants at each participatory level had gradually shrunk, while that of nonparticipants had increased. For example, the percentage of the respondents who engaged in at least one political act had declined from 62 percent (100 percent minus 38 percent) in 1995 to 53 percent (100 percent minus 47 percent) in 1999; the proportion of those who performed only one act had decreased from 46 percent in 1995 to 41 percent in 1999. The same pattern of decline appeared for those who engaged in two and three-to-four acts. In short, the overall level of political activism had declined for all political acts within the two major categories of mass participation.

I suspect that there could be at least two reasons for such a decline. One is that more and more people in urban China find these legitimate channels of participation to be ineffective in achieving their socioeconomic and political goals. The other reason is that people in today's China have less interest in and time for political acts, as they are more and more drawn into the rush to pursue their personal material well-being, which has been strongly encouraged by the government (Kristof and Wudunn 1994; Li 1997; Tang and Parish 2000, 41–3).

In sum, the empirical evidence presented above has indicated that while voting in the local People's Congress elections was still the most popular political act, voter turnout rates in such elections had gradually yet steadily decreased among our respondents; although contacting acts were not so common as voting, engagement in such acts (except contacting the people's deputy) had become more frequent over the period of our surveys. Moreover, the evidence has revealed that while more than half of the respondents in each sample still engaged in at least one of the political acts included in this study, overall political activism declined. What kinds of roles did the two dimensions—diffuse and specific—of attitudinal political support play in shaping people's political participation? This question will be the focus of the following analysis.

The Relationship between Political Support and Political Behavior

It has been assumed in this study that both specific support and diffuse support should variably affect different forms of political behavior and participation. Theoretically, as discussed in chapter 1, this is because these two dimensions of attitudinal political support have distinct sociopsychological

Table 6.3

The Expected Relationships between the Two Dimensions of Political Support and the Two Major Forms of Political Acts

Subjective Motivation	Voting Behavior	Contacting Behavior
Diffuse Support	+	0
Specific Support	0	−

characteristics that inevitably bring about variable impacts on different types of political acts. Empirically, some early studies of political participation in both Western societies (Muller 1970a and 1970b; Miller 1974b; Muller 1977; Muller and Jukam 1977; Muller, Jukam, and Seligson 1982; Erber and Lau 1990) and the former Soviet society (DiFranceisco and Gitelman 1984; Bahry and Silver 1990; Miller 1993) have confirmed the existence of the variable behavioral effects of different political attitudes, although some of them disagree on the particular directions of such effects. As Bahry and Silver (1990, 826–7) have noted in their study of mass political participation on the eve of Gorbachev's democratization, it is "not only that individual attitudes ought to matter in determining how much people participated but also that a different combination of them would come into play for each type of activism."

Table 6.3 summarizes the hypothesized relationships between each of the two dimensions of political support and the two major categories of political acts examined above. The sign indicates the expected direction of each relationship: positive, negative, or none. Specifically, I expect that diffuse support should be positively associated with voting behavior and not related to contacting behavior; specific support should not be correlated with voting behavior but negatively linked with contacting behavior. Furthermore, I expect these relationships to persist when controlling for some key sociodemographic factors and other important subjective orientations. The theoretical rationales behind each of these expected relationships are explained as follows.

Impact of Diffuse Support

To repeat what we have established for the purposes of the following discussion, diffuse support in this study is defined as the "diffused or generalized attachments" members of a polity have for the government and its normative principles. In other words, such support refers to citizens' deeply rooted beliefs about the norms and institutional structure of the prevalent political system in a certain society.

In their study of Soviet mass participation, Bahry and Silver (1990, 828) have argued that "people who concur with fundamental values of the Soviet regime should be more involved in compliant political and social activity, since they would have more of a normative stake in the system." Of the political activities examined in this study, voting in local People's Congress elections seems to be one of the best candidates for such a compliant act. This is because, as my earlier discussion indicates, the CCP's normative values and political leadership still prevail in these elections, and such elections in effect only legitimatize "the Party's claim to have established a democracy" (McCormick 1996, 41). Thus, voting in the elections can be considered compliance with these norms and the political leadership and help the Party legitimize its rule, especially when voting is not coerced by the government. Consequently, I expect that those who have strong diffuse support for the current political regime led by the CCP are more likely to vote in these local elections.

As mentioned earlier, contacting behaviors (including complaining to leaders at various levels, voicing concerns to local people's deputies and writing letters to the authority at any level) are engaged in to fulfill particularistic personal material needs. These activities are "typically personalized and nonideological" (Bahry and Silver 1990, 828) and hence not a suitable channel for people to express their normative values, such as their fundamental beliefs about the regime. Thus, I expect that diffuse support for the current political regime should not be related to the contacting behavior.

Impact of Specific Support

Again, specific support for the incumbent authorities in this study is measured by the citizens' evaluation of the "outputs and performance of the political authorities" (Easton 1975, 437). I hypothesize that those who have a lower evaluation of incumbent policies are more likely to contact officials and authorities at various levels through different channels. From the discussion above regarding the utilities and structural setting of contacting acts in contemporary China, one can infer at least three major reasons for this hypothesis. A first reason is that those who have a lower evaluation of incumbent policies are more motivated to ask the officials and authorities to correct specific policies or at least to have some explanations for the shortfalls or shortcomings of the policies (Jennings 1997). A second reason is that the government in such a socialist or transitional society as China still plays an imperative role in allocating major resources needed in everyday life through its public policies; people who feel negatively affected by the policies are more likely to contact government officials to seek changes. A third reason is that the government allows and often encourages citizens to contact officials about their concerns regarding specific policy issues related to citizens' personal and communal life, since such concerns hardly pose any serious threat to the political system.

Moreover, an empirical finding from a study of mass participation in the former Soviet Union apparently supports this hypothesis: that is, the complaints about government policies tend to be expressed by contacting specific government officials or agencies (Kaplan 1993). Based on all the reasons above and the empirical evidence, therefore, I expect specific support to be negatively associated with contacting behavior in our samples.

However, I expect that citizens' specific support for the incumbent authorities should not significantly affect their voting behavior one way or another. As discussed above, voters or nonvoters acquire only spiritual gains from elections for local People's Congresses, because the congresses and elected deputies are generally not able to deal with concrete policy issues effectively or to change political leaderships under the current political system. Thus, people's evaluations of incumbent policies should not be associated with their voting behavior in local People's Congress elections.

Impacts of Control Variables

Do the two dimensions of attitudinal political support influence people's political behaviors independently of some key demographic factors and other subjective orientations? To answer this question, I include in this analysis of behavioral impact of political support two categories of control variables: (1) respondents' sociodemographic attributes and (2) their attitudes toward some low- and high-politics issues.

Sociodemographic Attributes

Sociodemographic attributes here include age, sex, education, income, and Party membership. Some earlier empirical studies of mass political participation in urban China have found that these key sociodemographic attributes affect people's participation in various political activities (Shi 1997; Chen 2000; Tang and Parish 2000). In general, these studies suggest that such attributes may capture some of the effects that family, peer groups, generations, and social classes have on political socialization processes; socialization processes tend to have an impact on people's attitudes toward the political system and views on public policies that in turn influence their political behaviors. Thus, I suspect that the above-mentioned key socio-demographic attributes could affect the respondents' engagement in both voting and contacting behaviors.

Low- and High-Politics Orientations

I also selected and included in the analysis of behavioral impacts of attitudinal political support some of the low- and high-politics orientations (which have been examined as sources of political support in the previous chapters) as control variables. In the category of high-politics orientation, I chose interest in politics and democratic values; in the category of low-politics orientation, I selected personal life satisfaction and assessment of local policies. The reasons for the selection of these orientations as control variables are explained as follows.

First, the political interest variable refers to individual attentiveness to major national issues and politics as a whole. The empirical findings from studies of mass political participation in China as well as other countries have indicated that such attentiveness affects people's political behaviors, including voting and contacting (Bahry and Silver 1990; Shi 1999; Verba, Nie, and Kim 1978). These studies suggest that when given a choice, the most interested tend to participate in various political activities, simply because they are more inclined to view the government as an appropriate avenue for resolving individual problems (Bahry and Silver 1990, 827). Given that both voting and contacting acts are legitimate and not mandatory, engaging in these political acts is supposed to have a lot to do with individuals' interest in politics. Thus, I expect political interest to influence positively both categories of political acts.

Second, such democratic values as beliefs in true competitive elections and equal protection regardless of one's political beliefs might influence people's decisions to participate in both voting and contacting activities. Specifically, I suspect that those who support democracy could be more alienated by the severe political and ideological constraints (mentioned above) imposed by a single authoritarian party (i.e., the CCP) on the local People's Congress elections, since these constraints are incompatible with their democratic values. As a result, the democratic supporters tend to see voting in such elections as "going through a formality" (*zou xingshi*), which only serves the function of legitimizing undemocratic, one-party rule. As voting in these elections is no longer mandatory or coerced, therefore, it is reasonable to expect democratic supporters to express their discontent with the CCP's political and ideological constraints by abstaining from local People's Congress elections. This speculation about the relationship between democratic values and voting behavior has been confirmed by the empirical evidence from an earlier study of political participation in urban China (Chen and Zhong 2002).

Following a similar logic, I expect that those who share democratic values may *not* voice opinions to the authorities. This is because the democrats might see all or most officials simply as the product of a nondemocratic system, and hence they might refuse to turn to the officials in any way.

Third, I suspect that personal life satisfaction, defined as individuals' "subjective perceptions" of their personal material and social life, could affect people's political behavior. The empirical evidence from the former Soviet Union (Bahry and Silver 1990) and China (Jennings 1997) suggests that personal life satisfaction influences both voting and contacting behaviors. According to a study of mass participation in the former Soviet Union, for example, the most satisfied are more inclined to vote, since they are willing to maintain the status-quo by voting for more conservative candidates (who are supported by the Party) (Bahry and Silver 1990). According to studies of participation in both the Soviet Union and China, however, the dissatisfied are more likely to voice their concerns to authorities at various levels, since they would have more reason to turn to public officials for assistance (Bahry and Silver 1990; Jennings 1997). Thus, I expect that satisfaction with one's material and social life might influence both voting and contacting behaviors in our samples.

Finally, people's evaluation of local public policies might play a role in influencing their contacting behavior, while such evaluation may not have an impact on their voting behavior. This speculation has been supported by a finding from an earlier study of Chinese mass participation (Jennings 1997). According to this study, those who have a lower evaluation of local policies would be more likely to contact leaders, especially at the local levels, because they want to seek solutions to problems.

To summarize, I have hypothesized that diffuse support should have a positive impact on voting behavior, but it should have little effect on contacting behavior; specific support should not be associated with voting behavior but should be negatively connected with contacting behavior. In order to find whether diffuse support and specific support can independently affect political acts, moreover, I have selected some key sociodemographic attributes, and some low- and high-politics orientations as control variables.

The Multivariate Analyses

To test the hypothesized relationships between the two dimensions of attitudinal political support, on the one hand, and the two major categories of political acts, on the other hand, I conducted two sets of multivariate analyses. One set consists of logistic regression models[13] to estimate the impacts of two political-support dimensions on respondents' voting behavior (table 6.4) in the three surveys. The other set includes multiple regression models to capture the effects of the two political-support dimensions on respondents' contacting behavior (table 6.5). In order to assess whether the two dimensions of political support independently affect each of the two behavioral categories, I have included in each statistical model the control variables specified above: sociodemographic attributes and low- and high-politics orientations. Overall, the results from these two sets of multivariate statistic analyses are supportive of the earlier expectations regarding the relationship between attitudinal political support and political behavior in our samples.

First, as the results in table 6.4 indicate, even when the control variables were taken into account, diffuse support still had an independent and positive impact on respondents' voting behavior in all three surveys, and specific support did not exert such an impact. In other words, those who strongly supported the current regime, defined as a set of normative values and fundamental institutions, were more likely to vote in the elections for local People's Congresses; a person's evaluation of incumbent policies, however, did not affect his or her decision to vote in such elections. These results are consistent with the theoretical expectations explained above.

It is also worth noting that other sociopolitical characteristics of most likely voters, which are revealed by the results of some of the control variables in table 6.4, may supplement the findings on the behavioral impact of diffuse support. These characteristics include being a Party member, less

13. Since the dependent variable, voting, in each survey is a dichotomous variable, the logistic regression analysis is an appropriate statistical technique.

Table 6.4

Estimated Coefficients of Logistic Regressions of Voting Behavior by Diffuse Support and Specific Support, 1995, 1997, and 1999

Independent Variable	Voting at Local Elections		
	1995	1997	1999
Diffuse support	.39* (.11)	.19* (.07)	.26* (.10)
Specific support	.08 (.10)	.02 (.02)	.03 (.05)
Age	.04* (.01)	.05* (.00)	.03* (.00)
Age squared	−.01* (.00)	−.00* (.00)	−.00* (.00)
Sex[a]	−.17 (.18)	−.31 (.20)	−.16 (.14)
Education[b]	.13 (.16)	.23 (.24)	.18 (.14)
Income ($\times 10^{-4}$)[c]	−.03 (.02)	.00 (.00)	.01 (.06)
Party member[d]	.58* (.33)	.16* (.09)	.23* (.12)
Political interest	.19* (.09)	.21* (.05)	.23 (.18)
Democratic values	−.29* (.08)	−.34* (.11)	−.41* (.18)
Life satisfaction	.41* (.18)	.23* (.07)	.19* (.10)
Local policies	−.17 (.15)	−.08 (.10)	−.12 (.14)
Constant	−2.87* (.66)	−4.63* (1.06)	−3.67* (.10)
−2 Log likelihood	553.69	573.41	488.23
Model chi-square	56.68*	63.85*	53.44*
Degrees of freedom	11	11	11
N	590	591	610

Note: Numbers in parentheses are standard errors. *$p < 0.05$.
[a] Male = 1; female = 2.
[b] Illiterate or elementary = 1; junior high = 2; senior high = 3; college or higher = 4.
[c] Income is measured by Chinese currency, *yuan.*
[d] Non-member = 1; CCP member = 2.

supportive of democratic values, more interested in politics, and more satis-fied with one's personal material and social life. All these characteristics mirror those of most likely supporters of the current political regime, as demonstrated in chapter 4 (table 4.10). To a certain extent, therefore, the results from these control variables embody the findings about the effect of diffuse support on voting behavior: those who support the current political regime were more likely to vote, also because they were Party members, less democratic, more interested in politics, and more contented with their personal lives.

Second, as table 6.5 shows, when other variables were controlled for, respondents' specific support for incumbent authorities still had a signifi-cant and negative impact on their contacting behavior in all three surveys, and diffuse support had little independent impact. These results suggest that those

Table 6.5

Multiple Regression (OLS) of Contacting Behavior by Diffuse Support and Specific Support, 1995, 1997, and 1999

Independent Variables	Contacting Behavior								
	1995			1997			1999		
	b	s.e.	beta	b	s.e.	beta	b	s.e.	beta
Diffuse support	.13	.20	.04	.11	.18	.03	.29	.31	.06
Specific support	-.29*	.08	-.18	-.32*	.09	-.22	-.36*	.14	-.21
Age	.00	.02	.03	.00	.03	.02	.01	.02	.02
Age squared	-.01	.00	-.04	-.02	.02	-.03	-.00	.00	-.02
Sex[a]	-.21*	.12	-.09	-.23	.21	-.06	-.37*	.24	-.11
Education[b]	.18	.22	.04	.07	.15	.03	.14	.12	.06
Income (x 10^{-4})[c]	-.03	.02	-.03	-.00	.00	-.02	-.10	.11	-.05
Party member[d]	.21	.15	.07	.08	.12	.04	.31	.26	.06
Interest in politics	.30	.35	.07	.29*	.18	.09	.21	.17	.07
Democratic values	-.41*	.22	-.16	-.33*	.12	-.14	-.37*	.20	-.17
Life satisfaction	-.32*	.21	-.11	-.20*	.10	-.09	-.22*	.09	-.11
Local policies	-.45*	.27	-.15	-.38*	.16	-.17	-.34*	.12	-.16
Constant	.91*	.23		-1.12*	.44		-1.04*	.51	
R^2	.15			.18			.16		
Adjusted R^2	.14			.16			.14		
N	602			595			611		

Note: The dependent variable, contacting behavior, for each survey is the factor score derived from the factor analysis of three contacting acts (complaining to leaders at various levels, voicing concerns to local people's deputies, and writing letters to the authority at any level). In their study of mass participation in the former Soviet Union, Bahry and Silver (1990) have also used factor scores to measure various clusters of political acts. b refers to unstandardized coefficient, whereas beta stands for standardized coefficient. s.e. refers to standardized error. * $p < 0.05$.

[a] Male = 1; female = 2.

[b] Illiterate or elementary = 1; junior high = 2; senior high = 3; college or higher = 4.

[c] Income is measured by Chinese currency, yuan.

[d] Non-CCP member = 1; CCP member = 2.

who had lower evaluations of incumbent policies tended to contact leaders and government agencies at various levels, while people's attitudes toward the current political regime did not significantly influence their decisions to contact authorities. The findings are in accordance with the earlier expectations regarding different effects of the two dimensions of political support on people's contacting behavior.

Moreover, the results of some control variables included in table 6.5 help us understand the sociopolitical context in which specific support affects people's contacting behavior in contemporary China. As expected, those who were less satisfied with their personal material and social lives, and who had lower evaluations of local policies were more likely to contact government officials and agencies at various levels through different channels. As shown in chapter 5, these two groups were also less supportive of incumbent policies (see table 5.6). Thus, it appears that people who had lower support for incumbent policies tended to contact government officials and agencies, partially because they were less satisfied with their personal material and social life and local public policies.

In addition, as expected, democratic-value believers in our samples tended to be less likely to contact government officials and agencies at various levels. Since democratic values were not associated with specific support for incumbent policies as demonstrated in chapter 5 (table 5.6), therefore, one may suggest that, although both those who had high specific support and those who had strong democratic beliefs were less likely to engage in contacting behavior, they might not belong to the same political and ideological group. Those with high specific support were less likely to contact government officials probably because they were more satisfied with incumbent policies, whereas those with strong democratic beliefs were less likely to do so possibly because they distrusted the current nondemocratic government.

In sum, the results from the two sets of multivariate statistical models presented in tables 6.4 and 6.5 have confirmed the relationships specified earlier between the two dimensions of political support (i.e., diffuse support and specific support) and the two categories of political acts (i.e., voting behavior and contacting behavior). Diffuse support is positively linked with voting behavior but not related to contacting behavior; specific support has little impact on voting behavior but does have a negative effect on contacting behavior. Meanwhile, it has been shown that these hypothesized relationships persist even when some key demographic attributes and important subjective orientations are controlled for.

Summary and Conclusion

Does political support, defined as the two dimensions of attitudes toward the current political regime and incumbent authorities, affect people's political behavior or political participation? If so, how? These are the two central questions I have attempted to address in this chapter. To answer these questions, I have depicted the forms and intensity of mass political participation in Beijing, and then specified and tested the relationships between the two dimensions of political support, on the one hand, and two major categories of political acts, on the other hand. The findings from these analyses and their implications may be highlighted according to the two central questions raised in this chapter, as follows.

By now, the obvious answer to the first question of whether covert (i.e., attitudinal) political support affects mass political participation and behavior is that such covert support does influence participation and behavior. The answer to the second question of how political support influences people's political participation and behavior is that, under the current sociopolitical circumstances, the two dimensions of attitudinal political support exert different effects on each of the two categories of political behaviors. That is, a high level of diffuse support is likely to propel people to vote in local People's Congress elections, whereas this kind of support does not make a significant difference in people's decisions to contact government officials; a low level of specific support tends to give people an incentive to contact officials, while such support has no significant impact on people's voting behavior.

These findings have at least two important, general implications for the behavioral consequences of political support in contemporary China. First, given that "the overwhelming net outcomes of [the local People's Congress elections] have been very much in accordance with CCP's expectations" (Chen and Zhong 2002, 183) and the Party no longer coerces people to vote, the finding that those with strong diffuse support for the current political regime tend to vote in these elections implies that such elections still work to boost the legitimacy of the current political regime. Meanwhile, as the findings in table 6.4 indicate, the most likely regime supporters, such as those who are Party members, less supportive of democratic values, and more satisfied with personal material and social life, tend to express their support for the regime through these elections. Therefore, the voter turnout rate may serve as an important indicator of popular support for the current political regime. And it seems to be true that, in China, covert political support for the current political regime transforms into overt (i.e., behavioral) political support for the regime mainly through voting in the elections for local People's Congresses.

Second, given that, as discussed in the first section of this chapter, contacting behavior is often limited to specific policy issues and such behavior is generally allowed and even encouraged by the government, the finding that the level of specific support is associated with the level of engagement in this kind of behavior implies that, in urban China, the intensity of the contacting act serves as an important indicator of popular support for incumbent policies. Since specific support is found to be negatively associated with the contacting act, the lower the evaluation of incumbent performance by the public, the more contacting acts there will be. Thus, it can be argued that covert support for the incumbent authorities may change into overt support for the authorities mainly through avoiding contacting officials in China.

If the voter turnout rate and the frequency of contacting government officials serve as the indicators of diffuse support and specific support, respectively, one can detect the trends of the two kinds of support by examining aggregate, longitudinal data about the turnout rate and the contacting frequency. For example, the three Beijing surveys offer data of this sort, while they are limited to a single locale. As presented earlier in this chapter, there are two opposite trends of the two categories of political acts: one is that the voter turnout rates of the elections for local People's Congresses declined from 1995 to 1999, and the other trend is that the frequencies of contacting officials at various levels climbed during the same period. Apparently, these trends drawn from the three surveys suggest that diffuse support for the current political system and specific support for the incumbent authorities had both declined at least in such an urban area as Beijing.[14]

14. This conclusion is also supported by the evidence presented in chapter 3 (see, particularly, table 3.3).

Chapter 7

Conclusion: Empirical Findings and Their Implications

At the beginning of this book, a basic assumption was made: popular political support is critical for the functioning and persistence of any form of government. Even in such a nondemocratic system as the one in China where order is often maintained by coercion and the Party organization, the prolonged absence of political support may eventually bring about political instability and even the demise of the current political regime. Such an assumption gave rise to this study of mass political support in today's China.

I have sought to answer three fundamental questions about mass political support, using the data from the three Beijing surveys. (1) How much popular support does the current Chinese government enjoy? (2) Why do or do not Chinese citizens support the government? And (3) what impacts does attitudinal political support have on citizens' political behaviors? On the one hand, as explained in the first chapter, while the descriptive findings from the surveys about the first question—which mainly involves the intensity and change of popular political support—may not be directly generalized to other parts of China, they do offer needed benchmarks against which the descriptive findings from future studies in other regions can be compared. On the other hand, the findings about the other two questions—which largely pertain to the relationships between the two dimensions of political support and various sociopolitical variables—can directly apply to other parts of China, especially urban China.[1] In this chapter, I highlight empirical findings

---

1. For a detailed discussion about the generalizability of the findings about the relationships between variables from the Beijing surveys, see chapter 1 of this book.

from the previous chapters concerning these three questions and then elucidate the key political implications of the findings.

Major Empirical Findings

To answer the first question of how much popular support the current Chinese government enjoys, I have examined two dimensions of political support, which have been defined, according to the Eastonian conceptualization, as diffuse support for the political regime and specific support for the incumbent authorities. Specifically, my examination has been focused on the intensities and the trends of and the relationship between these two dimensions of political support.

First, in terms of the intensities of the two dimensions of political support, the average scores of the diffuse and specific support indexes for the three Beijing surveys suggest that the respondents had moderately high diffuse support (above the midpoint of the scale measuring diffuse support) for the current political regime during the second half of the 1990s, whereas their specific support for the incumbent authorities (as measured by citizens' evaluations of incumbent policy performance) was low during that period. Second, as for the trends of the two dimensions of political support, I have found that while the respondents' diffuse support had gradually declined from 1995 to 1999, their specific support had fluctuated, apparently in response to the socioeconomic consequences of incumbent policy performance. And finally, in respect to the relationship between these two dimensions, the empirical evidence presented earlier suggests that there was a weak association between citizens' evaluations of the incumbent authorities and their attitudes toward the political regime; this weak association persisted across such key sociodemographic divides as sex, age, education, and income.

In short, the picture portrayed here of mass political support in such an urban area as Beijing in the second half of the 1990s was complex. In terms of the intensity and change of the two dimensions of political support, a majority of people still supported the current political regime, although they assessed incumbent policy performance as mediocre; over time, people's support for the regime had steadily declined, whereas their assessment of policy performance was volatile. As for the relationship between the two dimensions of support, while people's assessment of policy performance did not translate to support for the regime in the short turn, such assessment was expected to affect support for the regime in the long run.

To answer the second question of why Chinese citizens do or do not support the government, I have explored the roles of three categories of factors—(1) sociodemographic attributes, (2) high-politics orientations, and (3) low-politics orientations—in shaping the two dimensions of political support. First, in terms of the effects of these three categories of factors on diffuse support for the current political regime, the empirical results indicate that both sociodemographic attributes and high-politics orientations exerted significant impacts on such support, while low-politics orientations did not. Specifically, as for the effects of sociodemographic attributes, I have found that those who were older, who were male, who were CCP members, who were government officials, who were less educated, and who had a high self-assessed economic status tended to be more supportive of the regime. As for the influences of high-politics orientations, the data revealed that those who expressed strong nationalist feelings and preference for stability and who had a high level of interest in politics were more supportive of the regime, whereas those who strongly believed in democratic values and who perceived the need for further political reform tended to be less supportive of CCP rule.

Second, in terms of the impacts of the three categories of factors on specific support for the incumbent authorities, the evidence from the surveys suggests that low-politics orientations played more important roles than did both sociodemographic attributes and high-politics orientations in influencing people's assessment of incumbent performance. In effect, such low-politics orientations as personal-life satisfaction and views of local policies were the most powerful factors in determining citizens' support for the incumbent authorities. Specifically, those who were more satisfied with their personal material and social lives and who had higher evaluations of local public policies tended to be more supportive of the incumbent authorities.

Within the categories of sociodemographic attributes and high-politics orientations, only the identities of middle class and government officials, interest in politics, and the perceived need for political reform played meaningful yet lesser (compared to low-politics orientations) roles in influencing people's assessment of incumbent performance. Specifically, those who belonged to the middle class, who were government bureaucrats, and who were interested in politics tended to be more positive about the incumbent authorities, while those who perceived the need for further political change were likely to be less positive.

Finally, to answer the third question about the impact of political support on citizens' political behaviors, I investigated the differing effects of diffuse support and specific support on two kinds of the most common political acts in today's China: (1) voting in the local People's Congress elections and (2) contacting government authorities at various levels through different channels. The data from the surveys indicate that a high level of diffuse support was most likely to motivate people to vote in local People's Congress elections, although this kind of support did not make a significant difference in people's decisions to contact government officials; a low level of specific support tended to give people an incentive to contact officials through various means, while such support had no significant impact on people's voting behavior. In other words, those who strongly supported the current political regime tended to express their support through participation in the local elections, while those who were dissatisfied with incumbent policy performance were more likely to vent their dissatisfaction by contacting government officials.

In sum, the data from the three Beijing surveys have provided us with a multifaceted picture of mass political support, with respect to its intensity, changing trend, sociopolitical sources, and behavioral consequences. What does this multidimensional picture imply for CCP rule as well as China's political development in general? This important question will be addressed as follows.

The Weakness and Strength of CCP Rule

The empirical findings presented in this book have important implications for the strength and weakness of CCP rule. Such strength and weakness not only pertain to the viability of the current political regime, but also relate to political stability in contemporary China.

The Strength of CCP Rule

The empirical findings from the three Beijing surveys indicate several areas of strength for CCP rule. First, the findings suggest that the CCP still enjoyed legitimacy, at least in urban areas such as Beijing, when the surveys were conducted. Most China scholars contend that since the 1989 Tiananmen crackdown, the communist regime has lost its moral legitimacy within the population, and as a result has been ruling the country almost solely by coercion and economic performance (Lieberthal 1995, 147; Chen and Deng

1995; Schoenhals 1999, 599; Wu 1999; Tiewes 2000). Contrary to these mainstream views, however, the results in this study indicate that an overwhelming majority of respondents still considered the current political regime legitimate, while they deemed incumbent policy performance mediocre (chapter 2). This suggests that the most potent popular base of CCP rule was diffuse support for the regime rather than specific support for incumbent policy performance. Thus, one may conclude that the CCP did not lose its legitimacy, at least among urban residents such as those in Beijing (if the concept of "legitimacy" in question is defined, according to the Eastonian conceptualization, as diffuse support mainly for the normative values and institutional structures).

Second, the relative stability of the aforementioned diffuse support or regime legitimacy may help sustain CCP rule at least in the short run. As described in chapter 3, people's diffuse support for the regime had been stable, although it had gradually declined within the four-year span of the surveys. This implies that at least in the near future, citizens' support for the current political regime will serve as a reliable popular base of CCP rule and that such support may not erode quickly to such a level that would endanger the viability of CCP rule.

Finally, the findings about the relationship between mass political support and political behavior imply that diffuse support or regime legitimacy could still translate into overt or behavioral support for (as opposed to overt alienation from) CCP rule at least in the near future. As demonstrated in chapter 6, the people who have stronger diffuse support are more likely to vote in local People's Congress elections. Voting in such elections can best be characterized as the expression of support for CCP rule, since the elections—in which people are no longer coerced to participate—have been dominated by the CCP politically and ideologically. By the late 1990s, as the data have shown, more than half of the eligible voters still voluntarily cast their votes in these elections in Beijing, even though the voter turnout rate in that city had gradually declined since the late 1980s. As diffuse support—which is one of the most powerful determinants for voting behavior—remains relatively stable, a sizable segment of the population will still go to the voting booth and register its support for CCP rule.

The Weakness of Current CCP Rule

The empirical findings from the three Beijing surveys have also revealed some areas of weakness for the CCP. First, the findings have indicated that diffuse support for the regime had declined by more than 6 percent[2] within the four years of the surveys, although the current level of such support remained in the positive territory. Since the three surveys cover a period of only four years, the empirical evidence from the surveys may not be conclusive enough to suggest that the falling of diffuse support would persist at the same rate (6 percent every four years).[3] Nonetheless, it is the downward direction of this trend that has posed a serious threat to CCP rule in the long run.

Second, the weakness of CCP rule also stems from the mediocre public evaluations of incumbent performance (specific support). Specifically, the findings have shown that throughout the second half of the 1990s, the levels of the evaluations in the samples were low (below the "so-so" level of the specific support index) on the average. Should such low levels of incumbent performance evaluations persist in most areas of China over time, the public's support for both the incumbent CCP leadership and the communist regime would significantly decline (because, as demonstrated in chapter 3, specific support and diffuse support are moderately yet positively associated).

Challenges for the CCP Leadership

What has been discussed about the strength and weakness of CCP rule can be understood to mean that at present and in the short run, the communist regime may be legitimate, although it faces serious problems in its incumbent policy performance. Nonetheless, in the long run, the prospects of CCP rule appear to be bleak unless the Party can reverse the downward trend of

2. This percentage results from the following equation: [1.22 (the difference between the mean score of the diffuse support index for the 1995 survey, 19.45, and that for the 1999 survey, 18.23) ÷ 19.45 (the mean score of the diffuse support index for the 1995 survey)] × 100 = 6.27. For the results of the mean scores of the diffuse indexes for all three surveys, see chapters 2 and 3.

3. Should diffuse support continue to decline at this rate for about fifteen years in most parts of China, such support would fall to the level at which CCP rule is no longer considered legitimate by the majority of the population. This level is the one below the point of "15" on the diffuse support index (which is a 6-to-24-point scale where "15" is the midpoint). For the details about the formation of the index, see chapter 2.

citizens' diffuse support for the current political regime and improve its policy performance in some socioeconomic areas.

Can the CCP succeed in reversing the trend and improving the performance? The findings from this study—especially those about the relationships between the two dimensions of political support on the one hand and various sociopolitical factors and political behavior on the other—have important implications for the challenges the Party will face in achieving these goals.

Challenges to the Improvement of Support for the Political Regime

There are at least two kinds of challenges that the CCP leadership has faced and will continue to face in its effort to improve (or reverse the downward trend of) diffuse support for the political regime within the population. One kind of challenge originates in citizens' high-politics orientations, which, as discussed in chapter 4, play powerful roles in shaping the people's support for the current political regime. The data here have indicated that those who believe in democratic values and who perceive the need for a further political reform tend to have a low level of diffuse support and hence are likely to challenge the current communist regime, while those who strongly embrace nationalism and who strongly prefer political stability are likely to have a high level of diffuse support. Thus, to improve diffuse support for the regime, not only should the CCP leadership continue its ongoing campaigns within the public to promote nationalism and patriotism and advocate the necessity of political stability, but it must convince those democratic believers and political-reform supporters that the current political regime deserves their support. Convincing the democratic and political-reform supporters, however, has presented a great challenge for the CCP leadership, although the Party's campaigns to promote nationalism and patriotism and popular preference for stability have been successful.

To meet this challenge, the Party has either to carry out a more fundamental reform in the current political system—a genuine democratization—or to provide the public with a more cohesive and convincing set of normative values to justify the existence of the current system. Thus far, the CCP leadership has seemingly put more of its efforts into the latter since the onset of post-Mao reform. In the wake of the drastic weakening of the old official ideology, Marxism-Leninism-Mao Zedong Thought, the Party had attempted to advance a set of "new" normative values by promoting the

Theory of Deng Xiaoping or Dengism,[4] which includes such ideological
principles as the so-called Four Cardinal Principles,[5] "socialism with Chinese characteristics," "socialist market economy," and some other specific
ideas on reform. Yet, it has been quite obvious that this set of values and
principles has not been able to serve as a unifying ideology for the entire
society, although it has been relentlessly promoted by the Party (Chen 1995;
Kalpana 1998).

In 2000 (one year after the last survey in Beijing), then–Party leader, Jiang
Zemin, initiated a nationwide campaign to promote another set of ideological principles, "three representations" (*sange daibiao*) in order "to transform
Party ideology" (Fewsmith 2001a, 232). This set of ideological principles
called for the Party to represent the most advanced force of production, the
most advanced culture, and the fundamental interests of the broadest masses
of the Chinese people (Jiang 2001). Of these three representations, the most
interesting seem to be the representations of the most advanced force of production and the fundamental interests of the broadest masses of the Chinese
people. According to some China observers, these two representations might
have signified the beginning of fundamental changes in the Party's ideology, if not in the political structure (Lo 2000; Xin 2002). As to the representation of the most advanced forces of production, in his important speech
at the meeting to celebrate the eightieth anniversary of the founding of the
CCP, Jiang Zemin (Jiang 2001) not only reiterated the belonging of the intellectuals to the working class[6] that is "the basic force to promote the force
of production" but also emphasized the extremely important role of intellectuals in the national economic development. As one China scholar (Fewsmith 2001a, 230) points out, "whereas Dengist doctrine made intellectuals
a part of the working class, Jiang Zemin seems to be coming close to say-
ing that intellectuals are the most advanced part of the working class." In
terms of the call for the representation of the fundamental interests of the

4. The Theory of Deng Xiaoping is a collection of Deng's remarks concerning major principles and policies of the post-Mao economic and political reforms. This collection has been published mainly in *Selected Works of Deng Xiaoping, 1975–1982* (Deng
1983) and *Deng Xiaoping wenxuan, 1982–1992* (Deng 1993).

5. The Four Cardinal Principles stand for: (1) supporting the CCP's leadership,
(2) adhering to socialism, (3) upholding Marxism-Leninism-Mao Zedong Thought, and
(4) maintaining the proletarian dictatorship (Wang 1999, 57).

6. According to Marxist ideology, the Communist Party should be the vanguard of
the working class. Thus, membership in the working class guarantees representation in
the party.

broadest masses of the Chinese people, Jiang Zemin (2001) emphasized that the Party "should carefully consider the interests of the masses in various classes and sectors" rather than those of only one class. According to Few-smith (2001a, 230), this call "moves away from traditional notions of the Communist Party representing the vanguard of the working class and to-ward the notion that it represents the interests of all the people. . . . [which] leaves the door open for political reform."

These new ideological principles have apparently left room for specula-tion about a potential loosening-up of the existing Party control. But they by no means indicate any fundamental changes in the current political sys-tem. Do these relatively new ideological principles have a stronger and broader appeal to the broad masses of the Chinese people, especially those who strongly believe in democratic values and who perceive the urgent need for a further political reform? This question—which directly relates to whether the current and future CCP leaderships can reverse the downward trend of citizens' diffuse support for the communist regime—remains to be answered.

The other kind of challenge to the CCP's efforts to improve diffuse sup-port is derived from the differences between the likely opponents and pro-ponents of the communist regime in their sociodemographic characteristics. As revealed in chapter 4, the most likely regime opponents come mainly from the more energetic and modern sectors of the population: they tend to be young and better educated, and are more likely to believe in democratic values and see the need for fundamental political change. On the other hand, the most likely regime proponents are mainly among the less resilient and more traditional or conservative sectors of the population: they tend to be older and less educated, and are more likely to have a strong preference for the political status quo. Thus, to improve diffuse support, not only should the CCP leadership consolidate the existing consent to the communist regime from the traditional sectors of the population, but it has to win support for the regime from the modern sectors. The latter task definitely presents a more serious challenge for the current and future CCP leadership.

Modernization theory has argued that ongoing economic modernization not only enlarges the size of the modern sector of the population but also increases the sociopolitical influence of this sector (Inkeles and Smith 1974; Inkeles and Diamond 1980; Inglehart 1997, 1990). According to this argu-ment, as economic development continues at a fast pace in China, more and more people will join the modern sector and gain more political power. Since people in the modern sector tend to be less supportive of the communist regime—as suggested by the data—the CCP will confront more opponents in the future unless it carries out a fundamental political change for democracy, which is demanded by the fast growing modern sector of the population.

As mentioned above, the Party's new set of ideological principles, the three representations, has called for the Party to represent the most advanced force of production, which presumably includes the modern sector of the population. Nonetheless, these principles do not advocate a transformation of the current political system. Consequently, the "representation" of the modern sector of the population is most likely to be confined within the old system. Thus, the call for such representation would not seem to diminish the opposition to the system by this modern sector.

Challenges to the Improvement of Support
for the Incumbent Authorities

As discussed in chapter 3, the prolonged deterioration of support for the incumbent authorities, measured by the popular evaluations of incumbent policy performance, will eventually erode popular diffuse support for the fundamental political system (or regime) to the level of crisis. Thus, in order to strengthen regime legitimacy, the current and future CCP leaderships must constantly improve their policy performance in some major socioeconomic areas. Yet, the data have predicated some formidable challenges for the CCP leadership to its improvement of policy performance particularly in urban China. Specifically, these challenges seem to come from at least three major policy areas—minimizing economic inequality, providing job security, and combating official corruption. Our respondents gave the lowest evaluations of incumbent performance in the late 1990s in all three policy areas.

First, as for the challenge to the minimizing of economic inequality, China's accession to the World Trade Organization (WTO) is very likely, at least in the short or medium term, to exacerbate the existing gap between rich and poor that has already widened since the onset of post-Mao reform. According to some independent sources outside China, for instance, de facto income inequality—measured by the Gini coefficient[7]—has reached the "alarming level" (Jianmin Wang 2002). Even in his government report

7. The Gini coefficient is a common measure of inequality, used by development economists. It ranges in value from "0" indicating perfect equality to "1" referring to absolute inequality.

to the National People's Congress in 2002, Zhu Rongji, China's premier at the time, admitted that there had existed a sizable "disadvantaged group" (*ruoshi qunti*)[8] in both the rural and the urban areas, whose economic status had been remarkably lower than that of the well-off (Zhu 2002). Moreover, according to some experienced China watchers, both intra- and interregional income inequalities will grow even more rapidly due to severer competition in various economic sectors, owing to China's entry into the WTO. Those who are younger, better educated, and hence more competitive will earn higher incomes than do those who are less blessed and less competitive (Wang 2000; Fewsmith 2001b).

Second, the provision of job security will be another serious challenge for the current and future CCP leadership in their efforts to improve the overall policy performance. Obviously, job security concerns the stability of employment as well as the opportunities of reemployment. Even without the WTO impact, as illustrated in chapter 2, not only had the unemployment rate already been increasing at a rapid pace but reemployment had become increasingly difficult. Although it is hard to obtain an accurate estimate of unemployment in China due to various technical and political obstacles,[9] most observers have agreed that the actual unemployment rate—which has been always substantially underestimated by the government—has increased dramatically since the mid 1990s. For example, Hu Angang, a leading Chinese development economist, has reported that the unemployment rate in urban areas increased from slightly below 4 percent in 1993 to over 8 percent in 1999.[10] The pressures of reemployment were also acute, even according to the figures published by the government: from 1998 to 2001, more than 25 million people were laid off, mostly from SOEs, and only 17 million of them had since found new jobs (State Council 2002). Based on a recent estimate, while about 13 million people enter China's labor market each year, only about 8 million new jobs a year are being created (Smith 2002).

Even worse, it has become more difficult to improve the current situations of unemployment and reemployment in China at least in the near future. The

8. The Chinese term, *ruoshi qunti,* has a more neutral and subtle connotation than the English term, "disadvantaged group." The Chinese term was said to be adopted in Zhu's speech to avoid potential political risk (Wang 2002).

9. For a penetrating and detailed discussion of different counts of unemployment and the difficulties in obtaining an accurate figure for unemployment in contemporary China, see the analysis by Solinger (2001).

10. Hu's estimate of the urban unemployment rate has been reported by Shaoguang Wang (2000, 833).

difficulties may come from at least two structural sources. One is the diminishing growth rate of new jobs, in spite of continuous economic expansion in China. According to some experienced observers, while each percentage point of GDP growth brought about a 0.14 percent increase in new jobs in the mid 1990s, it yielded only a 0.05 percent increase in employment by 1999 (Wang 2000, 383–4). This trend suggests that the growth of China's economy as such would not necessarily help to alleviate unemployment and increase reemployment.

The other structural source of the difficulties in improving employment conditions is the fierce competition in various economic sectors, brought about by China's entry into the WTO. WTO membership requires China to dismantle or reduce its remaining import barriers and to give foreign companies free access to Chinese markets. As a result, more Chinese producers in various economic and industrial sectors, which are less competitive than their foreign counterparts, will fail in the coming competition. Many analysts in and outside China have predicted that the failures of these Chinese producers in agriculture and industry will certainly generate a large number of the unemployed in both rural and urban areas at least in the short term (Wen 1999; Wang 2000; Qiao 2001; Fewsmith 2001b). For example, Shaoguang Wang has predicted that due to the competition resulting from China's participation in the WTO, "between 13 and 15 million growers of China's main agricultural crops will become unemployed between 2000 and 2010, among whom about 10 million will have to be transferred to nonagricultural sectors" (Wang 2000, 397). Meanwhile, however, the competition will force more Chinese firms (especially inefficient SOEs) in urban areas to downsize themselves or simply go out of business, laying off about 25 to 30 million employees (Wang 2000, 398). Thus, at least in the short term, China's WTO membership will create tremendous pressure on the labor markets in both the rural and the urban areas simultaneously, so that one could not supplement the other. In sum, the Party leadership will face serious challenges to its effort to create more job opportunities in the short or medium terms.

Finally, combating official corruption will continue to be one of the toughest battles that the CCP leadership must fight in order to improve its image. It is extremely difficult, if not totally impossible, however, for the central CCP leadership to win the battle within the current system, even though the leadership has launched a series of anticorruption campaigns since the early 1990s. This is not only because corruption has involved a large number of officials at various levels of the government but because the new, major form of corruption has made it extremely hard to win the battle. This relatively new form of corruption can be characterized as "organizational corruption." According to Xiaobo Lu (2000, 275), "organizational corruption refers to the actions of a public agency that, by exploiting its power in regulating the market or its monopoly over vital resources, are aimed at monetary or material gains," and such actions are "department-based and conducted in the name of an official unit equipped with legitimate discretion" to benefit all the members of the unit concerned. This type of official corruption has become increasingly widespread in China in recent years. For instance, about 60 percent of the corruption cases between 1995 and 1997 were of this type (Lu 2000, 276).

It can be argued that it is more difficult to fight organizational corruption than that of individual officials, even as organizational corruption has caused more discontent within the public. There are at least two major reasons to support this argument. First, as organizational corruption benefits a collective body of people rather than a few individuals, it tends to have support from a large number of organized participants. Such broader-based and organized support often turns into more powerful resistance to central-government sanctions against corruption. Second, since organizational corruption is conducted in the name of a government agency that has legal discretion to interpret and implement central policies and regulations, it often looks like a legitimate act. Such a disguise makes it harder to investigate and prosecute organizational corruption cases (Lu 2000, 275). Thus, to fight official corruption is one of the toughest challenges that the CCP leadership is facing.

Challenges from Overt Political Alienation

As described in chapter 6, our respondents' participation in such a regime support-oriented act as voting in local People's Congresses has declined, while their participation in such complaint-oriented acts as contacting authorities at various levels has increased. If these trends of mass political participation were to continue in most parts of China, the CCP leadership would not only lose overt support for the political regime expressed through the local elections, but also confront an increase in overt alienation manifested through either conventional or unconventional political activities.

Overt alienation reflected in such unconventional political acts as protest and demonstration is most likely to pose a direct threat to sociopolitical stability and even the survival of CCP rule. According to some early empirical studies of political participation in various sociopolitical settings (Muller 1977; Muller and Jukam 1977; Muller 1970b; Muller, Jukam, and Seligson 1982), there are both direct and indirect causes for mass participation in these unconventional political activities. The most important direct cause is a low level or absence of diffuse support for the current political regime, whereas prolonged discontent with incumbent performance in major socio-economic areas serves as a salient indirect cause. Therefore, on the one hand, the lack of diffuse support itself is sufficient to motivate people to participate in unconventional or aggressive activities; on the other hand, the discontent with incumbent performance (or lack of specific support) can propel people to do so when such discontent has been present over time and has been transformed into a low level of diffuse support.

The data from our surveys seem to suggest that both direct and indirect causes for unconventional political activities were in the making at least in such an urban area as Beijing. First of all, as indicated earlier, diffuse support for the current political regime among our respondents had declined in the second half of the 1990s, although the current level of such support remained moderately high. As a result, this downward trend of diffuse support might eventually set off a wave of participation in unconventional activities. Secondly, specific support for incumbent performance had already been quite low during our surveys. Should this low level of specific support last longer, it would turn into anti-regime sentiment that in turn will also motivate people to engage in unconventional political acts.

Unconventional political activities are not investigated in this study, because participation in such activities was "highly situational and rare in the general population" (Tang and Parish 2000, 193) at the time when our surveys were conducted and because questions regarding any intention to participate in these activities could carry some political risks. Nonetheless, some new evidence indicates that, since the late 1990s, mass participation in unconventional political activities is on the rise. For example, an independent source reported that in March 2002 about 100,000 SOE workers staged large-scale demonstrations in three heavy-industrial cities—Daqing, Liaoyang and Fushun (in Northeast China)—against their enterprises' decisions to lay off more workers and the poor treatment that the unemployed had received (*Mingpao* 2002). An increase in such incidents seems to suggest that both declining diffuse support and prolonged low specific support, respectively as direct and indirect causes, might have already been at work to motivate people—especially those who have suffered more and longer from the reform and who have become disillusioned about the current political system as a whole—to engage in such unconventional activities as mass demonstrations and protests. Widespread participation in such unconventional activities would threaten the sociopolitical stability and even the survival of CCP rule. The current and future CCP leadership will face serious challenges from the rise of overt alienation, unless it can reverse the declining trend of citizens' diffuse support for the regime and improve its policy performance.

To conclude, the post–Jiang Zemin leadership will inherit its predecessor's legacies in political support: both the existing strengths and existing weaknesses of the CCP as well as the coming sociopolitical challenges to its rule. The empirical findings presented in this study lead us to argue that whether the new leadership can succeed in meeting these challenges depends largely on whether it can take more substantive and decisive measures (1) to carry out a more fundamental political reform toward a democracy in order to reverse the downward trend of diffuse support for the political regime and (2) to address effectively such serious sociopolitical issues as official corruption, unemployment, and economic inequality in order to boost specific support for the incumbent authority.

Finally, I emphasize the need for more extensive and inclusive studies of popular political support in contemporary China. This is simply because as China's economy and politics inevitably become more modernized and liberalized, respectively, citizens' support for the predominant political system and the incumbent political leadership will play a more critical role in shaping the future of this dynamic country.

Appendix A

Reliabilities of the Diffuse and Specific Support Indexes

The Reliability of the Diffuse Support Index

While most of the questionnaire items in the diffuse support index were derived from previous survey studies of diffuse support in several non-Chinese settings (Muller and Jukam 1977; Finkel, Muller, and Seligson 1989), they were all pretested for their validity in Beijing before the formal surveys. To assess the reliability of this set of items for diffuse support, I examined the interitem correlations and reliability coefficients among these items across the three samples from Beijing. As table A.1 shows, while the item-scale correlations in each sample vary somewhat from item to item, the combination of the items for each sample produces desirable reliability coefficients (alpha): .80 in 1995, .84 in 1997, and .82 in 1995. These reliability coefficient scores indicate that this set of items is a reliable measure of diffuse support for the political regime. Moreover, the average interitem correlation (r) of this set of items for each sample is generally moderate: .39 in 1995, .47 in 1997, and .45 in 1999. Such a moderate interitem correlation means that it is from different angles that the items in the set measure the concept of diffuse support for the political regime.

But it is worth noting that one of the items, item 6 (regarding value congruence between the respondent and the government), correlates least closely with other items in all three samples (.44 in 1995, .50 in 1997, and .49 in 1999), while it does not detract from the overall scale reliability in each sample.[1]

1. The score of "alpha if item deleted" for this item does not exceed the score of "overall standardized item alpha" in each sample (table A.1). This result indicates that item 6 does not contribute to reducing the overall reliability of the index.

195

Table A.1

Reliability of the Diffuse Support Index: The 1995, 1997, and 1999 Beijing Samples

Item	1995 Sample		1997 Sample		1999 Sample	
	Item-Scale Correlation*	Alpha If Item Deleted	Item-Scale Correlation*	Alpha If Item Deleted	Item-Scale Correlation*	Alpha If Item Deleted
1. I am proud to live under the current political system.	.58	.75	.60	.82		
2. I have an obligation to support the current political system.	.52	.76	.67	.81	.64	.79
3. I respect the political institutions in China today.	.61	.74	.63	.82	.62	.82
4. I feel that the basic rights of citizens are protected.	.58	.75	.65	.81	.63	.80
5. I believe that the courts in China guarantee fair trials.	.51	.76	.69	.80	.68	.79
6. I feel that my personal values are the same as those advocated by the government.	.44	.78	.50	.84	.49	.82
Overall standardized item alpha:	.80		.84		.82	
Mean interitem correlation (r):	.39		.47		.45	

* The item-scale correlation is the correlation between the item and an additive scale built from all other items.

There are at least two possible reasons for this weak correlation between item 6 and the other items. One is that this item is more difficult than the others to respond to, because it requires sophisticated and abstract comparison between the respondent's own values and his or her perception of the government's values. Closely related to this, the other possible reason is that since the onset of post-Mao reform, the government's orientations toward some major sociopolitical issues—such as local elections, the Party's role at the grassroots level, and the direction of reform in state-own enterprises—have changed from time to time, although the regime has been consistent in adhering to the ruling position of the CCP at the national level. As Baum (1994, 5) has observed, the post-Mao leaders' political and ideological orientations have fluctuated between some extremes:

> They tended to follow each new round of liberalizing reform with an attempt to retain—or regain—control. Letting go (*fang*) with one hand, they instinctively tightened up (*shou*) with the other. Over time, the conflicting pressures and imperatives associated with fang and shou produced an oscillating pattern of policy initiative and response, as phases of reform and relaxation alternated with phases of relative restriction and retrenchment. The fluid ebb and flow of this recursive "fang/shou cycle" lent the process of political and economic reform a discontinuous, pulsating quality.

Due to this kind of uncertainty in the leadership's political and ideological orientations, therefore, it could be difficult for ordinary citizens to synthesize and conceptualize the regime's values and norms, and hence even more difficult for them to make a comparison between the government's norms/values and their own.

But, all in all, item 6 does not contribute negatively to the reliability of the entire index; rather it increases the reliability coefficient of the index by .02 in the 1995 sample. In other words, this item does help to measure the concept of diffuse support, together with other items. Therefore, I am inclined to include item 6 within the index.

The Reliability of the Specific Support Index

I have also assessed the reliability of the items for specific support by examining the interitem correlations and reliability coefficients among these

Table A.2

Reliability of the Specific Support Index: The 1995, 1997, and 1999 Beijing Samples

Item	1995 Sample		1997 Sample		1999 Sample	
	Item-Scale Correlation*	Alpha if Item Deleted	Item-Scale Correlation*	Alpha if Item Deleted	Item-Scale Correlation*	Alpha if Item Deleted
1. Controlling inflation	.52	.83	.44	.86	.51	.85
2. Providing job security	.60	.82	.65	.84	.62	.82
3. Minimizing the gap between rich and poor	.66	.81	.70	.84	.68	.83
4. Improving housing conditions for all	.56	.82	.52	.85	.57	.83
5. Maintaining order in society	.57	.82	.56	.85	.55	.82
6. Providing adequate medical care for all	.58	.82	.61	.85	.60	.83
7. Providing welfare services to the needy	.55	.82	.62	.85	.58	.83
8. Combating pollution	.55	.83	.64	.85	.65	.82
9. Fighting official corruption	.63	.83	.67	.84	.65	.82
Overall standardized item alpha:	.84		.87		.85	
Mean inter-item correlation (r):	.40		.42		.43	

* The item-scale correlation is the correlation between the item and an additive scale built from all other items.

items across the three samples. Table A.2 indicates that while the item-scale correlations in each sample vary somewhat from item to item, the combination of the items for each sample produces desirable reliability coefficients (alpha): .84 in 1995, .87 in 1997, and .85 in 1995. These reliability coefficients indicate that this set of items is a reliable measure of specific support for the political authorities. In addition, the average interitem correlation (r) of this set of items for each sample is generally moderate: .40 in 1995, .42 in 1997, and .43 in 1999. This kind of moderate interitem correlation establishes that the items in this set measure the same concept of specific support for the political authorities from multiple dimensions.

Appendix B

Supplemental Information about the Distributions of Diffuse Support and Specific Support

Table B.1

Distribution of Diffuse Support, 1995, 1997, and 1999

Item in the Index	(1)* Strongly Disagree (%)			(2)* Disagree (%)			(3)* Agree (%)			(4)* Strongly Agree (%)		
	1995	1997	1999	1995	1997	1999	1995	1997	1999	1995	1997	1999
1. Proud of system	.9	1.7	2.9	3.7	6.4	9.8	41.6	43.3	40.8	53.8	48.6	46.5
2. Obligated to system	.0	.7	2.5	2.5	6.6	12.1	35.3	45.3	43.9	62.2	47.3	41.5
3. Respect institutions	1.3	1.0	2.1	5.5	8.6	10.2	48.3	48.1	49.5	44.9	42.3	38.2
4. Basic rights protected	1.9	3.7	9.1	11.4	17.7	23.9	62.8	55.9	47.1	23.9	22.6	19.9
5. Fair courts	3.6	4.9	5.8	14.2	20.1	16.7	66.0	56.8	57.2	16.2	18.1	20.3
6. Personal vs. government values	1.8	2.4	6.6	18.2	23.9	27.5	61.0	54.7	50.1	19.0	17.2	15.8

* This is a numerical score assigned to each response.

Table B.2.

Distribution of Specific Support, 1995, 1997, and 1999

Item in the Index	(1)* Very Poor (%)			(2)* Poor (%)			(3)* So-So (%)			(4)* Good (%)			(5)* Very Good (%)		
	1995	1997	1999	1995	1997	1999	1995	1997	1999	1995	1997	1999	1995	1997	1999
1. Controlling inflation	11	6	2	37	11	6	39	50	36	10	19	38	3	13	18
2. Providing job security	6	11	18	27	33	34	54	43	38	10	8	5	4	5	4
3. Minimizing inequality	17	20	22	44	41	44	29	29	27	6	6	4	4	4	3
4. Improving housing	9	16	13	30	25	24	43	43	42	13	11	16	5	5	5
5. Maintaining order	9	9	9	29	23	25	40	42	41	14	18	17	8	9	8
6. Providing medical care	6	8	10	25	24	28	45	49	44	18	13	12	6	7	6
7. Providing welfare for the needy	4	6	5	19	23	22	49	42	44	21	20	22	8	9	7
8. Combating pollution	11	17	18	36	34	37	32	31	30	14	12	10	7	6	5
9. Fighting corruption	26	27	23	36	34	38	22	24	23	9	8	9	7	6	5

* This is a numerical score assigned to each response.

References

Abolfathi, Farid. 1980. "Threat, Public Opinion, and Military Spending in the United States, 1930–1990." In *Threats, Weapons, and Foreign Policy,* ed. Pat McGowan and Charles W. Kegley, Jr. Beverly Hills, Calif.: Sage.

Abramson, Paul R. 1974. "Generational Change in American Electoral Behavior." *American Political Science Review* 68 (March): 93–105.

———. 1989. "Generational Replacement, Ethnic Change, and Partisan Support in Israel." *Journal of Politics* 51 (June): 545–74.

Adamany, David, and Joel Grossman. 1983. "Support for the Supreme Court as a National Policymaker." *Law and Policy Quarterly* 5 (June): 405–37.

Alford, William P. 1993. "Double-edged Swords Cut Both Ways: Law and Legitimacy in the People's Republic of China." *Daedalus* 122 (Spring): 45–70.

Almond, Gabriel A., and Sidney Verba. 1963. *The Civic Culture: Political Attitudes and Democracy in Five Nations.* Princeton, N.J.: Princeton University Press.

Andors, Phyllis. 1983. *The Unfinished Liberation of Chinese Women, 1949–1980.* Bloomington: Indiana University Press.

Andrews, Frank M., and Stephen B. Withey. 1976. *Social Indicators of Well Being: Americans' Perceptions of Life Quality.* New York: Plenum.

Archive Research Office of the Central Committee of the Chinese Communist Party. 1994. *Deng xiaoping jianshe you zhongguo tesi de shehuizhuyi lunshu zhuanti zhaibian* (Special Digest of Deng Xiaoping's Works on Building Socialism with the Chinese Characteristics). Beijing: Central Archive Press.

Avery, William. 1988. "Political Legitimacy and Crisis in Poland." *Political Science Quarterly* 103 (Spring): 111–30.

Azrael, Jeremy R. 1965. "Soviet Union." In *Education and Political Development,* ed. James S. Coleman. Princeton, N.J.: Princeton University Press.

Bahry, Donna. 1987. "Politics, Generations, and Change in the USSR." In *Politics, Work, and Daily Life in the USSR: A Survey of Former Soviet Citizens,* ed. James R. Millar. Cambridge: Cambridge University Press.

Bahry, Donna, and Brian D. Silver. 1990. "Soviet Citizen Participation on the Eve of Democratization." *American Political Science Review* 48 (September): 820–47.

Banister, Judith. 1998. "Population, Public Health, and the Environment in China." *China Quarterly* 156 (December): 986–1015.

205

Barghoorn, Frederick C., and Thomas F. Remington. 1986. *Politics in the USSR.* Boston: Little, Brown.

Barker, Rodney. 1990. *Political Legitimacy and the State.* Oxford: Oxford University Press.

Barnes, Samuel. H., Barbara G. Farah, and Felix Heunks. 1979. "Personal Dissatisfaction." In *Political Action: Mass Participation in Five Western Democracies,* ed. Samuel H. Barnes and Max Kaase. Beverly Hills, Calif.: Sage.

Bauer, John, Wang Feng, Nancy E. Riley, and Zhao Xiaohua. 1992. "Gender Inequality in Urban China." *Modern China* 18 (July): 333–70.

Baum, Richard. 1994. *Burying Mao: Chinese Politics in the Age of Deng Xiaoping.* Princeton, N.J.: Princeton University Press.

———. 2000. "Jiang Takes Command: The Fifteenth National Party Congress and Beyond." In *China under Jiang Zemin,* ed. Hung-Mao Tien and Yun-Han Chu. Boulder, Colo.: Lynne Rienner.

Beetham, David. 1991. *The Legitimation of Power.* London: Macmillan.

———. 1993. "In Defense of Legitimacy." *Political Studies* 41 (September): 488–91.

Beijing Municipal Statistical Bureau. 1998. *Beijing Statistical Yearbook.* Beijing: China Statistical Publishing House.

Bialer, Seweryn. 1980. *Stalin's Successors: Leadership, Stability, and Change in the Soviet Union.* New York: Cambridge University Press.

Biers, Dan. 1994. "China's Rush to Boost Industry Causing Disastrous Pollution." *Associated Press* (April 28).

Bonin, Michel. 2000. "Perspectives on Social Stability after the Fifteenth Congress." In *China under Jiang Zemin,* ed. Hung-Mao Tien and Yun-Han Chu. Boulder, Colo.: Lynne Rienner.

Bottelier, Pieter. 2000. "How Stable Is China? An Economic Perspective." In *Is China Unstable? Assessing the Factors,* ed. David Shambaugh. Armonk, N.Y.: M.E. Sharpe.

Brugger, Bill, and Stephen Reglar. 1994. *Politics, Economy, and Society in Contemporary China.* Stanford, Calif.: Stanford University Press.

Brunner, Georg. 1982. "Legitimacy Doctrines and Legitimation Procedures in East European Systems." In *Political Legitimacy in Communist States,* ed. T. H. Rigby and Ferenc Feher. New York: St. Martin's.

Burg, Steven L., and Michael L. Berbaum. 1989. "Community, Integration, and Stability in Multinational Yugoslavia." *American Political Science Review* 83 (June): 535–54.

Burns, John P. 1999. "The People's Republic of China at 50: National Political Reform." *China Quarterly* 159 (September): 580–94.

———. 1988. *Political Participation in Rural China.* Berkeley: University of California Press.

Burton, Charles. 1990. *Political and Social Change in China since 1978.* New York: Greenwood.

Caldeira, Gregory A., and James L. Gibson. 1995. "The Legitimacy of the Court of Justice in the European Union: Models of Institutional Support." *American Political Science Review* 89 (June): 356–76.

Campbell, Angus. 1981. *The Sense of Well-Being in America.* New York: McGraw-Hill.

Campbell, Angus, Philip E. Converse, and Willard L. Rodgers. 1976. *The Quality of American Life: Perceptions, Evaluations, and Satisfactions.* New York: Russell Sage Foundation.

Casuck, Thomas R. 1999. "The Shaping of Popular Satisfaction with Government and Regime Performance in Germany." *British Journal of Political Science* 29 (September): 641–72.

Chan, Maria Hsia. 2001. *Return of the Dragon: China's Wounded Nationalism.* Boulder, Colo.: Westview.

Chan, Alfred L., and Paul Nesbitt-Larking. 1995. "Critical Citizenship and Civil Society in Contemporary China." *Canadian Journal of Political Science* 28, no. 2: 293–309.

Chan, Anita, and Robert A. Senser. 1997. "China's Troubled Workers." *Foreign Affairs* 76 (March/April): 104–17.

Chanley, Virginia A., Thomas J. Rudolph, and Wendy M. Rahn. 2000. "The Origins and Consequences of Public Trust in Government: A Time Series Analysis." *Public Opinion Quarterly* 64 (Fall): 239–56.

Chappell, Henry W., Jr., and William R. Keech. 1985. "A New View of Political Accountability for Economic Performance." *American Political Science Review* 79 (March): 10–27.

Chen, Feng. 1995. *Economic Transition and Political Legitimacy in Post–Mao China: Ideology and Reform.* Albany: State University of New York Press.

———. 2000. "Subsistence Crises, Managerial Corruption, and Labor Protests in China." *The China Journal* 44 (July): 41–63.

Chen, Feng, and Ting Gong. 1997. "Party versus Market in Post–Mao China: The Erosion of the Leninist Organization from Below." *Journal of Communist Studies and Transitional Politics* 13, no. 3: 148–66.

Chen, Jie. 1995. "The Impact of Reform on the Party and Ideology in China." *Journal of Contemporary China* 9 (Summer): 22–34.

———. 1999. "Comparing Mass and Elite Subjective Orientations in Urban China." *Public Opinion Quarterly* 63 (Summer): 193–219.

———. 2000. "Subjective Motivations for Mass Political Participation in Urban China." *Social Science Quarterly* 81 (June): 645–62.

———. 2001. "Urban Chinese Perceptions of Threats from the United States and Japan." *Public Opinion Quarterly* 65 (Summer): 254–66.

Chen, Jie, and Peng Deng. 1995. *China since the Cultural Revolution: From Totalitarianism to Authoritarianism.* Westport, Conn.: Praeger.

Chen, Jie, and Yang Zhong. 1998. "Defining the Political System of Post Deng China: Emerging Public Support for a Democratic Political System." *Problems of Post-Communism* 45 (January–February): 30–42.

———. 2002. "Why Do People Vote in Semicompetitive Elections in China?" *Journal of Politics* 64 (February): 178–97.

Chen, Jie, Yang Zhong, and Jan William Hillard. 1996. "Assessing Political Support in China: Citizens' Evaluations of Governmental Effectiveness and Legitimacy," presented at the annual meeting of the Western Political Science Association, San Francisco.

———. 1997. "The Level and Sources of Popular Support for China's Current Political Regime." *Communist and Post-Communist Studies* 30, no. 1: 45–64.

Chen, Minzhang. 1997. *Yearbook of Health in the People's Republic of China, 1997.* Beijing: People's Medical Publishing House.

Cheng, Xiaonong. 1999. "Breaking the Social Contract." In *Dilemmas of Reform in Jiang Zemin's China,* ed. Andrew J. Nathan, Zhaohui Hong, and Steven R. Smith. Boulder, Colo.: Lynne Rienner.

Cherrington, Ruth. 1979. "Generational Issues in China: A Case Study of the 1980s Generation of Young Intellectuals." *British Journal of Sociology* 48 (June): 302–20.

Chong, Dennis, Herbert McClosky, and John Zaller. 1985. "Social Learning and the Acquisition of Political Norms." In *The American Ethos,* ed. Herbert McClosky and John Zaller. Cambridge: Harvard University Press.

Christernsen, Thomas J. 1999. "China, the U.S.-Japan Alliance, and the Security Dilemma in East Asia." *International Security* 23 (Spring): 49–80.

Citrin, Jack. 1974. "Comment: The Political Relevance of Trust in Government." *American Political Science Review* 68 (September): 973–88.

Citrin, Jack, and Christopher Muste. 1999. "Trust in Government." In *Measures of Political Attitudes,* ed. John P. Robinson, Phillip R. Shaver, and Lawrence S. Wrightsman. San Diego: Academic.

Citrin, Jack, Herbert McClosky, J. Merrill Shanks, and Paul M. Sniderman. 1975. "Personal and Political Sources of Political Alienation." *British Journal of Political Science* 5 (January): 1–31.

Clarke, Harold D., Nitish Dutt, and Allan Kornberg. 1993. "The Political Economy of Attitudes toward Polity and Society in Western European Democracies." *Journal of Politics* 55 (November): 998–1021.

CND (China News Digest). 2001. "Public Opinion Survey on the Politburo Members." December 3 <http://www.cnd.org/HXWZExpress/01/12/011203-6.gb.html>.

Cohen, Raymond. 1979. *Threat Perception in International Crisis.* Madison: University of Wisconsin Press.

Converse, Philip. 1976. *The Dynamics of Party Support: Cohort-Analyzing Party Identification.* Beverly Hills, Calif.: Sage.

Cottam, Richard W. 1977. *Foreign Policy Motivation: A General Theory and a Case Study.* Pittsburgh: University of Pittsburgh Press.

Croll, Elizabeth J. 1983. *Chinese Women since Mao.* Armonk, NY: M. E. Sharpe.

———. 1999. "Social Welfare Reform: Trends and Tensions." *China Quarterly* 159 (September): 684–99.

Dahl, Robert A. 1971. *Polyarchy.* New Haven: Yale University Press.

———. 1989. *Democracy and Its Critics.* New Haven: Yale University Press.

Davidson, Robert H., and Glenn R. Parker. 1972. "Positive Support for Political Institutions: The Case of Congress." *Western Political Quarterly* 25 (December): 600–12.

Davis, Deborah. 1992. "Job Mobility in Post–Mao Cities: Increases in the Margins," *China Quarterly* 132 (December): 577–97.

Davis, E. E., M. Fine-Davis, and G. Meehan. 1982. "Demographic Determinants of Perceived Well-Being in Eight European Countries." *Social Indicators Research* 10 (November): 341–58.

Deng, Xiaoping. 1983. *Selected Works of Deng Xiaoping, 1975–1982.* Beijing: Foreign Language Press.

———. 1993. *Deng Xiaoping wenxuan* (Selected Works of Deng Xiaoping), 1982–1992, vol. 3. Beijing: Renmin chubanshe.

Deng, Young. 1998. "Chinese Conception of National Interests in International Relations." *China Quarterly* 154 (June): 308–29.

Denisovsky, Gennady M., Polina M. Kosyreva, and Mikhail S. Matskovsky. 1993. "Twelve Percent of Hope: Economic Consciousness and a Market Economy." In *Public Opinion and Regime Change: The New Politics of Post-Soviet Societies,* ed. Authur H. Miller, William M. Reisinger, and Vicki L. Heslie. Boulder, Colo.: Westview.

Dernberger, Robert F. 1999. "The People's Republic of China at 50: The Economy." *China Quarterly* 159 (September): 606–15.

Dickson, Bruce J. 2000a. "Political Instability at the Middle and Lower Levels: Signs of a Decaying CCP, Corruption, and Political Dissent." In *Is China Unstable? Assessing the Factors,* ed. David Shambaugh. Armonk, N.Y.: M. E. Sharpe.

———. 2000b. "Cooptation and Corporatism in China: The Logic of Party Adaptation." *Political Science Quarterly* 115 (Winter): 517–40.

Dickson, Bruce J., and Maria Rost Rublee. 2000. "Membership Has Its Privileges: The Socioeconomic Characteristics of Communist Party Members in Urban China." *Comparative Political Studies* 33 (February): 87–112.

DiFranceisco, Wayne, and Zvi Gitelman. 1984. "Soviet Political Cultural and 'Covert Participation' in Policy Implementation." *American Political Science Review* 78 (September): 603–21.

Ding, X. L. 1994. *The Decline of Communism in China's Legitimacy Crisis, 1977–1989.* New York: Cambridge University Press.

Dobson, Richard B. 1980. "Education and Opportunity." In *Contemporary Soviet Society: Sociological Perspectives,* ed. Jerry G. Pankhurst and Michael Paul Sacks. New York: Praeger.

Dorrill, William F. 1970. "Transfer of Legitimacy in the Chinese Communist Party: Origins of the Maoist Myth." In *Party Leadership and Revolutionary Power in China,* ed. John Wilson Lewis. Cambridge: Cambridge University Press.

Downs, Erica Strecker, and Phillip C. Saunders. 2000. "Legitimacy and the Limits of Nationalism: China and Diaoyu Islands." In *The Rise of China: An International Security Reader,* ed. Michael E. Brown et al. Cambridge: MIT Press.

Dreyer, June Teufel. 2000. *China's Political System: Modernization and Tradition.* New York: Longman.

Duara, Prasenjit. 1996. "De-Constructing the Chinese Nation." In *Chinese Nationalism,* ed. Jonathan Unger. New York: M. E. Sharpe.

Duch, Raymond M. 1993. "Tolerating Economic Reform: Popular Support for Transition to a Free Market in the Former Soviet Union." *American Political Science Review* 87 (September): 590–608.

Duckitt, John. 1989. "Authoritarianism and Group Identification: A New View of an Old Construct." *Political Psychology* 10: 63-84.

Easton, David. 1957. "An Approach to the Analysis of Political Systems." *World Politics* 9 (April): 383–400.

———. 1965. *A Systems Analysis of Political Life.* New York: Wiley.

———. 1975. "A Reassessment of the Concept of Political Support." *British Journal of Political Science* 5 (October): 435–57.

———. 1976. "Theoretical Approaches to Political Support." *Canadian Journal of Political Science* 9 (October): 431–48.

Edmonds, Richard L. 1994. *Patterns of China's Lost Harmony.* London: Routledge.

———. 1999. "The Environment in the People's Republic of China Fifty Years On." *China Quarterly* 159 (September): 640–9.

Epoch Times (da shiji shibao). 2001. "Workers from the Capital Steel Corporation Take on the Street on the Eve of China's Entrance into TWO." November 19: A3.

Epstein, Edward C. 1984. "Legitimacy, Institutionalization, and Opposition in Exclusionary Bureaucratic-Authoritarian Regimes: The Situation of the 1980s." *Comparative Politics* 16 (October): 37–54.

Erber, Ralph, and Richard Lau. 1990. "Political Cynicism Revisited: An Information-Processing Reconciliation of Policy-Based and Incumbency-Based Interpretations of Changes in Trust in Government." *American Journal of Political Science* 34 (April): 236–53.

Fainsod, Merle. 1961. *How Russia Is Ruled.* Cambridge: Harvard University Press.

Falkenheim, Victor C. 1978. "Political Participation in China." *Problems of Communism* 27 (May–June): 18–32.

Farah, Barbara G., Samuel H. Barnes, and Felix Heunks. 1979. "Political Dissatisfaction." In *Political Action: Mass Participation in Five Western Democracies,* ed. Samuel H. Barnes and Max Kaase. Beverly Hills, Calif.: Sage.

Fewsmith, Joseph. 2001a. *China since Tiananmen: The Politics of Transition.* New York: Cambridge University Press.

———. 2001b. "The Political and Social Implications of China's Accession to the WTO." *China Quarterly* 167 (September): 573–91.

Finifter, Ada. 1996. "Attitudes toward Individual Responsibility and Political Reform in the Former Soviet Union." *American Political Science Review* 90 (March): 138–52.

Finifter, Ada, and Ellen Mickiewicz. 1992. "Redefining the Political System of the USSR: Mass Support for Political Change." *American Political Science Review* 86 (December): 857–74.

Finkel, Steven E., Edward N. Muller, and Mitchell Seligson. 1989. "Economic Crisis, Incumbent Performance, and Regime Support: A Comparison of Longitudinal Data from West Germany and Costa Rica." *British Journal of Political Science* 19 (July): 329–51.

Fiorina, Morris P. 1981. *Retrospective Voting in American National Elections.* New Haven: Yale University Press.

Fitzgerald, John. 1994. "Reports of My Death Have Been Greatly Exaggerated." In *China Deconstructs: Politics, Trade, and Regionalism,* ed. David S. G. Goodman and Gerald Segal. New York: Routledge.

———. 1996. "The Nationless State: The Search for a Nation in Modern Chinese Nationalism." In *Chinese Nationalism,* ed. Jonathan Unger. New York: M. E. Sharpe.

Friedgut, Theodore H. 1979. *Political Participation in the USSR.* Princeton, N.J.: Princeton University Press.

Friedman, Edward. 1991. "Permanent Technological Revolution and China's Tortuous Path to Democratizing Leninism." In *Reform and Reaction in Post–Mao China: The Road to Tiananmen,* ed. Richard Baum. New York: Routledge.

———. 2000. "Globalization, Legitimacy, and Post-Communism in China: A Nationalist Potential for Democracy, Prosperity, and Peace." In *China under Jiang Zemin,* ed. Hung-Mao Tien and Yun-Han Chu. Boulder, Colo.: Lynne Rienner.

Gamson, William A., and Andre Modigliani. 1966. "Knowledge and Foreign Policy Opinions: Some Models for Consideration." *Public Opinion Quarterly* 30 (January): 187–99.

Geddes, Barbara, and John Zaller. 1989. "Sources of Popular Support for Authoritarian Regimes." *American Journal of Political Science* 33 (May): 319–47.

Gibson, James L., and Gregory A. Caldeira. 1992. "Blacks and the United States Supreme Court: Models of Diffuse Support." *The Journal of Politics* 54 (November): 1120–45.

Gibson, James L., Gregory A. Calderia, and Vanessa A. Baird. 1998. "On the Legitimacy of National High Courts." *American Political Science Review* 92 (June): 343–58.

Gibson, James L., and Raymond M. Duch. 1993. "Emerging Democratic Values in Soviet Political Culture." In *Public Opinion and Regime Change: The New Politics of*

Post–Soviet Societies, ed. Arthur H. Miller, William M. Reisinger, and Vicki L. Hesli. Boulder, Colo.: Westview.

Gibson, James L., Raymond M. Duch, and Kent L. Tedin. 1992. "Democratic Values and the Transformation of the Soviet Union." *The Journal of Politics* 54 (March): 329–71.

Gibson, James L., and Amanda Gouws. 2000. "Social Identities and Political Intolerance: Linkages within the South African Mass Public." *American Journal of Political Science* 44 (2): 272–86.

Gilison, Jerome. 1968. "Soviet Elections as a Measure of Dissent: The Missing One Percent." *American Political Science Review* 62 (September): 814–26.

Glaser, Bonnie S. 1993. "China's Security Perceptions: Interests and Ambitions." *Asian Survey* 33 (3): 252–71.

Gold, Thomas B. 1996. "Youth and the State." In *The Individual and the State in China,* ed. Brian Hook. New York: Oxford University Press.

Goldman, Merle. 1994. *Sowing the Seeds of Democracy in China.* Cambridge, Mass.: Harvard University Press.

———. 2000. "The Potential for Instability among Alienated Intellectuals and Students in Post–Mao China." In *Is China Unstable? Assessing the Factors,* ed. David Shambaugh. Armonk, N.Y.: M. E. Sharpe.

Goldstein, Avery. 1994. "Trends in the Study of Political Elites and Institutions in the PRC." *China Quarterly* 139 (September): 714–30.

Goldstone, Jack. 1995. "The Coming Chinese Collapse," *Foreign Policy* 99 (Summer): 43–8.

Gong, Ting. 1997. "Forms and Characteristics of China's Corruption in the 1990s: Change with Continuity." *Communist and Post-Communist Studies* 30 (3): 277–288.

Goodman, David S. G. 1985. "The Chinese Political Order after Mao: 'Socialist Democracy' and the Exercise of State Power." *Political Studies* 33, no. 2: 218–35.

Granberg, Donald, and Soren Holmberg. 1988. *The Political System Matters: Social Psychology and Voting Behavior in Sweden and the United States.* New York: Cambridge University Press.

Gurr, Ted. 1968. "Psychological Factors in Civil Violence." *World Politics* 20 (January): 245–78.

Gustafsson, Bjorn, and Wei Zhong. 2000. "How and Why Has Poverty in China Changed? A Study Based on Microdata for 1988 and 1995." *China Quarterly* 164 (December): 983–1006.

Halpern, Nina P. 1991. "Economic Reform, Social Mobilization, and Democratization in Post-Mao China." In *Reform and Reaction in Post-Mao China: The Road to Tiananmen,* ed. Richard Baum. New York: Routledge.

Hamrin, Carol Lee. 1987. "Conclusion: New Trends under Deng Xiaoping and His Successors." In *China's Intellectuals and the State: In Search of a New Relationship,* ed. Merle Goldman, Timothy Cheek, and Carol Lee Hamrin. Cambridge, Mass.: Council of East Asian Studies.

Harding, Harry. 1994. "The Contemporary Study of Chinese Politics: An Introduction." *China Quarterly* 139 (September): 699–703.

Hayek, Friedrich A. 1990. *The Road to Serfdom.* Chicago: University of Chicago Press.

Hermann, Richard. 1988. "The Empirical Challenge of the Cognitive Revolution: A Strategy for Drawing Inferences about Perceptions." *International Studies Quarterly* 32 (June): 175–203.

Herrmann, Richard K., James F. Voss, Tonya F. Schooler, and Joseph Ciarrochi. 1997.

"Images in International Relations: An Experimental Test of Cognitive Schemata." *International Studies Quarterly* 41 (September): 403–33.

Hetherington, Mark J. 1998. "Political Relevance of Political Trust." *American Political Science Review* 92 (December): 791–808.

Holland, Lorien. 2000. "Running Dry." *Far Eastern Economic Review* (February 3): 8.

Holsti, Ole R. 1962. "The Belief System and National Images: A Case Study." *The Journal of Conflict Resolution* 6 (December): 244–52.

———. 1996. *Public Opinion and American Foreign Policy.* Ann Arbor: University of Michigan Press.

Honig, Emily, and Gail Hershatter. 1988. *Personal Voices: Chinese Women in the 1980s.* Stanford, Calif.: Stanford University Press.

Hopple, Gerald W., Paul J. Rossa, and Jonathan Wilkenfeld. 1980. "Threat and Foreign Policy: The Overt Behavior of States in Conflict." In *Threats, Weapons, and Foreign Policy,* ed. Pat McGowan and Charles W. Kegley, Jr. Beverly Hills, Calif.: Sage.

HP. 2001. "Zhongguo xianfu qilai de nianqing ren rushi shuo" (What those of young people who have got rich ahead of others say). *China News Digest.* http://www.cnd.org (November 25).

Hu, Xiaobo. 2000. "The State, Enterprises, and Society in Post-Deng China." *Asian Survey* 40, no. 4: 641–57.

Hunt, Michael. 1994. "Chinese National Identity and the Strong State: The Late Qing-Republican Crisis." In *China's Quest for National Identity,* ed. Lowell Dittmer and Samuel S. Kim. Ithaca, N.Y.: Cornell University Press.

Huntington, Samuel P. 1991. *The Third Wave: Democratization in the Late Twentieth Century.* Norman: University of Oklahoma Press.

Hurwitz, Jon, and Mark Peffley. 1990. "Public Images of the Soviet Union: The Impact on Foreign Policy Attitudes." *Journal of Politics* 52 (February): 3–28.

Hurwitz, Jon, Mark Peffley, and Mitchell A. Seligson. 1993. "Foreign Policy Belief Systems in Comparative Perspective: The United States and Costa Rica." *International Studies Quarterly* 37 (September): 245–70.

Inglehart, Ronald. 1971. "The Silent Revolution in Europe: Intergenerational Change in Post-Industrial Societies." *American Political Science Review* 65 (December): 991–1017.

———. 1977. "Values, Objective Needs, and Subjective Satisfaction among Western Publics." *Comparative Political Studies* 9 (January): 429–58.

———. 1979. "Value Priorities and Socioeconomic Change." In *Political Action: Mass Participation in Five Western Democracies,* ed. Samuel H. Barnes and Max Kaase. Beverly Hills, Calif.: Sage.

———. 1990. *Culture Shift in Advanced Industrial Society.* Princeton, N.J.: Princeton University Press.

———. 1997. *Modernization and Postmodernization: Cultural, Economic, and Political Change in Forty-three Societies.* Princeton, N.J.: Princeton University Press.

Inkeles, Alex, and David Smith. 1974. *Becoming Modern: Individual Change in Six Developing Countries.* Cambridge, Mass.: Harvard University Press.

Inkeles, Alex, and Larry Diamond. 1980. "Personal Qualities as Reflection of National Development." In *Comparative Studies in Quality of Life,* ed. Frank Andrews and Alexander Szalai. London: Sage.

Jahiel, Abigail R. 1997. "The Contradictory Impact of Reform and Environmental Protection." *China Quarterly* 149 (March): 81–103.

————. 1998. "The Organization of Environmental Protection in China." *China Quarterly* 156 (December): 757–87.

Jennings, M. Kent. 1992. "Ideological Thinking among Mass Publics and Political Elites." *Public Opinion Quarterly* 56 (Winter): 419–41.

————. 1996. "Cohort Differences in the Chinese Countryside." Presented at the annual meeting of the American Political Science Association, San Francisco.

————. 1997. "Political Participation in the Chinese Countryside." *American Political Science Review* 91 (June): 361–72.

————. 1998. "Gender and Political Participation in the Chinese Countryside." *Journal of Politics* 60 (November): 954–73.

Jennings, M. Kent, and Richard Niemi. 1981. *Generations and Politics: A Panel Study of Young Adults and Their Parents*. Princeton, N.J.: Princeton University Press.

Jervis, Robert. 1976. *Perception and Misperception in International Politics*. Princeton, N.J.: Princeton University Press.

————. 1989. "Perceiving and Coping with Threat." In *Psychology and Deterrence*, ed. Robert Jervis, Richard N. Lebow, and Janice Stein. Baltimore: Johns Hopkins University Press.

Jiang, Zemin. 1997. "Hold High the Great Banner of Deng Xiaoping Theory for an All-Around Advancement of the Cause of Building Socialism with Chinese Characteristics into the Twenty-First Century." Speech at the Fifteen National Congress of the CCP. *Beijing Review* (October 6–12): 10–33.

————. 2001. "The Speech at the Meeting to Celebrate the Eightieth Anniversary of the Founding of the CCP." *People's Daily* (July 2).

Johnson, Chalmers. 1971. "The Changing Nature and Locus of Authority in Communist China." In *China: Management of a Revolutionary Society*, ed. John M. H. Lindbeck. Seattle: University of Washington Press.

Johnson, Todd M., Feng Liu, and Richard Newfarmer. 1997. *Clear Water, Blue Skies: China's Environment in the New Century*. Washington, D.C.: World Bank.

Kalpana, Misra. 1998. *From Post-Maoism to Post-Marxism: The Erosion of Official Ideology in Deng's China*. New York: Routledge.

Kaplan, Cynthia S. 1993. "New Forms of Political Participation." In *Public Opinion and Regime Change: The New Politics of Post-Soviet Society*, ed. Arthur H. Miller, William M Reisinger, and Vicki L. Hesli. Boulder, Colo.: Westview.

Kegley, Charles W., Jr., and Eugene R. Wittkoph. 1996. *American Foreign Policy: Pattern and Process*. New York: St. Martin's.

Key, V. O. 1961. *Public Opinion and American Democracy*. New York: Knopf.

Khan, Azizur Rahman, and Carl Riskin. 1998. "Income and Inequality in China: Composition, Distribution, and Growth of Household Income, 1988 to 1995." *China Quarterly* 154 (June): 221–53.

————. 2001. *Inequality and Poverty in China in the Age of Globalization*. New York: Oxford University Press.

Klingemann, Hans D. 1979. "The Background of Ideological Conceptualization." In *Political Action: Mass Participation in Five Western Democracies*, ed. Samuel H. Barnes and Max Kaase. Beverly Hills, Calif.: Sage.

Knorr, Klaus. 1976. "Threat Perception." In *Historical Dimensions of National Security Problems*, ed. Klaus Knorr. Lawrence: University Press of Kansas.

Kornberg, Allan, and Harold D. Clarke. 1992. *Citizens and Community: Political Support in a Representative Democracy*. New York: Cambridge University Press.

Kristof, Nicholas, and Sheryl Wudunn. 1994. *China Wakes: A Struggle for the Soul of a Rising Power.* New York: Times Books.

Kwong, Julia. 1997. *The Political Economy of Corruption in China.* Armonk, N.Y.: M. E. Sharpe.

Lane, Christel. 1984. "Legitimacy and Power in the Soviet Union through Socialist Ritual." *British Journal of Political Science* 14 (April): 219–32.

Leung, Joe C. B. 1995. "The Political Economy of Unemployment and Unemployment Insurance in the People's Republic of China." *International Social Work* 38 (April): 139–49.

Levine, Steven I. 1995. "Perception and Ideology in Chinese Foreign Policy." In *Chinese Foreign Policy: Theory and Practice,* ed. Thomas W. Robinson and David Shambaugh. Oxford: Oxford University Press.

Lewis, Paul G. 1984. "Legitimation and Political Crisis: East European Developments in the Post-Stalin Period." In *Eastern Europe: Political Crisis and Legitimation,* ed. Paul G. Lewis. New York: St. Martin's.

Li, Bobai, and Andrew G. Walder. 2001. "Career Advancement as Party Patronage: Sponsored Mobility into the Chinese Administrative Elite, 1949–1996." *American Journal of Sociology* 106, no. 5: 1371–1408.

Li, Cheng. 1997. *Rediscovering China: Dynamics and Dilemmas of Reform.* Lanham, Md.: Rowman and Littlefield.

Li, Lianjiang, and Kevin J. O'Brien. 1996. "Villagers and Popular Resistance in Contemporary China." *Modern China* 22 (January): 28–34.

Li, Wen. 1999. "China's Environmental Conditions in 1998." *Beijing Review* (July 12):15.

Li, Wen-Lang. 1989. "Changing Status of Women in the PRC." In *Changes in China: Party, State, and Society,* ed. Shao-chuan Leng. New York: University Press of America.

Liao, Xin. 2000. "Corruption: Tip-Offs from the General Public." *Beijing Review* (February 28): 16.

Lieberthal, Kenneth. 1995. *Governing China: From Revolution through Reform.* New York: W. W. Norton.

———. 1997. "Domestic Forces and Sino-U.S. Relations." In *Living with China: U.S./China Relations in the Twenty-First Century,* ed. Ezra F. Vogel. New York: W. W. Norton.

Link, Perry. 1992. *Evening Chats in Beijing: Probing China's Predicament.* New York: W. W. Norton.

———. 1993. "China's 'Core' Problem." *Daedalus* 122 (Spring): 189–206.

Lipset, Seymour Martin. 1959. "Some Social Requisites of Democracy: Economic Development and Political Legitimacy." *American Political Science Review* 53 (March): 69–105.

———. 1981. *Political Man: The Social Bases of Politics.* Baltimore: Johns Hopkins University Press, 1960. Reprint, Garden City, N.Y.: Doubleday.

———. 1994. "The Social Requisites of Democracy Revisited: 1993 Presidential Address." *American Sociological Review* 59 (February): 1–22.

Liu, Alan P. L. 1996. *Mass Politics in the People's Republic: State and Society in Contemporary China.* Boulder, Colo.: Westview.

Liu, Chun. 1998. *Quanli de dajiun: dangdai zhongguo fan fubai lun* (Answer from the power: anti-corruption campaign in contemporary China). Beijing: The Party School of the CCP's Central Committee Press.

Lo, Bin. 2000. "Jiang Zemin's Self-Promotion of Jiang Zemin Thought." *Zhengming* (Hong Kong) 271 (May): 12–14.

Lo, Carlos Wing Hung, and Sai Wing Leung. 2000. "Environmental Agency and Public Opinion in Guangzhou: The Limits of a Popular Approach to Environmental Governance." *China Quarterly* 163 (September): 677–704.

Lock, Jean. 1989. "The Effect of Ideology in Gender Role Definition: China as a Case Study." *Journal of Asian and African Studies* 24 (July): 228–38.

Locke, John (1632–1704). 1967. *Two Treatises of Government.* London: Cambridge University Press.

Loewenberg, Gerhard. 1971. "The Influence of Parliamentary Behavior on Regime Stability: Some Conceptual Clarifications." *Comparative Politics* 3 (January): 177–200.

Louie, Kam. 2001. "Sage, Teacher, Businessman: Confucius as a Model Male." In *Chinese Political Culture: 1989–2000,* ed. Shiping Hua. New York: M. E. Sharpe.

Lowenthal, Richard. 1976. "The Ruling Party in a Mature Society." In *Social Consequences of Modernization in Communist Societies,* ed. Mark G. Field. Baltimore: Johns Hopkins University Press.

Lu, Xiaobo. 2000. "Booty Socialism, Bureau-Preneurs, and the Sate in Transition: Organizational Corruption in China." *Comparative Politics* 32 (April): 273–95.

Lujan, Herman D. 1974. "The Structure of Political Support: A Study of Guatemala." *American Journal of Political Science* 18 (February): 23–43.

MacKuen, Michael B., Robert S. Erikson, and James A. Stimson. 1992. "Peasants or Bankers? The American Electorate and the U.S. Economy." *American Political Science Review* 86 (September): 597–611.

Macridis, Roy C. 1986. *Modern Political Regimes.* Boston: Little, Brown.

———. 1992. *Contemporary Political Ideologies: Movements and Regimes.* New York: Harper Collins.

Macridis, Roy, and Steven L. Burg. 1991. *Introduction to Comparative Politics: Regimes and Change.* New York: Harper Collins.

Manheim, Jarol B., and Richard C. Rich. 1986. *Empirical Political Analysis: Research Methods in Political Science.* New York: Longman.

Manion, Melanie. 1994. "Survey Research in the Study of Contemporary China: Learning from Local Samples." *China Quarterly* 139 (September): 741–65.

———. 1996. "The Electoral Connection in the Chinese Countryside." *American Political Science Review* 90 (December): 736–48.

———. 1998. "Issues in Corruption Control in Post-Mao China." *Issues and Studies* 34, no. 9: 1–21.

Markus, Maria. 1982. "Overt and Covert Modes of Legitimation in East European Societies." In *Political Legitimacy in Communist States,* ed. T. H. Rigby and Ferenc Feher. New York: St. Martin's.

Marsh, Alan, and Max Kaase. 1979. "Background of Political Action." In *Political Action: Mass Participation in Five Western Democracies,* ed. Samuel H. Barnes and Max Kaase. Beverly Hills, Calif.: Sage.

Mason, David. 1995. "Attitudes towards the Market and Political Participation in the Postcommunist States." *Slavic Review* 54 (Summer): 385–406.

McClosky, Herbert, and Alida Brill. 1983. *Dimensions of Tolerance,* New York: Basic.

McCormick, Barrett L. 1996. "China's Leninist Parliament and Public Sphere: A Comparative Analysis." In *China after Socialism: In the Footsteps of Eastern Europe or*

East Asia? ed. Barrett L. McCormick and Jonathan Urger. Armonk, N.Y.: M. E. Sharpe.

McDonough, Peter, Samuel H. Barnes, and Antonio Lopez Pina. 1986. "The Growth of Democratic Legitimacy in Spain." *American Political Science Review* 80 (September): 735–60.

McGowan, Pat, and Charles W. Kegley, Jr. 1980. *Threats, Weapons, and Foreign Policy.* Beverly Hills, Calif.: Sage.

Meaney, Connie Squires. 1991. "Market Reform and Disintegrative Corruption in Urban China." In *Reform and Reaction in Post-Mao China: The Road to Tiananmen,* ed. Richard Baum. New York: Routledge.

Metzger, Thomas A. 1996. *Transcending the West: Mao's Vision of Socialism and the Legitimization of Teng Hsiao-ping's Modernization Program.* Stanford, Calif.: Hoover Institution on War, Revolution, and Peace.

Millar, James R., and Elizabeth Clayton. 1987. "Quality of Life: Subjective Measures of Relative Satisfaction." In *Politics, Work, and Daily Life in the USSR: A Survey of Former Soviet Citizens,* ed. James R. Millar. Cambridge: Cambridge University Press.

Miller, Arthur H. 1974a. "Political Issues and Trust in Government, 1964–1970." *American Political Science Review* 68 (September): 951–72.

———. 1974b. "Rejoinder to 'Comment' by Jack Citrin: Political Discontent or Ritualism." *American Political Science Review* 68 (September): 989–1001.

———. 1993. "In Search of Regime Legitimacy." In *Public Opinion and Regime Change: The New Politics of Post–Soviet Societies,* ed. Arthur H. Miller, William M. Reiginger, and Vicki L. Hesli. Boulder, Colo.: Westview.

Miller, Arthur H., Vicki L. Hesli, and William M. Reisinger. 1994. "Reassessing Mass Support for Political and Economic Change in the Former USSR." *American Political Science Review* 88 (June): 399–411.

———. 1995. "Comparing Citizen and Elite Belief Systems in Post–Soviet Russia and Ukraine." *Public Opinion Quarterly* 59 (Spring): 1–40.

Miller, Arthur H., William M. Reisinger, and Vicki L. Hesli. 1990–1991. "Public Support for New Political Institutions in Russia, the Ukraine, and Lithuania." *Journal of Soviet Nationalities,* no 4: 82–107.

———. 1996. "Understanding Political Change in Post–Soviet Societies: A Further Commentary on Finifter and Mickiewicz." *American Political Science Review* 90 (March): 153–66.

Mingpao. 2002. "Almost a Half of Workers Losing Jobs." *Mingpao,* March 27.

Mueller, John. 1973. *War, Presidents, and Public Opinion.* New York: Wiley.

Muller, Edward N. 1970a. "The Representation of Citizens by Political Authorities: Consequences for Regime Support." *American Political Science Review* 64: 1149–1166.

———. 1970b. "Correlates and Consequences of Beliefs in the Legitimacy of Regime Structures." *Midwest Journal of Political Science* 14 (August): 392–412.

———. 1977. "Behavioral Correlates of Political Support." *American Political Science Review* 71 (June): 454–67.

———. 1979. *Aggressive Political Participation.* Princeton, N.J.: Princeton University Press.

Muller, Edward N., and Thomas O. Jukam. 1977. "On the Meaning of Political Support." *American Political Science Review* 71 (December): 1561–95.

Muller, Edward N., Thomas O. Jukam, and Mitchell A. Seligson. 1982. "Diffuse Political Support and Antisystem Political Behavior: A Comparative Analysis." *American Journal of Political Science* 26 (May): 240–64.

Muller, Edward N., and Carol J. Williams. 1980. "Dynamics of Political Support-Alienation." *Comparative Political Studies* 13 (month): 33–59.

Nathan, Andrew J. 1985. *Chinese Democracy.* New York: Alfred A. Knopf.

———. 1997. *China's Transition.* New York: Columbia University Press.

Nathan, Andrew J., and Robert S. Ross. 1997. *The Great Wall and the Empty Fortress: China's Search for Security.* New York: W. W. Norton.

Nathan, Andrew J., and Tianjian Shi. 1993. "Cultural Requisites for Democracy in China: Findings from a Survey." *Daedalus* 122 (Spring): 95–123.

National People's Congress (of the PRC). 1982. "The Constitution of the People's Republic of China." *Beijing Review* 52 (December 27): 10–52.

Naughton, Barry. 1996. "China's Macroeconomy in Transition." In *China's Transitional Economy,* ed. Andrew G. Walder. New York: Oxford University Press.

O'Brien, Kevin J. 1990. *Reform without Liberalization: China's National People's Congress and the Politics of Institutional Change.* New York: Cambridge University Press.

———. 1994. "Chinese People's Congresses and Legislative Embeddedness: Understanding Early Organizational Development." *Comparative Political Studies* 27 (April): 80–109.

O'Kane, Rosemary H. T. 1993. "Against Legitimacy." *Political Studies* 41 (September): 471–87.

Overholt, William. 1993. *The Rise of China: How Economic Reform Is Creating a New Superpower.* New York: W. W. Norton.

Paal, Douglas H. 1997. "China and the East Asian Security Environment: Complementarity and Competition." In *Living with China: U.S./China Relations in the Twenty-First Century,* ed. Esra F. Vogel. New York: W. W. Norton.

Pakulski, Jan. 1986. "Legitimacy and Mass Compliance: Reflections on Max Weber and Soviet-Type Societies." *British Journal of Political Science* 16 (January): 35–56.

Palma, Giuseppe di. 1991. "Legitimation from the Top to Civil Society: Political-Cultural Change in Eastern Europe." *World Politics* 44 (October): 49–80.

Pan, Phillip P., and John Pomfret. 2002. "Critics Scoff as Chinese Premier Defends Record." *Washington Post* (March 16): A18.

Pearson, Margaret M. 1997. *China's New Business Elite: The Political Consequences of Economic Reform.* Berkeley: University of California Press.

Peffley, Mark, and Jon Hurwitz. 1992. "International Events and Foreign Policy Beliefs: Public Response to Changing Soviet-U.S. Relations." *American Journal of Political Science* 36 (May): 431–61.

Pei, Minxin. 1994. *From Reform to Revolution: The Demise of Communism in China and the Soviet Union.* Cambridge, Mass.: Harvard University Press.

———. 1998. "Is China Democratizing?" *Foreign Affairs* 77 (January/February): 68–82.

Pomfret, John. 2001. "In China, Anti-U.S. Sentiment Unfettered." *Washington Post* (September 14): A26.

Pruitt, D. G. 1965. "Definition of the Situation as a Determinant of International Action." In *International Behavior,* ed. Herbert G. Kelman. New York: Holt, Rinehart, and Winston.

Pye, Lucian W. 1971. "The Legitimacy Crisis." In *Crises and Sequences in Political*

Development, ed. Leonard Binder, James S. Coleman, Joseph LaPalombara, Lucian W. Pye, Sidney Verba, and Myron Weiner. Princeton, N.J.: Princeton University Press.

———. 1990. "China: Erratic State, Frustrated Society." *Foreign Affairs* 69 (January/February): 56–74.

———. 1991. *China: An Introduction,* 4th ed. New York: Harper Collins Publishers.

Qiao, Jian. 2001. *Jiaru WTO beijing xia de Zhongguo Zhigong Zhuangkuang* (China's employment situation viewed against the background of joining WTO). In *2001 nian: Zhongguo shehui xingshi fenxi yu yuce* (2001: Analysis and Predictions of the Situation in China's Society). Beijing: Shehui kexue wenxian.

Qiao, Lijun, and Tianze Chen. 1994. *China Cannot Afford Chaos.* Beijing: Chinese Party School Press.

Qu, Geping, and Jinchang Li. 1990. *An Outline Study on China's Population: Environmental Issues.* Beijing: National Environmental Protection Agency.

Razi, G. Hossein. 1987. "The Nexus of Legitimacy and Performance: The Lessons of the Iranian Revolution." *Comparative Politics* 20 (July): 453–69.

Reef, Mary Jo, and David Knoke. 1999. "Political Alienation and Efficacy." In *Measures of Political Attitudes,* ed. John P. Robinson, Phillip R. Shaver, and Lawrence S. Wrightsman. San Diego: Academic.

Remington, Thomas F. 1993. "Afterward to Part Two: Agendas—Researching the Emerging Political Cultures." In *Public Opinion and Regime Change: The New Politics of Post-Soviet Societies,* ed. Arthur H. Miller, William M. Reisinger, and Vicki L. Hesli. Boulder, Colo.: Westview.

Reuters. 1999. "Nine of the World's Top Ten Worst-Polluted Cities in China: Report." *South China Morning Post* (January 25).

Rigby, T. H. 1982. "Introduction: Political Legitimacy, Weber, and Communist Mono-organizational Systems." In *Political Legitimacy in Communist States,* ed. T. H. Rigby and Ferenc Feher. New York: St. Martin's.

Riskin, Carl. 1987. *China's Political Economy: The Quest for Development since 1994.* New York: Oxford University Press.

Robinson, Jean C., and Kristen Parris. 1990. "The Chinese Special Economic Zones, Labor, and Women." In *Political Implications of Economic Reform in Communist Systems: Communist Dialectic,* ed. Donna Bahry and Joel Moses. New York: New York University Press.

Roeder, Philip G. 1989. "Modernization and Participation in the Leninist Developmental Strategy." *American Political Science Review* 83 (September): 859–84.

Rogowski, Ronald. 1983. "Political Support for Regime: A Theoretical Inventory and Critique." In *Political Support in Canada: The Crisis Years,* ed. Allan Kornberg and Harold D. Clarke. Durham: Duke University Press.

Rose, Richard, and William Mishler. 1994. "Mass Reaction to Regime Change in Eastern Europe: Polarization or Leaders and Laggards." *British Journal of Political Science* 24 (April): 159–81.

———. 2000. *Regimes Support in Non-Democratic and Democratic Contexts.* Glasgow: University of Strathclyde.

Rosen, Stanley. 1991. "The Rise (and Fall) of Public Opinion in Post-Mao China." In *Reform and Reaction in Post–Mao China: The Road to Tiananmen,* ed. Richard Baum. New York: Routledge.

———. 1992. "Students and the State in China: The Crisis in Ideology and Organization." In *State and Society in China: The Consequences of Reform,* ed. Arthur Lewis Rosenbaum. Boulder, Colo.: Westview.

———. 1993. "Women and Politics in China." *Chinese Law and Government* 26 (January): 3–87.

———. 1995. "Women and Political Participation in China." *Pacific Affairs* 68 (Summer): 315–42.

Saich, Tony. 1994. "The Search for Civil Society and Democracy in China." *Current History: The People's Republic of China* 93 (September): 260–72.

Schaar, John H. 1981. *Legitimacy in the Modern State.* New Brunswick, N.J.: Transaction.

Schoenhals, Michael. 1999. "Political Movements, Change, and Stability: The Chinese Communist Party in Power." *China Quarterly* 159 (September): 595–605.

Schram, Stuart R. 1970. "The Party in Chinese Communist Ideology." In *Party Leadership and Revolutionary Power in China,* ed. John Wilson Lewis. Cambridge: Cambridge University Press.

Schumpeter, Joseph A. 1947. *Capitalism, Socialism, and Democracy.* New York: Harper.

Schwartz, Benjamin I. 1970. "The Reign of Virtue: Some Broad Perspectives on the Leader and Party in the Cultural Revolution." In *Party Leadership and Revolutionary Power in China,* ed. John Wilson Lewis. Cambridge: Cambridge University Press.

Seligson, Mitchell A., and Edward N. Muller. 1987. "Democratic Stability and Economic Crisis: Costa Rica, 1978–1983." *International Studies Quarterly* 31 (September): 301–26.

Shambaugh, David. 1993. "Losing Control: The Erosion of State Authority in China." *Current History: The People's Republic of China* 93 (September): 253–9.

———. 1996. "The Soldiers and the State in China: The Political Work System in the People's Liberation Army." In *The Individual and the State in China,* ed. Brian Hook. New York: Oxford University Press.

———. 1997. "The United States and China: Cooperation or Confrontation?" *Current History* 96 (September): 241–5.

———. 2000. "The Chinese State in the Post–Mao Era." In *The Modern Chinese State,* ed. David Shambaugh. Cambridge: Cambridge University Press.

Shanks, J. Merrill, and Warren E. Miller. 1990. "Policy Direction and Performance Evaluation: Complementary Explanations of the Reagan Elections." *British Journal of Political Science* 20 (April): 143–235.

———. 1991. "Partisanship, Policy, and Performance: The Reagan Legacy in the 1988 Election." *British Journal of Political Science* 21 (April): 129–97.

Shen, Xiaomin, J. F. Rosen, and S. M. Wu. 1996. "Childhood Lead Poisoning in China." *Science of the Total Environment* 181 (March 15): 101–9.

Shi, Tianjian. 1996. "Survey Research in China." In *Research in Micropolitics: Rethinking Rationality,* vol. 5, ed. Michael X. Delli Carpini, Leonie Huddy, and Robert Y. Shapiro. Greenwich, Conn.: JAI.

———. 1997. *Political Participation in Beijing.* Cambridge, Mass.: Harvard University Press.

———. 1999. "Voting and Nonvoting in China: Voting Behavior in Plebiscitary and Limited-Choice Elections." *Journal of Politics* 61 (November): 1115–39.

———. 2001. "Cultural Values and Political Trust: A Comparison of the People's Republic of China and Taiwan." *Comparative Politics* (July): 401-419.

Shi, Weimin, and Jingxuan Lei. 1999. *Zhijie xuanju: Zhidu yu chengxu* (Direct elections: the system and procedure). Beijing: Chinese Academy of Social Sciences Press.

Shue, Vivienne. 1988. *The Reach of the State: Sketches of the Chinese Body Politics.* Stanford, Calif.: Stanford University Press.

Silver, Brian D. 1987. "Political Beliefs of the Soviet Citizen: Source of Support to Regime Norms." In *Politics, Work, and Daily Life in the USSR: A Survey of Former Soviet Citizens,* ed. James R. Millar. Cambridge: Cambridge University Press.

Sinkule, B., and L. Ortolano. 1995. *Implementing Environmental Policy in China.* London: Praeger.

Smil, Vaclav. 1993. *China's Environmental Crisis: An Inquiry into the Limits of National Development.* Armonk, N.Y.: M. E. Sharpe.

Smith, Craig S. 2001. "'Strike Hard' Campaigns against Crimes: Torture Hurries New Wave of Executions in China." *New York Times* (September 9).

———. 2002. "China Faces Problems of Creating Jobs, Official Says." *New York Times* (April 30).

Solinger, Dorothy J. 2001. "Why We Cannot Count the 'Unemployed.'" *China Quarterly* 167 (September): 671–88.

———. 1999. "Demolishing Partitions: Back to Beginnings in the Cities?" *China Quarterly* 159 (September): 629–39.

Solomon, Richard. 1973. "From Commitment to Cant: The Evolving Functions of Ideology in the Revolutionary Process." In *Ideology and Politics in the Contemporary Press,* ed. Chalmers Johnson. Seattle: University of Washington Press.

Song Qiang, Zhang Zangzang, and Qiao Bian. 1996. *Zong Guo Keyi Shuo Bu* (China can say: No!). Beijing: Press of the Industrial and Commercial Association of All China.

Soutman, Barry. 1992. "Sirens of the Strongman: Neo-Authoritarianism in Recent Chinese Political Theory." *China Quarterly* 129 (March): 72–102

SPSS. 1997. *SPSS Base 7.5 Applications Guide.* Chicago: SPSS.

State Council (PRC). 2002. "The Conditions of Labor and Social Security in China: White Paper." *People's Daily* (April 30).

State Statistical Bureau (PRC). 1991–2000. *China Statistical Yearbooks.* Beijing: China Statistical Publishing House.

Sun Keqin, and Cui Hongjian. 1996. *Ezhi zhongguo* (Containing China). Beijing: Zhongguo Yanshi.

Swafford, Michael. 1987. "Perception of Social Status in the USSR." In *Politics, Work, and Daily Life in the USSR: A Survey of Former Soviet Citizens,* ed. James R. Miller. Cambridge: Cambridge University Press.

Tajfel, Heni. 1978. "Social Categorization, Social Identity and Social Comparison." In *Differentiation between Social Groups: Studies in the Social Psychology of Intergroup Relations,* ed. Henri Tajfel. New York: Academic.

Tang, Wenfang. 2001. "Political and Social Trends in the Post–Deng Urban China: Crisis or Stability." *China Quarterly* 168 (December): 890–909.

Tang, Wenfang, and William L. Parish. 2000. *Chinese Urban Life under Reform: The Changing Social Contract.* Cambridge: Cambridge University Press.

Teiwes, Frederick C. 1984. *Leadership, Legitimacy, and Conflict in China: From a Charismatic Mao to the Politics of Succession.* London: Macmillan.

———. 2000. "The Problematic Quest for Stability: Reflections on Succession, Institutionalization, Governability, and Legitimacy in Post–Deng China." In *China under Jiang Zemin,* ed. Hung-Mao Tien and Yun-Han Chu. Boulder, Colo.: Lynne Rienner.

Thomassen, Jacques J. A. 1990. "Economic Crisis, Dissatisfaction, and Protest." In *Continuities in Political Action: A Longitudinal Study of Political Orientations in Three Western Democracies,* ed. M. Kent Jennings and Jan W. van Deth. New York: Walter de Gruyter.

Tian, Guoqiang, and Hong Liang. 1999. "What Kind of Privatization?" In *Dilemmas of Reform in Jiang Zemin's China,* ed. Andrew J. Nathan, Zhaohui Hong, and Steven R. Smith. Boulder, Colo.: Lynne Rienner.

Townsend, James R. 1967. *Political Participation in Communist China.* Berkeley : University of California Press.

UNDP (United Nations Development Program). 1999. *The China Human Development Report.* New York: Oxford University Press.

Verba, Sidney, and Norman H. Nie. 1972. *Participation in America: Political Democracy and Social Equality.* New York: Harper and Row.

Verba, Sidney, Norman H. Nie, and Jae-On Kim. 1978. *Participation and Political Equality: A Seven Nation Comparison.* Cambridge: Cambridge University Press.

Vermeer, Eduard B. 1998. "Industrial Pollution in China and Remedial Policies." *China Quarterly* 156 (December): 952–85.

Walder, Andrew G. 1986. *Communist Neo-Traditionalism: Work and Authority in Chinese Industry.* Berkeley: University of California Press.

———. 1995. "Career Mobility and the Communist Political Order." *American Sociological Review* 60 (June): 309–28.

———. 1996. "Workers, Managers, and the State: The Reform Era and the Political Crisis of 1989." In *The Individual and the State in China,* Brian Hook. New York: Oxford University Press.

———. 1998. "Zouping in Perspective." In *Zouping in Transition: The Process of Reform in Rural North China,* ed. Andrew G. Walder. Cambridge, Mass.: Harvard University Press.

Walder, Andrew G., Bobai Li, and Donald J. Treiman. 2000. "Politics and Life Chances in a State Socialist Regime: Dual Career Paths into the Urban Chinese Elite, 1949 to 1996." *American Sociological Review* 65 (April): 191–209.

Wan, Ming. 1998. "Chinese Opinion on Human Rights." *Orbis: A Journal of World Affairs* 42 (Summer): 361–74.

Wang, Gungwu, and Zheng Yongnian. 2000. "Introduction: Reform, Legitimacy, and Dilemmas." In *Reform, Legitimacy and Dilemmas: China's Politics and Society,* ed. Wang Gungwu and Zheng Yongnian. Singapore: Singapore University Press.

Wang, James C. F. 2002. *Contemporary Chinese Politics: An Introduction.* Upper Saddle River, N.J.: Prentice Hall.

———. 1999. *Contemporary Chinese Politics.* Upper Saddle River, N.J.: Prentice Hall.

Wang, Jianmin. 2002. "Zhenshi pinfu chaju, guanzhu ruoshi qunti" (Confront the gap between rich and poor, care for the weak group." *Yazhou Zhoukan* (Asia weekly) (Hong Kong) (March 24).

Wang, Shaoguang. 2000. "The Social and Political Implications of China's WTO Membership." *Journal of Contemporary China,* no. 25: 373–405.

Wang, Shaoguang, and Angang Hu. 2000. *The Political Economy of Uneven Development: The Case of China.* Armonk, N.Y.: M. E. Sharpe.

Wang, Zhongtian. 1998. *Xingde bi'an: Zouxiang 21ˢᵗ shiji de zhongguo minzhu* (A new horizon: marching toward the Chinese democracy in the twenty-first century). Beijing: The Party School of the CCP's Central Committee Press.

Wank, David. 1995. "Private Business, Bureaucracy, and Political Alliance in a Chinese City." *Australian Journal of Chinese Affairs* 33 (January): 55–71.

Wasserstrom, Jeffrey N., and Elizabeth J. Perry. 1992. *Popular Protest and Political Culture in Modern China: Learning from 1989.* Boulder, Colo.: Westview.

Wen, Tiejun. 1999. "Zhong-Mei WTO tanpan zhong nongye tiaokuan dui woguo de yingxiang" (The impact that the terms in the WTO negotiations between China and the United States involving agriculture will have on our country). *Nongcun jingji daokan* (Journal of Agricultural Economy) (China) 6 (February): 4–10.

White, Gordon. 1993. *Riding the Tiger: The Politics of Economic Reform in Post–Mao China.* Stanford, Calif.: Stanford University Press.

White, Gordon, and Xiaoyuan Shang. 1996. "Social Security Reforms in Urban China: A Preliminary Research Report." In *Issues and Answers: Reforming the Chinese Social Security System,* ed. Gordon White and Xiaoyuan Shang. Brighton, England: Institute of Development Studies.

White, Stephen. 1986. "Economic Performance and Communist Legitimacy." *World Politics* 38 (3): 462–82.

Whiting, Allen S. 1996. "The PLA and China's Threat Perceptions." *China Quarterly* 146 (June): 596–615.

Whyte, Martin K. 1984. "Sexual Inequality under Socialism: The Chinese Case in Perspective." In *Class and Social Stratification in Post–Revolutionary China,* ed. James L. Watson. Cambridge: Cambridge University Press.

———. 2000. "Chinese Social Trends: Stability or Chaos?" In *Is China Unstable: Assessing the Factors,* ed. David Shambaugh. Armonk, N.Y.: M. E. Sharpe.

Willerton, John P., and Lee Sigelman. 1993. "Perestroika and the Public: Citizens' Views of the 'Fruits' of Economic Reform." In *Public Opinion and Regime Change: The New Politics of Post–Soviet Societies,* ed. Arthur H. Miller, William M. Reisinger, and Vicki L. Hesli. Boulder, Colo.: Westview.

Wolf, Margery. 1985. *Revolution Postponed.* Stanford, Calif.: Stanford University Press.

Wong, Christine. 1994. "China's Economy: The Limits of Gradualist Reform." In *China Briefing 1994,* ed. William A. Joseph. Boulder, Colo.: Westview.

World Bank. 1991. *Efficiency and Environmental Impact of Coal Use in China.* Washington, D.C.: World Bank.

———. 1998. *World Development Indicators 1998.* Washington, D.C.: World Bank.

Wu, Guoguang. 1999. "Legitimacy Crisis, Political Economy, and the Fifteen Party Congress." In *Dilemmas of Reform in Jiang Zemin's China,* ed. Andrew J. Nathan, Zhaohui Hong, and Steven R. Smith. Boulder, Colo.: Lynne Rienner.

Xin, Yong. 2002. "Inside Account: The Reason for Proposing Jiang Zemin's 'Three Representations.'" *The Mirror* (Hong Kong) 275 (June): 20–2.

Xu, Xinxin, and Li Peilin. 1999. "1998–1999 nian: zhongguo jiuye shouru he xinxi chanye di fenxi he yuce" (Employment, income, and IT industry: analyses and forecasts, 1998–1999). In *Shehui lanpishu: zhongguo shehui xingshi fenxi yu yuce* (Social Bluebook: Analyses and Forecast of Social Situation in China), ed. Ru Xin et al. Beijing: Shehui kexue wenxian chubanshe (Social Science Literature Press).

Yahuda, Michael. 1979. "Political Generations in China." *China Quarterly* 80 (September): 793–805.

Young, Steven M. 1995. "Post-Tiananmen Chinese Politics and the Prospects for Democratization." *Asian Survey* 35 (July): 652–67.

Yu, Gouming. 1998. "Zhonggou ren yanzhong de riben he qita goujia: Zhonggou gongzhong dui riben ji qita goujia yinxiang de daocha fenxi baogao (Japan and other countries in the eyes of the Chinese people: Surveys of the Chinese public's images of Japan and other countries)." *International News Media* (January): 21–31.

Yu, Guoming, and Xiayang Liu. 1994. *Zhongguo Minyi Yanjiu* (Research of Public Opinion in China). Beijing: People's University Press.

Yue, Daiyun, and Jin Li. 1994. "Women's Life in New China." In *Women and Politics Worldwide,* ed. Barbara Nelson and Najma Chowdhury. New Haven: Yale University Press.

ZGFLNJ. 1993 and 1994. *Zhongguo falu nianjian* (China legal yearbook). Beijing: China Legal Yearbook Publishing House.

Zhao, Suisheng. 1997. "Chinese Intellectuals' Quest for National Greatness and Nationalistic Writing in the 1990s." *China Quarterly* 152 (December): 725–45.

———. 1998. "A State-Led Nationalism: The Patriotic Education Campaign in Post-Tiananmen China." *Communist and Post–Communist Studies* 31 (September): 287–302.

———. 2000. "Chinese Nationalism and Its International Orientations." *Political Science Quarterly* (Spring): 1–33.

Zheng, Yongnian. 1994. "Development and Democracy: Are They Compatible in China?" *Political Science Quarterly* 109 (Spring): 35–59.

———. 1999. *Discovering Chinese Nationalism in China.* Cambridge: Cambridge University Press.

Zhong, Yang. 1996. "Legitimacy Crisis and Legitimization in China." *Journal of Contemporary Asia* 26 (2): 201–20.

Zhong, Yang, Jie Chen, and John Scheb. 1998. "Mass Political Culture in Beijing: Findings from Two Public Opinion Surveys." *Asian Survey* 38, no. 8 (August): 763–83.

Zhou, Xueguang. 2000. "Economic Transformation and Income Inequality in Urban China: Evidence from Panel Data." *American Journal of Sociology* 105 (March): 1135–74.

Zhu, Rongji. 2002. "Zhu rongji zongli zai jiujie qunguo renda wuci huiyi shang de zhengfu gongzuo baogao" (Premier Zhu Rongji's government work report to the fifth session of the ninth National People's Congress). *Renmin Ribao* (People's daily) (March 6).

Zimmermann, E. 1979. "Crises and Crises Outcomes: Towards a New Synthetic Approach." *European Journal of Political Research* 7 (March): 67–115.

Zweig, David. 1999. "Undemocratic Capitalism: China and the Limits of Economism." *National Interest* 56 (Summer): 63–72.

Index

age: and behavioral consequences of political support, 170–171; and diffuse support, 7, 78–80, 88, 118; and specific support, 122–124, 152
air pollution, 46–47
Almond, Gabriel A., 82, 101
authoritarian party, 171. *See also* Chinese Communist Party (CCP)
authoritarian regime, 22, 83, 99, 106
authoritarianism. *See* new authoritarianism
anti-regime sentiment, 192. *See also* diffuse support; legitimacy; political regime.

Bahry, Donna, 94, 168, 169
Bauer, John, 81
behavioral consequences of political support, 11–14, 154–178, 182; and democratic beliefs, 171–173; and high-politics orientations, 171–173; impact of control variables on, 170–173; impact of diffuse support on, 168–169, 182; impact of specific support on, 169–170, 182; and low-politics orientations, 171–173; and mobilization model, 12; and motivation model, 12; multivariate analyses of, 173–176; and political awareness, 171–173; relationship between, and political support, 167–168; and sociodemographic attributes, 170–171. *See also* mass political participation
Beijing surveys, 15–17, 21–53; and conventional views, 36–48; democratic norms, questions on, 100; diffuse support

in, 27–36; empirical results from, 28–33, 48–51; and mainstream views, 27–28; political reform, questions on need for, 105; political stability, results on, 106; specific support in, 36–51. *See also specific subject areas of survey questions*
Bialer, Seweryn, 94, 111, 136
bureaucrats: and diffuse support, 86, 88, 119, 120, 181; and specific support, 128, 135, 152; and standard of living, 90
Burg, Steven L., 69–70

CCP. *See* Chinese Communist Party
challenges facing CCP leadership, 184–193; in improving support for incumbent authorities, 188–191; in improving support for regime, 185–188; and overt political alienation, 191–193
Chan, Alfred L., 78
Chen Xitong, 28
Chinese Communist Party (CCP): ban on engaging in profit-making business by, 37; challenges facing, 184–193; control of local elections by, 156–159; control over private lives of citizens by, 98; and diffuse support, 185–188; and egalitarianism, 44; fear of chaos exploited by, 106; and Fifteenth National Congress policy on state-owned enterprises, 40–41; gender differences in support of, 78–80, 120, 124–126; liberalization viewed cautiously by, 103; and modernization theory, 187–188; stability provided by, public opinion

225

Chinese Communist Party (CCP) (*continued*): favoring, 32, 106; strength of current rule of, 182–183; support for, 1, 71–72, 74, 119; weakness of current rule of, 183–184; youth's attitude toward, 78–80. *See also* ideology; Party membership

Clayton, Elizabeth, 126

college students: and diffuse support, 86, 88, 107, 118; and specific support, 128, 129, 135; of journalism and sociology, 17

connection hypothesis and high-politics orientation, 137–138

consistency of diffuse vs. specific support, 61–64, 74

constitution of PRC, 98, 160

contacting political behavior, 161–164, 169–170, 172, 178, 182; frequency of, 164–166

correlations between diffuse and specific support, 6–11, 64–67

corruption, 37–38, 190–191, 193; effect on CCP, 28; incumbent authority rated for handling of, 49, 50

crime-combating campaigns, 10

crisis of faith in the post-Tiananmen era, 27–28

data, 15–18; from Beijing surveys, 15–17; generalizability of, 17–18

Democracy Movement (1989), 83, 88

democratic beliefs: and behavioral consequences of political support, 171–173; and diffuse support, 96–99, 119, 193; and specific support, 139, 140

demonstrations, 86, 191, 192

Deng PRC: motivation model in, 12; need to replace old official ideology in, 63–64, 185–186; political reform in, 103

Deng Xiaoping, 13, 37, 45, 103, 156, 157, 186. *See also* Dengism

Dengism, 186. *See also* Deng Xiaoping; Deng PRC; ideology

Dickson, Bruce J., 89, 134

diffuse support, 54–75; and age, 78–80, 88, 118, 181; behavioral consequences of, 11, 168–169, 182; in Beijing surveys, 27–36, 180; from bureaucrats, 86, 88, 119, 120, 181; CCP need to improve, 185–188; from college students, 86, 88; consistency levels of, 61–64, 74; correlations between, and

specific support, 6–11, 64–67; current political system's reliance on, 52; definition of, 3–4; and democratic beliefs, 96–99, 119; differences between, and specific support, 54–64; and economic status, 89–92, 118, 181; and education, 82–84, 85, 118, 181; and gender differences, 80–82, 118, 120, 181; high-politics orientations, impact on, 8–9, 96–108, 181; index of, 23–24, 34–36, 195–197; and local issues and politics, interest in, 111–113, 181; low-politics orientations, impact on, 10, 108–113, 181; from military personnel, 86, 88; multivariate analysis of, 113–118; and occupation, 84, 86–89, 119; and Party membership, 93–96, 118, 181; and personal material satisfaction, 109–111, 112, 181; and political awareness, 99–102, 181; political reform, perceived need for, and, 103–104, 119; for political regime, 23–24, 28–33, 52; political stability and interaction between diffuse and specific support, 69–73, 74; from private entrepreneurs, 88–89; relationship between, and specific support, 5–6, 64–69; sociodemographic impact on, 7–8, 67–69, 77–95, 181; and socioeconomic satisfaction, 109–111, 112, 181; from SOE workers, 86, 120; sources of, 76–120; stability of, 55–61, 73–74; supplemental information about distributions of, 202; truthfulness of responses to index of, 34–36

disconnection hypothesis and high-politics orientation, 137–138

diseases, 47

dissidents: oppression of, 96–98

Eastern European countries, 2

Easton, David. *See* Eastonian theory

Eastonian theory, 55, 180, 183; dimensions of, 4–5; on erosion in popular support of regime, 73; as framework for analysis, 2–3; on regime legitimacy, 23; on spillover effects, 10; on weak relationship between diffuse and specific support, 64

economic status: and diffuse support, 89–92, 118, 181; and specific support, 131–134

economic reform: and diffuse support, 88; and inequality, 44; and job security, 40; purpose of, 38; and social welfare, 42; .

economy: and inflation, 38–39; socialist-market, 38, 186; and stable government, 106. *See also* economic reform; World Trade Organization accession

education: and behavioral consequences of political support, 170–171; and diffuse support, 82–84, 85, 118, 181; patriotic campaign in, 107; and specific support, 126–127, 152

elections: abstention from voting in, 159–160, 165, 177; competitive systems in, 96–97; decline in voter turnout in, 165, 167, 177, 183; and electoral law, 156; and local election committees, 157; local-level, 14, 25, 103, 156–161, 169, 177–178, 183

environment, 9, 46–48

Environment Protection Law of 1998, 48

equal protection and rights, 97, 137

fear of chaos, 106

fear of political persecution, 34–36

Fewsmith, Joseph, 186, 187

Finifter, Ada, 78

former Soviet Union. *See* USSR

Four Cardinal Principles, 158, 186

free markets: and private entrepreneurs, 88–89

freedom of press, 97–98

Geddes, Barbara, 99

gender: and behavioral consequences of political support, 170–171; and diffuse support, 80–82, 118, 120; and specific support, 124–126, 152

generational differences, 7-8. *See also* age

Goldstein, Avery, 27

government bureaucrats. *See* bureaucrats

government performance, evaluation of. *See* specific support

health care, 42–43

high-politics orientations, 8–9; and behavioral consequences of political support, 171–173; definition of, 8; and diffuse support, 96–108, 181; and specific support, 136–140; and mass political participation, 14; in multivariate analysis for diffuse support, 113–118

Hu Angang, 189

Huntington, Samuel P., 97

ideology, 9; Dengism as, 186; Four Cardinal Principles as, 158, 186; Jiang's approach to, 186–187; neutrality of, in developing survey instruments, 21–23; old official, 63, 185–186; and women's interests, 80

income: and behavioral consequences of political support, 170–171. *See also* economic status; income inequality

income inequality, 43–45, 193; growth of, 188–189; incumbent authority rated for handling of, 49, 50

inflation, 38–39; incumbent authority rated for handling of, 49, 50, 61

Inglehart, Ronald, 109, 119, 137

Institute of Economics of the Chinese Academy of Social Sciences, 40

intellectuals: and challenge to authoritarian regimes, 83; and specific support, 129, 135

interest in politics. *See* political awareness

Jiang Zemin, 28; and anticorruption campaign, 37; transformation of Party ideology by, 186–187; on welfare for needy, 41

job security, 39–41, 189–190

Jukam, Thomas O., 23, 54–55

Kaase, Max, 92

Khan, Azizur Rahman, 45

labor issues. *See* job security; unemployment

lead poisoning, 47

legitimacy of political system. *See* diffuse support; political regime

Letters and Visits Offices/Departments/Bureau, 163

Lieberthal, Kenneth, 38, 94

life satisfaction. *See* personal material satisfaction

Lipset, Seymour Martin, 23, 70, 71, 72

local elections. *See* elections

local issues and politics, interest in: and diffuse support, 111–113, 181; and specific support, 144–147

Locke, John, 97

low-politics orientations, 9–11; and behavioral consequences of political support, 171–173; definition of, 9; and diffuse support, 10, 108–113, 181; and specific support, 9–10, 141–147; and mass political participation,

low-politics orientations (*continued*): 14, 161; and multivariate analysis for diffuse support, 113–118
Lu, Xiaobo, 191

Macridis, Roy C., 69–70
Maoist PRC: consumer goods prices in, 38; egalitarianism in, 44; ideology of and belief in, 63, 95; job security in, 39; and mobilization model, 12; political intolerance in, 97
Marsh, Alan, 92
mass political participation, 12, 13–14, 154–167; and contacting behavior, 161–164, 169–170, 172, 178, 182; demonstrations as, 86, 191, 192; frequency of, 164–166; intensity of, 164–167; major forms of, 155–156; spread of, 166–167; and voting behavior, 156–161, 163, 177–178
May Fourth Movement, 83
McCormick, Barrett L., 160
measurement of political support, 21–26. *See also* political support
medical care, 42–43
Mickiewicz, Ellen, 78
military personnel: and diffuse support, 86, 88; and specific support, 128, 135
Millar, James R., 126
mobilization model, 12
modernization and likelihood to support political change, 119–120;
modernization theory and CCP, 187–188
motivation model, 12
Muller, Edward N., 23, 54–55
multivariate analyses: of behavioral consequences of political support, 173–176; of diffuse support, 113–118; of specific support, 147–151

Nathan, Andrew, 159
nationalism: Beijing survey results on, 31, 108; and diffuse support, 106–108; and specific support, 139, 140; state-led, 107
Nesbitt-Larking, Paul, 78
new authoritarianism, 106, 107

occupation: and diffuse support, 84, 86–89, 119; and specific support, 128–131, 135
Office of Environmental Protection, 47
overt political alienation, 191–193

Parish, William L., 26, 123, 125, 126, 161
particularistic political activities, 161
Party membership: and behavioral consequences of political support, 170–171; and diffuse support, 93–96, 118, 181; and specific support, 134–135, 152
patriotism. *See* nationalism
People's Congress: local, 156–161; as mere facade of democracy, 160
People's Liberation Army (PLA), 88
personal material satisfaction: and diffuse support, 109–111, 112, 181; and political participation, 167; and specific support, 141–143; subjectivity of, 172
political authorities: challenge to improve support for, 188–191; decline in specific support for, 192; measurement of support for, 24–25; and specific support, 25–26
political awareness: and behavioral consequences of political support, 171–173; and diffuse support, 99–102, 181; and specific support, 137, 139
political reform, 13; need for, and diffuse support, 103–104, 119; need for, and specific support, 137, 139; and need to replace old official ideology, 63
political regime: Beijing survey data on, 28–33; challenge to improve support for, 185–188; and diffuse support, 23–24, 52, 63; loss of moral support for, 28, 52; majority support for, 180; measurement of support for, 21–23; declining trends in support for, 71–72, 192. *See also* authoritarian regime; Chinese Communist Party (CCP); diffuse support
political support: definition of, 3–5; measurement of, 21–26
political stability. *See* stability
pollution. *See* environment
postmaterialist values, 137
private entrepreneurs: and diffuse support, 88–89; and specific support, 128, 131, 135; and standard of living, 90
protests. *See* demonstrations
Public Opinion Research Institute (PORI), 15, 17
public policy issues of concern, 25–26, 37; and specific support, 49; and stability trends of specific support, 58–59. *See also*

specific issues (e.g., corruption, job security, etc.)

regime legitimacy. *See* political regime; diffuse support
retirees, and diffuse support, 88, 118; and economic status, 90–91; and specific support, 129, 135
revolutionary climate, 1–2
Riskin, Carl, 45
Rublee, Maria Rost, 134

SEPA (State Environment Protection Administration), 47–48
sex discrimination, 80–82, 124–126. *See also* gender
Shaoguang Wang, 190
Shi, Tianjian, 25, 78, 111, 136, 144, 162
Silver, Brian D., 94, 109, 110, 168, 169
socialist market economy, 38, 186
sociodemographic attributes, 7–8; age as one of, 78–80, 88, 118, 122–124, 152, 181; and behavioral consequences of political support, 170–171; and correlation between diffuse and specific support, 67–69; economic status as one of, 89–92, 118, 131–134, 181; education as one of, 82–84, 85, 118, 126–127, 152, 181; effect of, on diffuse support, 77–95, 118–119, 181; effect of, on specific support, 122–135; gender as one of, 80–82, 118, 120, 124–126, 152, 181; in multivariate analysis for behavioral consequences of political support, 173–176; in multivariate analysis for diffuse support, 113–118; in multivariate analysis for specific support, 147–151; occupation as one of, 84, 86–89, 119, 128–131, 135; Party membership as one of, 93–96, 118, 152, 181
SOEs. *See* state-owned enterprises
Soviet Union. *See* USSR
specific support, 54–75; and age, 122–124, 152; behavioral consequences of, 11, 169–170, 182; in Beijing surveys, 36–51, 180; from bureaucrats, 128, 135, 152; from college students, 128, 129, 135; consistency levels of, 61–64; correlations between, and diffuse support, 6–11, 64–67; definition of, 4; and democratic beliefs, 139, 140; differences between, and diffuse support, 54–64;

and economic status, 131–134; and education, 126–127, 152; and gender differences, 124–126, 152; high-politics orientations, impact on, 9, 136–140; index of, 26, 197–199; from intellectuals, 129, 135; and local issues and politics, interest in, 144–147; low-politics orientations, impact on, 9–10, 141–147; measurement of, 24–26; from military personnel, 128, 135; multivariate analysis of, 147–151; and nationalism, 139, 140; and occupation, 128–131, 135; from Party membership, 134–135, 152; and personal material satisfaction, 141–143; and political authorities, 25–26; and political awareness, 137, 139; and political reform, need for, 137, 139; political stability and interaction between, and diffuse support, 69–73, 74; from private entrepreneurs, 128, 131, 135; relationship between, and diffuse support, 5–6, 64–69; sociodemographic impact on, 7–8, 67–69, 122–135; and socioeconomic satisfaction, 141–143; from SOE workers, 128, 129, 131; sources of, 121–153; stability of, 55–61, 73–74; supplemental information about distributions of, 203
stability of Chinese political system, 2, 52–53, 63, 73–74; Beijing survey results about, 31–32, 104, 106, 108; and interaction between diffuse and specific support, 69–73, 74; and specific support, 139, 140
stability of diffuse vs. specific support, 55–61
stability of European countries' political systems, 70
State Environment Protection Administration (SEPA), 47–48
state-owned enterprises (SOEs): Fifteenth National Congress policy on, 40–41; and medical care, 42–43; unemployment and reform policies in, 39–41, 125; workers of, and diffuse support, 86, 120; workers of, and specific support, 128, 129, 131; and WTO, 189–190

Tang, Wenfang, 26, 123, 125, 126, 128, 161
technocratic leaders: likelihood of support for, 152
theoretical framework, 2–14; *See also* Eastonian theory

Tiananmen crackdown, 97, 103; crisis of faith after, 27–28, 182; and new authoritarianism, 106
traditional Chinese culture: fear of chaos in, 106; governmental control of morality in, 98; inequality in, 97; women's status in, 80, 81
truthfulness of responses to diffuse support index, 34–36

unemployment, 39–42, 189–190, 193; demonstrations over, 192; and women, 82, 125
USSR, 2; and behavioral consequences of political support, 168, 169, 172; and Communist Party membership as factor in support of political regime, 94; and education as factor in supporting democratic change in, 83, 126, 127; in Gorbachev era, 12, 13; high-politics orientation in, 136; local politics in, 144; mobilization model applied to, 12; motivation model applied to, 12; personal material satisfaction in, 109

Verba, Sidney, 82, 101
voting. *See* elections

Wang Baosen, 28
water pollution, 46–47
welfare, 41–42; to alleviate urban poverty, 92; incumbent authority rated for handling of, 49, 50
women's support of current political regime, 80–82, 120, 124–126
worker demonstrations, 86
World Bank report on income inequality, 45
World Health Organization (WHO) on air pollution, 46
World Trade Organization accession, 188, 189, 190

youth. *See* generational differences; age

Zaller, John, 99
Zhu Rongji, 189

The authorized representative in the EU for product safety and compliance is:
Mare Nostrum Group
B.V Doelen 72
4831 GR Breda
The Netherlands

www.ingramcontent.com/pod-product-compliance
Lightning Source LLC
Chambersburg PA
CBHW020346270326
41926CB00007B/333

9 780804 750578